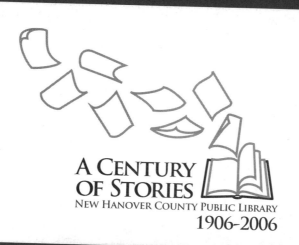

The Crossway Illustrated Bible Handbook

EDITED BY TIM DOWLEY

Contributors:

Stephen Motyer

David Payne   Mary Evans

Robert Backhouse

The Crossway Illustrated Bible Handbook
Copyright © 2005 by LionHudson plc/Tim Dowley and Peter Wyart trading as Three's Company

First published in the USA in 2005 by Crossway Books,
a publishing ministry of Good News Publishers
Wheaton, Illinois

Published in the UK as *The Candle Bible Encyclopedia*, by Candle Books, a publishing imprint of Lion/Hudson plc.

First printing 2005
Printed in Singapore

Unless otherwise noted, Scripture quotations are from *The Holy Bible, English Standard Version*™, copyright © 2001 by Crossway Bibles, a publishing ministry of Good News Publishers. Used by permission. All rights reserved.

Scripture references marked NIV are from the *Holy Bible: New International Version*. ® Copyright <\#169> 1973, 1978, 1984 by International Bible Society. Used by permission of Zondervan Publishing House. All rights reserved.

The "NIV" and "New International Version" trademarks are registered in the United States Patent and Trademark Office by International Bible Society. Use of either trademark requires the permission of International Bible Society.

Scripture quotations marked KJV are from the King James Version of the Bible.

Book Design: Peter Wyart
Worldwide co-edition produced by Lion Hudson plc, Mayfield House,
256 Banbury Road, Oxford OX2 7DH, England.
Telephone: +44 (0) 1865 302750. Fax: +44 (0) 1865 302757.
Email: coed@lionhudson.com. www.lionhudson.com

Picture acknowledgments

Photographs:
Tim Dowley: pp. 12, 13, 14, 21, 25, 30 bottom, 42, 51, 52, 55, 73, 79, 87, 90, 98, 100, 104, 106 bottom, 109, 113 top, 115, 118, 119, 122, 124, 130, 140, 141 top, 158, 166-67, 179, 186, 1900, 191, 199, 216, 219, 227, 228 Peter Wyart: pp. 9, 17, 19, 24, 30 top, 31, 72, 80, 83, 94, 97, 103, 106 top, 113 bottom, 114 top, 119 inset, 120, 126, 141 bottom, 163, 168-69, 184, 196, 203, 221, 226

Maps: Hardlines
Timeline: Tony Cantale

Illustrations:
Frank Baber: p. 160 top
Brian Bartles: pp. 142-43, 217
Shirley Bellwood: p. 95
Peter Dennis: pp. 1, 2, 3, 9, 10 bottom, 13, 15, 16 top, 17, 18, 19, 22, 23 top

Jeremy Gower: pp. 29, 152 top
James Macdonald: pp. 54, 65, 76, 92, 100, 227, 234
Bob Moulder: pp. 172-73
Trevor Parkin: pp. 43, 56, 136-37
Alan Parry: pp. 72, 79, 91, 93, 128, 129, 131, 132, 133, 134, 135, 144-45, 146, 147, 149, 152 bottom, 153, 156-57, 158-59, 160 bottom, 161, 164-75, 180-81
Kate Pascoe: p. 185
Francis Phillipps: p. 78
David Price: p. 23 bottom
Richard Scott: pp. 8, 10 top, 16 bottom, 45, 55, 68, 69, 89, 104, 115, 116, 139, 140, 164, 165, 179, 193, 194, 196, 197, 198, 200, 201, 202, 203, 204, 206, 207, 208, 209, 210-11, 211, 212, 213, 214, 215, 216, 217, 218, 219, 232, 233
Annabel Spenceley: pp. 81, 231
Paul Wyart: p. 184

Library of Congress Cataloging-in-Publication Data
The Crossway illustrated Bible handbook / edited by Tim Dowley ; contributors, Stephen Motyer ... [et al.].
    p. cm.
  Includes index.
  ISBN 1-58134-693-X (hc : alk. paper)
  1. Bible--Introductions. I. Dowley, Tim. II. Motyer, Stephen, 1950-
  BS475.3.C75 2005
  220.6'1--dc22   2005009875

16   15   14   13   12   11   10   09   08   07   06   05

15   14   13   12   11   10   9   8   7   6   5   4   3   2   1

Contents

How the Bible Came to Us   5

The History of Bible Times   25

Introducing the Old Testament   43

Introducing the New Testament   77

Living in Bible Times   127

Religion in Bible Times   163

Men and Women of the Bible   193

Some Bible Facts and Figures   221

Index   236

How the Bible Came to Us

What is the Bible?	6
How the Bible was written down	7
The languages of the Bible	8
Who wrote the Bible?	10
Scrolls from the Dead Sea	12
The book arrives	14
How the Bible came down to us	16
The first translations	17
Precious books	18
The Bible for the people	20
No more copying!	22
Two great translators	23
Changing language for a changing world	24

What is the Bible?

The Bible is made up of a "library" of 66 books, 39 in the Old Testament, 27 in the New. The writings of the **OLD TESTAMENT** first appeared as separate scrolls in Hebrew; we do not know how or when they were first gathered into a single volume. The 39 books of the Old Testament vary in authorship and style and can be divided into four major groupings:

Law
Sometimes called the Pentateuch, or "five scrolls."

History
Tracing the story of God's people from their entry into the Promised Land to the Exile.

Poetry and Wisdom
Full of psalms, proverbs, riddles, parables, warnings, and wise sayings.

Prophecy
God's prophets explained what had happened in the past, spoke out against evil in the present, and told of what God would do in the future.

The Apocrypha
The Apocrypha is a collection of books and additions to the Old Testament books written between 300 B.C. and A.D. 100. They were not accepted by the Jews as part of the Old Testament Scripture, and most Protestant denominations do not accept them as part of genuine Scripture.

The books are interesting documents that range from valuable historical narratives to pious fiction.

The 27 books of the **NEW TESTAMENT** were written in Greek and can also be divided into different types of writing:

History
The book of Acts and the four Gospels. The Gospels, however, are not simply historical records; they were also written to persuade readers to believe in Jesus, and form portraits of Jesus as the Messiah.

Letters
These include Paul's letters to churches in various cities, his letters to individual Christians, and letters written by other apostles.

Revelation
This book opens with letters to seven churches in Asia Minor, but continues with visions about the Last Days that foretell the ultimate victory of Christ and his Church.

How the Bible was written down

Clay tablets
In ancient Babylonia clay for writing was shaped into thin, flat, rectangular bricks. Words were pressed into the soft clay with a wedge-shaped stylus, and the clay then baked in the sun. Archaeologists have found whole "libraries" of these clay tablets.

Papyrus
Before the pyramids were built, the ancient Egyptians had learned to make papyrus paper from the pith (or inner stalk) of Nile papyrus reeds, which grew in marshy areas around Egypt. Still wet, the thick stems were laid out in rows on top of each other and beaten until they melded together into a flat paper surface. (Our word "paper" comes from "papyrus.") When this sheet had dried in the sun, it could be written on. Papyrus was expensive—but it could be reused by washing, or by scraping.

Egyptian pens were brushes made from reeds, and ink was derived from plants and insects.

Stone
The first permanent writing surface was stone. In the Bible, the first reference to writing is to the Ten Commandments, which were written on stone. The first pen was a chisel.

Ordinary people often used broken bits of pottery, called "sherds," to write memos, bills, and even shopping lists.

Ink was made from soot mixed with oil or gum.

Waxed boards
Writing boards were made from pieces of wood or ivory covered with wax. They were used by the Assyrians, Greeks, and Romans. Two boards were sometimes hinged together. Any pointed stick made a pen.

Leather
The skins of sheep, goats, calves, and antelopes were dried, scraped, and cleaned to make a smooth material called parchment. (The Hebrew word for book means "scrape.") Then the skins were stretched and beaten flat, ready for writing on.

Pens were made from reeds, with one end cut to a sloping edge and then split.

The languages of the Bible

Writing

The first writing consisted of simple pictures, with one picture for each word. Writing like this, with over 800 pictures, has been found in Babylonia (modern Iraq) and is over 5,000 years old.

Hieroglyphs

The Egyptians made up their own little pictures to represent words, or parts of words. They painted them on papyrus sheets—and on walls.

Cuneiform writing

The Babylonians did not have access to papyrus, and it was not easy to draw on clay. For this reason their pictures became increasingly simplified, until words became standard shapes pressed into the clay with wedge-shaped sticks. The word "cuneiform" means wedge-shaped.

The alphabet

In Canaan about 1500 B.C. someone had the clever idea of making up a symbol—a letter—for each sound in the language. They found that they needed about 25 letters.

There was now no longer any need to learn hundreds of different shapes for hundreds of different words. Any word could be written down just by listening to its sounds and choosing the matching letters. This simple idea quickly spread to other languages.

A Jewish rabbi teaches boys to read the Scripture. They are using writing boards; he is reading from a scroll.

The Hebrew alphabet:

a, b, g, d, h, w, z, h, t, y, k

l, m, n, s, p, s, q, r, s, t

Hebrew

The Old Testament tells the story of the Israelite people. Their language was Hebrew, and most of the Old Testament is written in Hebrew. The Hebrew alphabet has 22 consonants, but no vowels (vowel sounds had to be added by the reader). Hebrew is read from right to left, so the first page of the Hebrew Bible is our last page.

A Hebrew scroll

Aramaic

Aramaic was spoken by the Persians, who were the major power in the Middle East for 200 years from about 550 B.C. Aramaic became the language used by traders in that region. Parts of the Old Testament books of Daniel, Ezra, and Jeremiah were written in Aramaic.

By New Testament times, Aramaic was the everyday language of the Jews, and Jesus would have spoken it. However, Hebrew remained the language for prayer and worship. Educated people still understood Hebrew, but when the Hebrew Bible was read aloud in synagogue services, a translator often gave the meaning in Aramaic.

Some manuscripts of parts of the Old Testament in Aramaic, called "Targums," have survived. They help us to discover the words of the original Hebrew.

The Greek alphabet

A	A	K	K
B	B	L	L
Γ	G	M	M
Δ	D	N	N
E	E	Ξ	U
Y	Y	O	O
Z	Z	Π	P
H	H	P	R
Θ	TH	Σ	S
I	I	T	T

Greek

In 331 B.C. the Greek general Alexander the Great conquered Persia. He now ruled the known ancient world, and "common" Greek became the language that most people understood.

When the followers of Jesus wrote the New Testament, they wanted the whole known world to hear the good news. So they wrote in Greek, translating the Aramaic spoken by Jesus into the Greek language. In just a few places they retained original Aramaic words. For example "abba" is an Aramaic word meaning Dad.

When Jesus spoke to Jairus's daughter, he said, "*Talitha cumi*"— these were his actual Aramaic words. The Gospel writers gave us a Greek translation, which in English is, "Little girl . . . arise" (Mark 5:41).

There are 24 letters in the Greek alphabet, which was the first alphabet to include letters for vowels. Sentences—and books—were written from left to right.

In Revelation, God says: "I am the Alpha and the Omega"—the first and last letters of the Greek alphabet—"who is and who was and who is to come" (Revelation 1:8).

The earliest evidence

Possibly the earliest part of the New Testament so far discovered is a papyrus fragment, only 6 x 9 centimeters (2 x 3 inches), containing a few lines from John's Gospel. It is written in Greek, dates from about A.D. 130, and is known as the "John Rylands fragment."

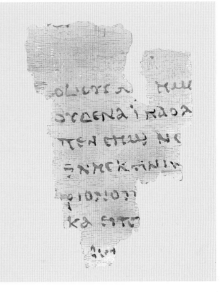

Who wrote the Bible?

The Bible we have today is usually in the form of one very thick book of more than 1,000 pages. But different parts of the Bible were written by different people over a very long period of time—probably more than 1,500 years. It was only later that the many different parts were collected together into a single book.

Oral tradition

The first stories in the Bible happened long before writing was invented. They were passed on in the same way as children's playground songs are passed on today—by being constantly repeated. Passing stories on in this way is often called oral (or spoken) tradition. Around the campfires in the evenings, at worship, at work or at war, people sang the songs and told the stories that they had learned as children. Because these stories were about God, they were treated with great respect. Every word was important and had to be repeated correctly.

Jewish scribe

In writing

Scholars are not sure when the books of the Old Testament were first written down; the period of their writing covered several centuries. By the third century B.C. the Jews recognized a number of their books as "holy" and directly inspired by God. They were formally recognized at the Synod of Jamnia in A.D. 90 and are the books we know as the Old Testament—though we have them in a different order.

What about the New Testament?

Jesus of Nazareth was born hundreds of years after the writings mentioned earlier, just 2,000 years ago. But stories about Jesus were at first passed on by word of mouth too. Matthew, Mark, Luke, and John wrote the four Gospels based on eye-witness accounts of Jesus' life. The stories about Jesus' birth at Bethlehem, his life and miracles, which we know from the Gospels of Matthew, Mark, Luke, and John, were all written down before A.D. 100.

The apostle Paul and others wrote letters to explain to believers about the faith and instruct them in Christian behavior. The first of these letters appeared before the Gospels, around A.D. 50.

As the apostles and first generation of Christians began to die, the younger believers began the attempt to assemble a collection of authentic writings that would preserve a more permanent record of Jesus and his teachings. By A.D. 100, most of the individual writings we now know as the New Testament were recognized by the Church as inspired; and by about A.D. 200 the New Testament as we know it today, with its 27 books, was recognized.

The contents of various Old Testaments

The Jewish Bible, the Septuagint (an early Greek translation of the Old Testament), the Roman Catholic Old Testament, and the Protestant Old Testament all vary a little in the number of their constituent books and in the order of those books. The chart helps compare the four different versions. (See also page 76.)

RABBINIC CANON 24 BOOKS	SEPTUAGINT 51 BOOKS	ROMAN CATHOLIC O.T. 46 BOOKS	PROTESTANT O.T. 39 BOOKS
The Law	*Law*	*Law*	*Law*
Genesis	Genesis	Genesis	Genesis
Exodus	Exodus	Exodus	Exodus
Leviticus	Leviticus	Leviticus	Leviticus
Numbers	Numbers	Numbers	Numbers
Deuteronomy	Deuteronomy	Deuteronomy	Deuteronomy
The Prophets	*History*	*History*	*History*
The Former Prophets			
Joshua	Joshua	Joshua	Joshua
Judges	Judges	Judges	Judges
1–2 Samuel	Ruth	Ruth	Ruth
1–2 Kings	1 Kingdoms (1 Samuel)	1 Samuel (1 Kingdoms)	1 Samuel
The Latter Prophets	2 Kingdoms (2 Samuel)	2 Samuel (2 Kingdoms)	2 Samuel
Isaiah	3 Kingdoms (1 Kings)	1 Kings (3 Kingdoms)	1 Kings
Jeremiah	4 Kingdoms (2 Kings)	2 Kings (4 Kingdoms)	2 Kings
Ezekiel	1 Paralipomena (1 Chronicles)	1 Chronicles (1Paralipomena)	1 Chronicles
The Twelve:	2 Paralipomena (2 Chronicles)	2 Chronicles (2 Paralipomena)	2 Chronicles
Hosea	1 Esdras (Apocryphal Ezra)	Ezra	Ezra
Joel	2 Esdras (Ezra-Nehemiah)	Nehemiah	Nehemiah
Amos	Esther (with Apocryphal additions)	Tobit	Esther
Obadiah	Judith	Judith	
Jonah	Tobit	Esther (with additions)	
Micah	1 Maccabees	1 Maccabees	
Nahum	2 Maccabees	2 Maccabees	
Habakkuk	3 Maccabees		
Zephaniah	4 Maccabees	*Poetry*	*Poetry*
Haggai		Job	Job
Zechariah	*Poetry*	Psalms	Psalms
Malachi	Psalms	Proverbs	Proverbs
	Odes (including the prayer of Manasseh)	Ecclesiastes	Ecclesiastes
The Writings	Proverbs	Song of Solomon	Song of Solomon
Poetry	Ecclesiastes	Wisdom of Solomon	
Psalms	Song of Solomon	Ecclesiasticus (The Wisdom of	
Proverbs	Job	Jesus the son of Sirach)	
Job	Wisdom (of Solomon)		
Rolls–"the Festival Scrolls"	Sirach (Ecclesiasticus or The Wisdom	*Prophecy*	*Prophecy*
Song of Solomon	of Jesus the son of Sirach)	Isaiah	Isaiah
Ruth	Psalms of Solomon	Jeremiah	Jeremiah
Lamentations		Lamentations	Lamentations
Ecclesiastes	*Prophecy*	Baruch (including the	Ezekiel
Esther	Hosea	Letter of Jeremiah)	Daniel
Others (History)	Amos	Ezekiel	Hosea
Daniel	Micah	Daniel (including Susanna, The Song of	Joel
Ezra-Nehemiah	Joel	the three young men, Bel and Dragon)	Amos
1–2 Chronicles	Obadiah	Hosea	Obadiah
	Jonah	Joel	Jonah
	Naham	Amos	Micah
	Habakkuk	Obadiah	Nahum
	Zephaniah	Jonah	Habakkuk
	Haggai	Micah	Zephaniah
	Zechariah	Nahum	Haggai
	Malachi	Habakkuk	Zechariah
	Isaiah	Zephaniah	Malachi
	Jeremiah	Haggai	
	Baruch	Zechariah	
	Lamentations	Malachi	
	Letter of Jeremiah		
	Ezekiel		
	Daniel (with apocryphal additions, including the Prayer of Azariah, the Song of the Three Children, Susanna, and Bel and the Dragon)		

Scrolls from the Dead Sea

In 1947 a Bedouin shepherd boy tending his flock in the barren hills west of the Dead Sea noticed a hole in nearby cliffs. He tossed a stone inside and heard the sound of breaking crockery. Intrigued, he went to explore and found a number of earthenware jars. Exploring further, he discovered that inside the jars were rolls of leather parchment covered in ancient Hebrew writing. At first no one was interested in his find; but when some archaeologists saw the scrolls, there was real excitement.

Eventually about 400 scrolls were found in caves near a place called Qumran. They turned out to be the library of a Jewish religious sect called the Essenes, and they include parts of every book in the Hebrew Old Testament except Esther. The ascetic Essene community lived nearby around the time of Christ and built a settlement that has been excavated to reveal a watchtower, refectory, scriptorium—where the Dead Sea Scrolls were probably copied—ritual baths, pottery, and a cemetery.

Carbon 14 dating has shown that the Dead Sea Scrolls were written between 200 B.C. and A.D. 70. The Isaiah Scroll is almost complete and is 1,000 years older than our next oldest surviving copy of Isaiah; yet the two texts are almost identical. This shows how accurate the copyists were— and how seriously they took their job.

Qumran
Plan of settlement

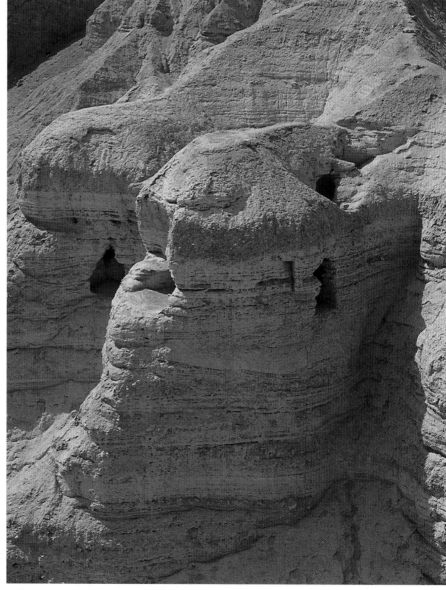

In these caves near Qumran a Bedouin shepherd found the Dead Sea Scrolls.

Some of the Dead Sea Scrolls are now housed in the Shrine of the Book, in Jerusalem.

A number of the Dead Sea Scrolls were made of copper.

Excavated remains of the Essene community at Qumran, near the Dead Sea

Part of the Isaiah Scroll, the oldest and longest of the Dead Sea Scrolls.

The scroll

When the Bible was written, books with pages did not exist. Instead, people wrote on scrolls. These were made from sheets of papyrus, parchment, or even thin copper, sewn or glued together to form a long strip, up to 30 feet long and 12 inches wide. Each end was wound around a wooden rod, and the reader unrolled the scroll with one hand and rolled it up with the other. When not in use, scrolls were wrapped in cloths and stored in tall jars to preserve them.

The apostle Paul wrote from prison in Rome asking Timothy to bring him his "scrolls, especially the parchments" (2 Timothy 4:13, NIV).

The earliest Christian writings were on papyrus scrolls.

The Qumran scrolls were found in jars like this.

The book arrives

Scrolls were cumbersome to carry, and it was time-consuming to find a short Bible passage on a long scroll.

In the second century Christians collected together the books of the New Testament. They were probably the first people to do away with the scroll. Instead, they hit on the idea of collecting together several sheets of papyrus or parchment, folding them in half, sewing along the fold, and then adding more folded sheets. This forerunner of our "book" was sometimes also given a harder cover. This early type of book was called a codex (plural codices).

The book had arrived.

Above: St. Catherine's Monastery, Sinai
Below: Overall view of St. Catherine's

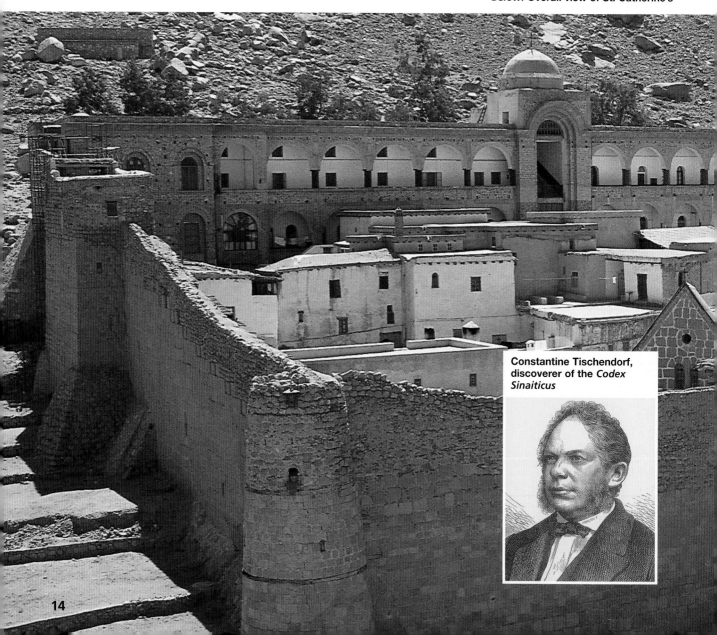

Constantine Tischendorf, discoverer of the *Codex Sinaiticus*

Codex Sinaiticus

Our earliest complete copy of the New Testament was written out not long after A.D. 300. It is called *Codex Sinaiticus* because it was found at the foot of Mount Sinai, in St. Catherine's Monastery.

In 1844 a German scholar called Constantine Tischendorf was visiting this remote monastery and discovered some parchments with early Greek writing. The manuscripts turned out to be part of the Old Testament and dated from the fourth century A.D. Excited by his discovery, Tischendorf made a return visit to the monastery and eventually found enough sheets to make an almost complete Bible. Today the *Codex Sinaiticus* is preserved in the British Museum, in London.

Other important early manuscripts of the Bible in Greek include the *Codex Vaticanus*, now in the Vatican Library, in Rome, and the *Codex Alexandrinus*, also in the British Museum.

Pages of the *Codex Sinaiticus*

A page from the *Codex Sinaiticus*

How the Bible came down to us

Copying was lengthy and laborious.

Jewish scribes

The Jewish scribes were important figures, because in early times they were often the only people who could read and write. They drew up wills and other legal documents and kept records.

When new copies of Old Testament scrolls were needed, every word had to be written out by hand. The scribes had the sacred task of preserving, copying out, and explaining the teaching of the Old Testament.

To make sure that each scribe understood the importance of his work, and to prevent his making mistakes, careful rules were followed. For example:
• *Each day he had to start his work with prayer.*
• *The name of God had to be left blank, to be filled in later by a different scribe, using a "purer" ink.*
• *At the end of a section of a book, the scribe counted the lines, the words, and the letters in the original and checked them with his copy. He also found and checked the middle word of each section.*

Sometimes mistakes were made. But it has been computed that mistakes averaged only one mistake in every 1,580 letters.

Septuagint

The Old Testament was first translated from Hebrew into Greek in the second and third centuries B.C. This translation was known as the Septuagint. "Septuagint" comes from the Latin for 70; there is a tradition that 70 (or perhaps 72) scholars made this translation. It is sometimes written as LXX (70 in Roman numerals).

Jewish people had spread all over the Mediterranean world and often spoke Greek rather than Hebrew. This translation was made in Alexandria, Egypt, for the legendary great library there.

Monks

The word "monk" comes from a Greek word meaning "someone who lives alone." The first Christian monk was Antony, who lived by himself in the deserts of Egypt from about A.D. 270 to 290. Others followed his example. More often men (and, separately, women) lived in a group in a monastery, spending their days in prayer, Bible study, and useful work such as farming or nursing.

Copyists

During the Dark Ages, after the Roman Empire had collapsed, the monks protected and passed on the Bible. When a Bible was worn out, they spent years making a fresh copy. Every codex had to be copied out by hand. This was a long and laborious process.

Mistakes were sometimes made, perhaps by the monk or scribe becoming tired, or because of the poor light in which he was working. Sometimes the scribe would even change things deliberately because he wanted to put the Scriptures into his own words or make them fit his own point of view.

Often the monks worked in a scriptorium, or writing room, each monk writing in silence at his desk. Because of the danger of fire destroying the manuscripts, the room had no heat and no lighting. The work was tiring. There was a saying, "Two fingers hold the pen, but the whole body toils."

A medieval monk copies a page of the Bible.

The first translations

By A.D. 300 the New Testament had been translated into several languages, including Latin and Syriac—a language spoken in what is today Turkey. The Syriac Bible was called the Peshitta, or "simple" version. Syriac missionaries took the gospel—and the Bible—as far as China, India, Armenia, and Georgia.

The Armenian and Georgian alphabets were probably created to allow the Bible to be translated into both these languages. The Bible was also translated into Coptic, a form of ancient Egyptian—the language of the North African Christians—and Sahedic, a dialect of Coptic.

A book for the Goths

By the fourth century, the language of the Germanic Ostrogoths had never been written down. Around A.D. 350 Bishop Ulfilas translated the Bible

Jerome translated the Vulgate in Bethlehem.

into the language of the Ostrogoths and committed it to writing.

Jerome

A scholar named Jerome, born in northern Italy in about A.D. 345,

A leather-bound copy of the Vulgate

became very concerned about copyists' mistakes. He traveled widely, learning many languages and transcribing many parts of the Scriptures.

Around A.D. 382, Pope Damasus asked Jerome to make a completely new translation of the Gospels, the Psalms, and other Old Testament books in an attempt to get rid of mistakes that had crept in.

The Vulgate

At this time most Christians in the West spoke Latin and found it hard to understand the Greek New Testament. Many Latin translations had been made, but they were neither well-written nor accurate. So Jerome, who went to live in seclusion in a monastery in Bethlehem in 386, set about translating into Latin the original Hebrew and Greek texts of the entire Bible. A Jewish rabbi helped him learn Hebrew and translate directly from the Old Testament. His task was to take him 23 years.

Jerome's translation gradually increased in popularity. Known as the Vulgate, meaning "Common Version," from the eighth century until 1609 it was the only Bible used by the Roman Catholic Church.

Jerome translated the Bible with the help of a Jewish rabbi.

Precious books

Irish monks traveled to Scotland, taking with them their faith and their Bibles.

and northern England, wandering from place to place explaining their Christian faith and setting up monasteries. These monks brought with them the skills to create beautiful and imaginative Celtic designs. Superbly decorated books were produced in remote monasteries on bleak cliffs and islands. A monk might spend his whole life working on one book, thus demonstrating his love for God.

The Book of Kells
In the Irish Book of Kells one small design, only ¼ square inch in size, is made up of 158 tiny interlaced shapes. This illuminated book of the Gospels in Latin is perhaps the greatest masterpiece of Celtic and Anglo-Saxon art. It was begun in the seventh century in the monastery at Iona, western Scotland. After a Viking raid, it was taken for safe-keeping to the monastery of Kells in Ireland, where it was completed. It consists of 339 leaves, 13 x 10 inches in size, and every page is richly decorated. The Book of Kells is today preserved at Trinity College in Dublin, Ireland.

Decorating the book
Books were made from parchment (the skin of a calf, sheep, or goat) or from vellum (a very fine parchment). After a monk had finished copying out the Latin words in a beautiful, elegant script, his work was checked.

In time, instead of merely copying the Latin words, the monks began to decorate the page as well. The resulting decorated books are known as illuminated manuscripts.

Sometimes the copyists would add a painted border with an intricate pattern to the page. Also the first letter of a paragraph or chapter would be enlarged almost to fill the page, and then be decorated with patterns, flowers, or even little figures. The monks created intricate, interlocking designs of curves, spirals, scrolls, shields, and tiny detailed paintings of animals and birds. They used watercolor paints that they had to make up themselves, and sometimes gold leaf was added for a rich effect.

Quill pens—made from sharpened feathers—and very basic brushes were the only tools available, but the results were exquisite.

Irish tradition
In the fifth and sixth centuries Irish monks traveled to Scotland

Copying a page of Scripture by hand

The first page of Luke's Gospel, from the Lindisfarne Gospels

An ornamented page from the Lindisfarne Gospels

Ruins of the monastery of Lindisfarne in northeast England

Lindisfarne Gospels

In A.D. 635 a monastery was set up on Lindisfarne, a small island off the coast of northeast England.

The Lindisfarne Gospels, particularly fine examples of illuminated manuscripts, were copied out and illuminated there around A.D. 700. A priest named Aldred added an Anglo-Saxon translation between the lines of Latin text some 300 years later.

The Golden Gospels

The Golden Gospels are a magnificent series of illuminated manuscripts of the Gospels, created in eighth-century France under the guidance of Alcuin, who came from York, England. The lettering in these manuscripts was mainly in gold, and the decoration in silver and gold, all on purple-stained vellum.

A sixth-century copy of Ulfilas's translation of the Bible for the Goths was similarly written in gold and silver on a purple-painted parchment.

Bibles in chains

Most Bibles were much less ornate than the Book of Kells or the Golden Gospels. But even plain books took years to copy and then bind with leather into a huge, heavy volume. They were also very valuable; so when a finished Bible was put on display in a monastery chapel or in a cathedral, it would often be chained to the reading desk to prevent anyone from stealing it.

A medieval monk reads from a chained illuminated Bible.

The Bible for the people

Peter Waldo

In the Middle Ages most Bibles, however beautiful, were still written in Latin—a language that ordinary people did not understand. Some men were determined to change this—by translating the Bible into the vernacular.

Waldo's versions
About 1175, Peter Waldo, a wealthy merchant living in Lyons, France, became a Christian. Taking Jesus' words literally, he gave away all his possessions.

Waldo's followers, called Waldensians, translated the Bible into the Provençal language— and probably also into Italian, German, Piedmontese (north Italian), and Catalan (spoken in northeast Spain).

An alphabet for Russia
In the ninth century Cyril and Methodius, two Christian brothers from Thessalonica in Greece, embarked on a mission to the Slavs of Eastern Europe. As part of their task, they translated the Bible into the Old Slavonic language. To write out their

John Wycliffe

The very first translation of any part of the Bible into Anglo-Saxon was a version of the Psalms, made about A.D. 700 by Bishop Aldhelm of Sherborne. Later the Venerable Bede, abbot at Jarrow, in northeast England, translated part of John's Gospel before his death in 735.

Heresy!
John Wycliffe (1329–1384) longed for the Bible to be translated into English, so that ordinary people could understand its message. It angered him that priests could decide which part of the Bible to read and how to interpret it. Wycliffe taught at Oxford University until he was thrown out for attacking these and other failings in the Church.

translation, they invented an alphabet that was the forerunner of the Cyrillic alphabet—named after Cyril— still used today in southeast Europe and Russia.

Here are the names of the Gospel writers in Russian, in Cyrillic script:

Матфея

Марка

Луки

Иоанна

John Hus

In fifteenth-century Prague, the capital of Bohemia (now part of the Czech Republic), John Hus (1374–1415), rector of Charles University, began to speak out against the greed, immorality, and ambition of priests. He was greatly influenced by Wycliffe's teachings. As a result of his outspoken views, Hus was accused of heresy, imprisoned, and eventually burned at the stake.

However, Hus's followers started to translate the Bible into Czech, and a Czech New Testament was published in 1475.

John Hus, the Czech reformer

Wycliffe was later tried as a heretic, and some of his precious books were thrown onto a public bonfire.

Wycliffe's Bible
Some of Wycliffe's followers, such as Nicholas of Hereford and John Purvey, translated the entire Bible into English, a task they finished in 1384. In 1408 this "Wycliffe Bible" was banned, but hundreds of copies were made and secretly sold.

Ordinary people could rarely read, so Wycliffe's followers—poor priests or "Lollards"—traveled from town to town reading and explaining the Bible. Some were burned at the stake as heretics, with Bibles tied around their necks. However, some 170 copies of this version still survive today.

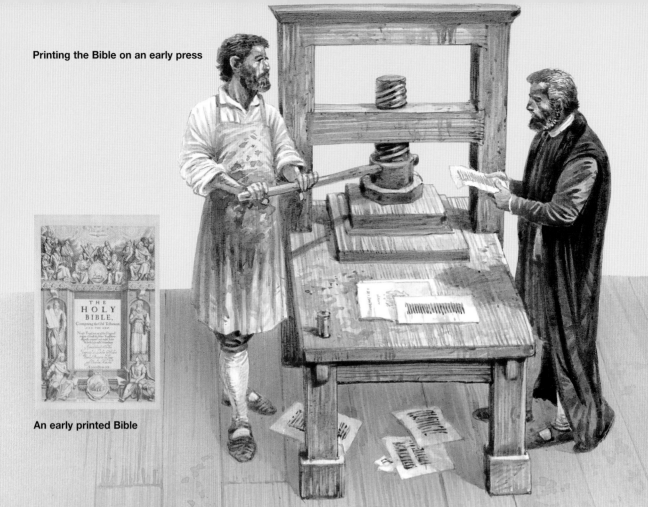

Printing the Bible on an early press

An early printed Bible

No more copying!

In 1450 an event occurred that was radically to affect the story of the Bible: printing was invented. (Or reinvented—the Chinese had been printing books since A.D. 868.)

In Mainz, Germany, Johann Gutenberg discovered that he could print onto parchment with wooden letters dipped in dye. Using this method, he could make hundreds of printed books, instead of just one hand-written volume.

Gutenberg next experimented with metal type: the age of printed books had begun.

The first complete book printed by Gutenberg was the Latin Bible, in 1456. In 1978 one of the few surviving Gutenberg Bibles was bought for $2.4 million.

Although Johann Gutenberg and the people of Mainz tried to keep their invention secret, word soon got out, and before long presses were springing up all over Europe, from Rome and Paris to Kracow and London. The first printing press in England was set up by William Caxton in London in 1476.

Soon there were printed Bibles everywhere. The first printed Hebrew Old Testament appeared at Soncino, Italy, in 1488, produced by a group of Italian Jews.

Greek Testament

A famous Dutch scholar, Desiderius Erasmus, prepared the first printed edition of the Greek New Testament, which was printed in Basel, Switzerland, in 1516. This formed the basis for many modern European translations of the New Testament, including important English and German translations.

Erasmus of Rotterdam, c.1466–1536

Two great translators

The great reformer
In the fifteenth and sixteenth centuries huge changes took place in Europe. More people were being educated, forming their own opinions about society and religion. Things were badly awry in the Church: many priests were dishonest or lazy, some teaching their own ideas without reference to the Bible.

One person prepared to stand up and criticize this was a German priest named Martin Luther, born in 1483. Becoming a monk, Luther strove to lead a good life, but felt he could never be as good as God wanted. While reading the book of Romans, he suddenly recognized that salvation is by grace through faith in Jesus Christ. It was a breakthrough!

Church doors were often used as notice-boards, and in October 1517 Martin Luther nailed to the door of a Wittenberg church a list of 95 religious reforms that he believed needed implementing. Because of his stand, Luther became known as a "reformer," and his actions led to the huge changes in the Church which we call the Reformation.

Fugitive
Luther was declared an outlaw for his stand, and he fled into hiding at Wartburg Castle. There he began to translate the Bible into German; he wanted others to experience the joy he had found through reading it.

Luther believed that a good translation had to be made directly from the original language and that it should be in everyday speech. The complete "Luther Bible" was published in 1532, one of the first in the language of ordinary people. Even today Luther's translation remains the best-loved of German Bibles, and it helped shape the modern German language.

A Bible for plowboys
Although Wycliffe's Bible had been in English, it was handwritten and contained many mistakes of translation and copying. Even after the invention of printing, there was still no printed Bible that English people could read in their own language.

Leaders in church and state thought it dangerous for ordinary people to read the Bible for themselves and decide what to believe. So it was illegal to translate or print any part of the Bible. But the Englishman William Tyndale declared to a priest, "If God spare my life . . . I will cause the boy that drives the plow to know more of the Bible than you do."

Bible smugglers
William Tyndale (1494–1536) was the greatest English Bible translator. Exiled in Germany, he

William Tyndale

translated the New Testament from the original Greek. In 1526 printed copies were smuggled into England hidden in sacks of grain and crates of fish; King Henry VIII ordered them to be burned. Before Tyndale could finish translating the Old Testament, he was betrayed, ambushed, and burned at the stake in Belgium. As he died, he prayed, "Lord, open the King of England's eyes."

Martin Luther

Changing language for a changing world

For 300 years English-speaking Protestants read the King James Version of the Bible. Recently many new translations have come out. Why do we have new translations? One reason is that language changes over the years.

Today Bible society translators often retranslate the Bible into languages in which the Scriptures are already available. They are eager to ensure that the translation is as accurate as possible. For this reason, translation is usually done by native speakers, with advice from missionaries and trained linguists. A native speaker can help ensure that the translation sounds natural.

The language used in a Bible translation should not sound old-fashioned or be difficult to understand. A good Bible translation will accurately convey the words and meanings of the original authors, but it will also be as fresh and meaningful for today's readers as it was for the people who first read it in Greek 2,000 years ago.

The Bible must be as fresh today as it was for its original readers.

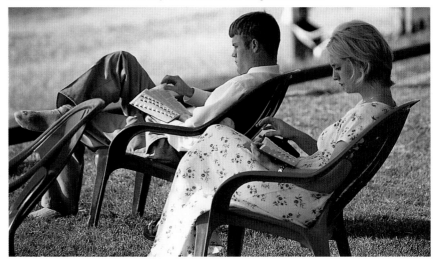

John 3:16 worldwide

English Standard Version
For God so loved the world, that he gave his only Son, that whoever believes in him should not perish but have eternal life.

Modern German
Gott liebte die Menschen so sehr, dass er seinen einzigen Sohn hergab. Nun wird jeder, der sich auf den Sohn Gottes verlässt, nicht zugrunde gehen, sondern ewig leben.

Malay
Karena demikianlah Allah mengashi isi doienia ini sewhingga dikaroeni-akannja Anaknja jang toenggal itoe, soepaja barang siapa jang partjaja akan Dia djangan binasa, melainkan beroléh hidoep jang kekal.

Modern French
Car Dieu a tellement aimé le monde qu'il a donné son Fils unique, afin que tout homme qui croit en lui ne meure pas mais qu'il ait la vie éternelle.

Modern Spanish
Pues Dios amó tanto al mundo, que dio a su Hijo único, para que todo aquel que cree en él, no perezca, sino que tenga vida eterna.

Tahitian
I aroha mai te Atua I to te ao, e ua tae roa I te horoa mai I ta 'na Tamaiti fanau tahi, ia ore ia pohe te faaroo ia 'na ra, roiaa ra te ora mure ore.

Setswana
Gonne Modimo o ratile lehatshe yalo, oa ba oa naea Morwa òna eo o tsecweñ a le esi, gore moñwe le moñwe eo o dumèlañ mo go èna a se ka a hèla, me a nè le botshelò yo bo sa khurleñ.

Aymara
Cunalaycutejja Diosaji uqhama acapacharu muni, jupa sapa jathata Yokaparu churi, take qhitití juparu iyausisqui ucajja, jan chhakhtasiñap-ataqui, ucatsipana wiñaya jacañaniñapataqui.

RULES FOR TRANSLATORS

When translating the Bible into another language:
- *Do not add anything*
- *Do not leave anything out*
- *Do not alter the meaning*
- *Find words that communicate to new readers the words and meaning of the original*

The History of Bible Times

The Bible and archaeology	26
How archaeologists work	28
The Bible and history	30
Lands of the Bible	32
Bible timeline	34
Israel today	42

The Bible and archaeology

Archaeological milestones

Probably the earliest recorded attempt at what might be called archaeological excavation was made in 1738 at Herculaneum in southern Italy. Herculaneum, like Pompeii, which was first excavated in 1748, was covered when Mount Vesuvius erupted in A.D. 79. The "excavations" consisted of tunnels into the hardened mud lava, allowing the excavators to remove treasures from the buried city. There was none of the systematic, scientific removal of layers of earth— carefully recorded, measured, drawn, and reported—that characterizes modern archaeological excavations.

The search for ancient treasure was extended to the Middle East in 1799 with the discovery, by a Napoleonic officer, of a stone with a trilingual inscription, the famous "Rosetta Stone," which, once deciphered, unlocked the language and history of ancient Egypt, written in previously undecipherable hieroglyphics on its buildings and tombs. Throughout the nineteenth century, entrepreneurs filled the museums of Europe with antiquities taken from the Middle East. Expeditions also went to Mesopotamia. Paul Botta ravaged Khorsabad, ten miles north of Nineveh, in 1842, and filled the Louvre in Paris with antiquities from the reign of Sargon II, an Assyrian monarch. From 1845, Sir Austen Layard filled the British Museum with treasures from Nineveh, from the reign of another Assyrian king, Ashurnasirpal II.

Reading the tablets

Between 1846 and 1855, Sir Henry Rawlinson deciphered the cuneiform script of the Old Persian language on the trilingual Behistun Rock, the "Rosetta Stone of the East." Soon the Elamite and Akkadian languages were also deciphered, and the history of Assyria and Babylonia was opened to the world, through the translation of stone inscriptions and clay tablets, approximately 500,000 of which have now been discovered.

Since Palestine itself, the land comprising present-day Jordan, Israel, and Syria seemed to be largely devoid of valuable artifacts, the first scholars there undertook geographical surveys and the identification of ancient sites. Palestinian excavation began in Jerusalem in 1850, but the early work was not scientific.

Homer's Troy

Heinrich Schliemann, the German excavator of Homer's Troy and Mycenae, first introduced scientific methodology into archaeology. At Troy, in 1870, Schliemann discovered that the distinctive mounds which dot the countryside of the Middle East are the accumulated layers of

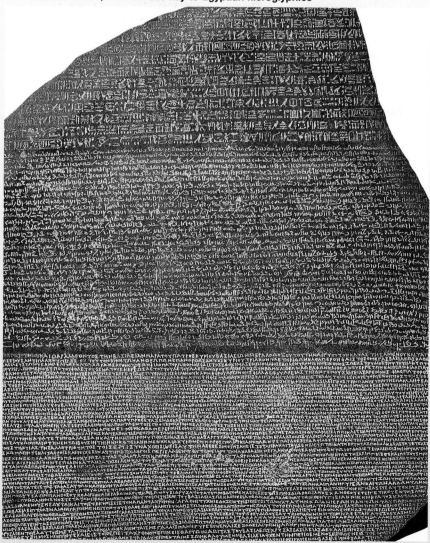

The "Rosetta Stone," the famous key to Egyptian hieroglyphics

Heinrich Schliemann (*top*) addresses a London meeting.

Sir Henry Lagard supervises the removal of a giant bull from Nineveh.

ancient cities, which have been destroyed and rebuilt time and again over the centuries. Beneath each mound (or *tell*, as they are called in Hebrew and Arabic) lay an ancient city or portion of a city. By cutting through these layers, as one might slice a cake, the history of the site could be uncovered from the most recent period of occupation (at the surface) to the earliest (at the bottom). Then 20 years later, the English Egyptologist Sir Flinders Petrie, working briefly at Tell Hesi in Palestine, observed that each layer in the tell contained its own unique type of ceramic pottery. By carefully recording the pottery in each layer, he observed changes in cultural occupation. He saw that some of the pottery had different forms, which he recognized from his work in Egypt, where he had found similar pottery in contexts that could be dated from inscriptions found at the levels in which the pottery was discovered. In this way originated "ceramic typology," the most important technique in modern Palestinian archaeology for dating stratigraphic levels that do not contain inscriptions or coins.

Pots and dates

Petrie's discovery was revolutionary. Since ancient people often made their own pottery, when they moved on they did not bother to take it with them because it was so inexpensive. Since pottery was virtually imperishable, every layer of a tell contains an abundance of potsherds. Once this was recognized, a chronology based on ceramic typology had to be established, so that more precise dates could be given to the changes in pottery styles, which could be distinguished as precisely as changes in car models today.

The man who recognized this was the preeminent Middle-Eastern archaeologist William Foxwell Albright. Working at Tell Beit Mirsim in southern Palestine from 1926–32, he excavated a well-stratified mound with enough pottery in each stratum to record scientifically the typological and chronological evolution of their major forms. His work remains the basis of all modern ceramic typology.

Some of the largest excavations in Palestine—for example, at Jerusalem, Samaria, Jericho, Tanaach, Megiddo, Gezer, Lachish, and Hazor—were carried out before this method of dating had matured. Most of these sites have been reexcavated since World War II by archaeologists using not only a highly refined pottery chronology but also modern scientific techniques.

Three legendary archaeologists

Three of the greatest archaeologists of the twentieth century are regarded as biblical archaeologists.

• W. F. Albright, of Johns Hopkins University, was perhaps the greatest archaeological mind in history. His work was often directed against radical German critics, who attacked the historical credibility of the Bible.

• Nelson Glueck, one of Albright's students, was an ordained rabbi, and he described how he used the Bible as a map when making his archaeological surveys.

• Another of Albright's students, Professor G. Ernest Wright, was one of the greatest authorities on archaeological methodology. He pointed out that the biblical archaeologist "must be . . . concerned with stratigraphy and typology, upon which the methodology of modern archaeology rests . . . yet his chief concern is not with methods or pots or weapons in themselves alone. His central and absorbing interest is the understanding and exposition of the Scriptures."

How archaeologists work

The methods of archaeology have come a long way since the tunnels into ancient Herculaneum, and much progress has been made since the early part of the twentieth century, when well-meaning but ill-equipped diggers attacked sites with spades and wheelbarrows, with the help of hundreds of hired laborers who were paid at the current market price for every artifact found.

A scientific approach
The techniques of excavation have evolved into what is now a highly scientific, carefully controlled, and very expensive operation. The cost, and the demand for ever greater accuracy, have helped transform excavation into an organization of highly specialized experts pooling their skills in an expedition resembling an outdoor scientific laboratory. There are five major tasks in modern archaeological expeditions: surveying, excavating, recording, interpreting, and publishing. First, every new site must be approached by surveying for miles around to discover as much as possible about the geographical and historical setting in which the site evolved.

The grid method
Following the survey of the surrounding area, the site chosen is plotted from above, on a grid divided into 15-foot squares. Each square will be numbered, and only a representative number of squares are dug—not the whole site. This allows later excavators to check and correct errors, if necessary, as archaeological methods continue to improve. Many sites have been "re-dug" in this way, including Gezer, Jericho, Hazor, and Lachish. The squares are dug in successive strata, peeling off one layer at a time, including any pits that penetrate into lower levels. This method is known as the Kenyon-Wheeler method (after the British archaeologists Dame Kathleen Kenyon and Sir Mortimer Wheeler) and provides the greatest possible control. The work is done under the eye of area supervisors, one to each square, who keep careful records of everything that happens in that square.

Any object or small area that needs to be identified separately and recorded by itself is known as a *locus*, which may be a mere change in the color of the soil, or something as large as a stone floor or wall. Each *locus* is given a number, and all data relevant to it will be recorded under that number.

Recording the dig
Top-plans are drawn, showing the square from a bird's-eye view as it appears at the end of each working day, and listing all the *loci* visible at that time. Dig photos are taken of important stages and are later used for publication. When the digging is finished, the baulk, or exposed wall of a square, is carefully drawn and becomes the guide to the analysis of the chronological history of the square.

By putting all the baulk drawings together, the archaeologist has the basis for analyzing the entire excavated site. Just as the number of layers in a cake can be determined by cutting a slice, so the history of a site exists in its stratigraphy. This is the single most important index to the site, and for this reason the baulks are kept trimmed and their *loci* identified by sticking tags with *locus* numbers onto their walls.

Nothing is more important than keeping careful records on a dig. By its nature, archaeology is systematic destruction, and nothing will ever be seen again exactly the way it was when it was dug. Thus photography,

Workers open a new square during a recent dig at Capernaum, Israel.

Archaeological methods

Excavated squares

Stepped trench

Successive occupation levels

Archaeologist's soundings

Tell or occupation mound

elevations, scale drawings, supervisors' observations, and impressions kept in diaries are essential elements in modern excavations.

Understanding the dig
All of this is necessary for the next step—interpretation. This is, of course, the ultimate purpose of any dig, and the most difficult part of the process. Normally, supervisors, volunteer diggers, and excavation directors interpret the data in the same way.

The "new archaeology"
Recent decades have seen the use of many advanced scientific techniques in field archaeology: ground and aerial photo-grammetry, magnetometers and resistivity instruments, laser-guided and computerized transits for shooting elevations and making surveys, infrared photography, neutron activation analysis of pottery, thin section and petrographic analysis of temper and clay, thermoluminescence, flotation

of pollen samples, and settlement pattern analysis. All these are part of the "new archaeology" and have helped transform excavation techniques.

It is now possible to date discoveries more accurately than years ago. In addition to noting the stratum in which an artifact or structure appears (the successively lower strata are progressively earlier, if the strata are scaled and undisturbed), we can now place that object in a related pottery chronology which dates the stratum for us.

Dates and coins
The discovery of coins is very important to dating, because coins carry names, and often dates, on them. Carbon 14 may be applied to organic matter, which, once a portion is burned, gives off radioactive carbon 14 at a rate which may be measured by a type of Geigercounter. Under ideal conditions, a dating accurate to +/-200 years may be obtained

from the amount of carbon detected. Potassium argon dating may be used for much older inorganic materials. For sites later than the Hellenistic period, a chronological typology for glass similar to that for ceramic pottery is being developed.

Interpreting the data
The interpretation of archaeological data is usually done by parallelism. This indispensable procedure requires knowledge of what has already been dug at sites elsewhere with similar timeframes. A particular find is compared to these parallel sites, which hopefully will have been adequately dated, and may thus increase confidence in the interpretation given to that object at the site in question. Caution must be used, or a fruitless cycle of circular reasoning and conjecture may result. Computers are increasingly being used to catalog finds, and they make the retrieval of otherwise unknown parallels rapid and effective.

The Bible and history

There are limits to the achievements of archaeology. Much has been achieved since Heinrich Schliemann dug at Troy, but archaeology remains an inexact science. The data extracted from an excavation can often be interpreted in a number of different ways and can be dated only within relative degrees of certainty. Absoluteness is rare. How old is man? How old is the earth? When did Abraham live? What was the date of the Exodus? Was the conquest of Canaan an invasion or just a social upheaval within the land itself? Neither biblical criticism nor archaeological excavation has been able to answer these and other issues conclusively.

At times archaeology and biblical scholarship seem to work against each other. Part of the problem lies in a failure adequately to understand the biblical text, and part in a misunderstanding of the archaeological evidence. Some sites may be wrongly identified, while others may be inadequately dug or erroneously evaluated. Archaeology can often help us understand something more clearly, but it rarely injects certainty into biblical uncertainties. To claim too much for it is to misunderstand its contribution.

The acts of God
The Bible is a collection of many books written over hundreds of years. Its authors' primary purpose was not to write history in the modern sense; their purpose was to faithfully record the words and actions of God in Jewish history.

Archaeology's main contribution to the study of the Bible is as an important means of clarifying and dramatizing the history in which the biblical faith originated.

The Bible was not written in a vacuum, nor did the events it records take place in a vacuum. The Jews interacted with the ancient cultures with which they came into contact; the Bible records those interactions, both good and bad. Biblical archaeology penetrates and clarifies that area of ancient history which gave birth to the Bible.

What do these stones mean?
What is the value of archaeological discoveries to the reader of the Bible? Archaeology's major contribution is not apologetic. Certainly, some difficulties are clarified by the results of archaeological work. For instance, stone inscriptions were found in Thessaloniki, Greece, containing

Sennacherib's prism records events of his reign.

Herodion, site of Herod the Great's stronghold and palace

Part of the extensive excavations at Masada, near the Dead Sea in Israel

the term *politarch*, a term which Luke used in Acts 17:6 in referring to Roman authorities, but which critics of the Bible had rejected as erroneous because no record of such a term existed prior to the discovery. On the other hand, attempts to find Joshua's Jericho or Solomon's Jerusalem have been largely disappointing.

Exciting discoveries
Nevertheless, many exciting discoveries have been made that illustrate the Bible beautifully: the Clay Prism of Sennacherib, mentioning the Judean king Hezekiah; the Black Obelisk of Shalmanezer portraying Jehu, the Jewish king, bowing before him; the Babylonian Chronicle, providing the basis for dating the destruction of the Temple in Jerusalem in 587 B.C.; the Cyrus Cylinder, showing the Persian monarch's policy of assisting nations like the Jews to return and rebuild their cities and temples; the inscription in the pavement of the theater courtyard in Corinth containing the name of Erastus, the city treasurer, who is probably mentioned in Romans 16:23; the winter palace of Herod

the Great in Jericho, and the site where he was buried in Herodium.

The value of archaeology
The great value of archaeology to the student of the Bible lies in its ability to place our biblical faith in its historical setting, and to demonstrate the cultural setting in which biblical events took place. For those who love the Bible, there is no experience like standing on the Mount of Olives in Jerusalem and looking out over the results of archaeological excavation in the Holy City: here is part of Nehemiah's rebuilt walls; there are the steps that led up to the Temple during the days of Jesus; here is Hezekiah's tunnel, leading to the Pool of Siloam, where Jesus made the blind man see; there are the beautiful stones on the pinnacle of the Temple which the disciples pointed out to Jesus. And what a thrill to walk through the remains of the chariot city of Solomon and Ahab at Megiddo; to linger among the ruins of Caesarea Maritima, Herod the Great's magnificent city on the Mediterranean; and to stroll among the pools built by the

Essenes at Qumran, where the Dead Sea Scrolls were found. The aqueducts of Caesarea, the bathhouses of Masada and Jericho, the synagogues of Galilee, the water tunnels of Megiddo, Hazor, Gezer, and Jerusalem, the fortifications of Lachish, the altars of Beersheba and Mount Ebal, the *fora* and temples of Samaria and Jerash, the theaters of Amman and Ephesus, all create an indelible impression of the civilization that once inhabited these ruins. We are hence able to reconstruct in our minds these cities as they existed in the time of Abraham, Solomon, Jesus, and Paul.

A historical context
The story of Jesus does not begin, "Once upon a time in a faraway land . . . ," but rather, "After Jesus was born in Bethlehem in Judea, in the days of Herod the king . . ." (Matthew 2:1). What a thrill it is to traverse the hills of Judea and walk the streets of Bethlehem, to wander through Nazareth and take a boat ride on the Sea of Galilee and walk the streets of Jerusalem's Old City. How exciting to watch each turn of the archaeologist's spade, knowing that it was here, in these very places, here in historical and geographical reality, that the most precious heritage of human history was bequeathed to humankind. This is the value of biblical archaeology—its ability to locate the faith in the realities of ancient history.

Economy of the Ancient Near East

Copper

Salt

Copper

Copper (Tabriz)

Iron

Tarsus

Haran

Carchemish

Nineveh

Iron

ELISHAH

Ugarit

Ivory

Timber

Papyrus

Nuzi

Ivory

Copper

Copper Dyes, Coin minting

Euphrates

Tigris

Mari

GREAT SEA

Iron

Tyre

Damascus

Timber

Hazor

Papyrus

Babylon

Susa

Iron

Gaza

Salt

Metalwork

Copper

Iron

Noph (Memphis)

Elath

LOWER SEA

Ur

Nile

Akhetaton (El-Amarna)

Turquoise, Copper

RED SEA

Thebes

Ivory, Gold

Perfume

Sheep farming

Horse breeding

Camel breeding

Fishing

Textile production

Grain production (wheat, barley)

Fruit growing (dates, figs, olives)

BLAC

TUR

TAURUS MOUNTAINS

CYPRUS

Mt. Lebanon △

LEBANON

ISRAEL

Jordan

DEAD SEA

JORDAN

GREAT SEA (MEDITERRANEAN SEA)

Lands of the Bible

Palestine was situated at the crossroads of the ancient world and has been fought over countless times across the centuries. It lies at the western end of the Fertile Crescent, the great arc of low-lying, well-watered, cultivable land stretching from the Persian Gulf to the Nile Delta. Mesopotamia, "the land between the rivers," makes up a large part of the Crescent and was one of the cradles of civilization.

E G Y P T

Nile

LOWER SEA (THE GULF)

RED SEA

CASPIAN SEA

SEA

Mt. Ararat △

K E Y

S Y R I A

M E S O P O T A M I A

Tigris

Euphrates

I R A N

Z A G R O S   M O U N T A I N S

I R A Q

S A U D I   A R A B I A

KUWAIT

PERSIAN GULF

0	250	500 km
0	100	200	300 miles

Fertile land
Desert
IRAQ Modern state

Bible timeline

Abraham, the first of Israel's patriarchs, receives God's call to leave his home in Ur, Mesopotamia, and go in search of a new home. This will be Israel, the land promised by God for the Israelites. Abraham is further called by God to sacrifice his son

1950–1550 Middle Bronze Age

Beginning of Egyptian Middle Kingdom—second great age of Egypt **2134**

Great pyramids built in Egypt **c.2685**

■ Wooden ships developed in Crete **c.2000**

■ Settlement of Melanesia by immigrants from Indonesia **c.2000**

■ Stonehenge started in Britain **c.2000**

■ Hittite Empire founded **c.2000**

Code of Hammurabi—first written set of laws

ISRAEL / THE JEWS

The patriarchs

Jacob **1800–1700** ●

■ Abram leaves Ur **c.1925**

● Isaac **1900–1720**

Note on dating:
Insufficient historical sources mean that sometimes dates of events and lives of figures cannot be corroborated. In these instances dating must be conjectural.

Dates of national leaders refer to their reigns, and single dates of individuals refer to their births.

Key

■ Significant events

♜ Hebrew/Jewish kings

♜ All other colors—non-Hebrew rulers/kings

● Hebrew/Jewish people other than rulers

● Non-Hebrew people other than rulers

✦ Battles/points of conflict

2100 B.C.

2000

1900

1800

34

Isaac as a test of his loyalty to God. Jacob, grandson of Abraham, fathers twelve children, who become the ancestors of the tribes that settle in Canaan and form the new nation of Israel. Joseph, one of Jacob's sons, is sold into slavery and taken to Egypt. He rises to power and becomes a high official under Pharaoh. Joseph's brothers come to Egypt at a time of famine in the Middle East and the family of Jacob is reunited. The community of Israelites lives near the Nile Delta. They become slaves of the Egyptian Pharaoh and build the store city of Rameses. The Israelites live in Egypt for some 400 years.

Shang ideograms from China. Clockwise from top left: city– a man kneeling in submission beneath an earthen enclosure; city wall; chariot.

Hyksos rule in Egypt *c.*1640–1570 ■

First urban civilization in China *c.*1600 ■

merian epic of gamesh **?**

Palace at Knossos destroyed and rebuilt **1720**

New Kingdom begins in Egypt —Egypt's greatest era **1552** ■

Development of Brahma worship *c.*1450 ■

Ideographic script in use in China *c.*1500 ■

Greek language written down for the first time *c.*1450 ■

Israel in Egypt *c.*1700–1280

Joseph **1750–1640**

1700

1600

1500

Moses champions the cause of freedom and leads the Exodus of Israelites from Egypt by crossing the sea. They begin a 40-year period in the wilderness, during which they receive a God-given law code, which includes the Ten Commandments, at Mount Sinai.

Joshua succeeds Moses and leads the Israelites across the River Jordan into Canaan. Military leaders, known as judges, fight campaigns against neighboring enemies such as the Canaanites, Midianites, and Israel's greatest foe, the Philistines, whom Samson challenges. Eli and then Samuel preside over the priesthood at Shiloh, but Israel lacks military leadership and looks for a king, who is found in the person of Saul. But it is David who unites the Israelites to defeat the Philistines. He captures Jerusalem and makes it the new state capital and national center of worship, lasting over 400 years. The Temple at Jerusalem is built by David's successor Solomon, who expands David's empire to its greatest extent. Unrest between the north and south of Israel results in civil

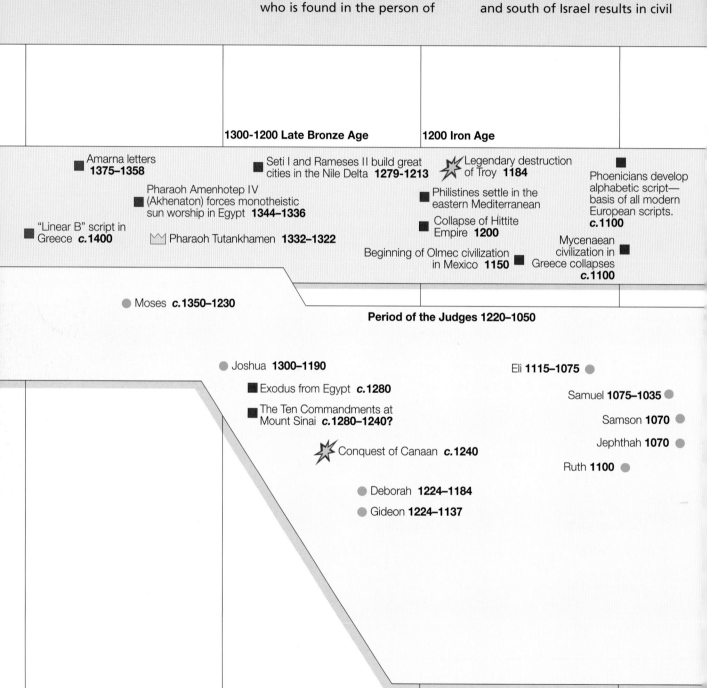

1300-1200 Late Bronze Age

1200 Iron Age

Amarna letters **1375–1358**

Seti I and Rameses II build great cities in the Nile Delta **1279-1213**

Legendary destruction of Troy **1184**

Phoenicians develop alphabetic script—basis of all modern European scripts. **c.1100**

Pharaoh Amenhotep IV (Akhenaton) forces monotheistic sun worship in Egypt **1344–1336**

Philistines settle in the eastern Mediterranean

Collapse of Hittite Empire **1200**

"Linear B" script in Greece **c.1400**

Pharaoh Tutankhamen **1332–1322**

Beginning of Olmec civilization in Mexico **1150**

Mycenaean civilization in Greece collapses **c.1100**

Moses **c.1350–1230**

Period of the Judges 1220–1050

Joshua **1300–1190**

Eli **1115–1075**

Exodus from Egypt **c.1280**

Samuel **1075–1035**

The Ten Commandments at Mount Sinai **c.1280–1240?**

Samson **1070**

Jephthah **1070**

Conquest of Canaan **c.1240**

Ruth **1100**

Deborah **1224–1184**

Gideon **1224–1137**

1400

1300

1200

1100

war and the division of the land into two kingdoms: Israel (north) and Judah (south). Jerusalem remains the capital of Judah, and Samaria emerges as the northern capital.

Elijah typifies Israel's prophets in their crusade against idolatry, especially the worship of the Canaanite god Baal. Amos and Hosea condemn Israel's social injustice and religious complacency, and they foretell political disaster. This is fulfilled in the invasion by the Assyrians, who capture Samaria and take many Israelites into exile. The smaller state of Judah also becomes subject to the Assyrian king, Sennacherib. Hezekiah of Judah tries to rebel but loses half his kingdom. The prophet Isaiah comforts the Judeans during this time.

With the waning of Assyrian power Josiah instigates religious reform in Judah. First the Egyptians then the Babylonians emerge as major powers in the Middle East. Under Nebuchadnezzar Babylon besieges Jerusalem and in 587 destroys the city and Temple.

Phoenician characters representing an ox (left) and a bow.

K W

Etruscans arrive in Italy **c.1000**

Phoenicians found Carthage **814**

Golden age of Tyre (Phoenicia) **c.900**

Indo-Aryans reach Ganges Valley and start to lay basis of urban civilization **c.800**

Homer composes *Iliad* and *Odyssey* **c.750**

Damascus falls to Assyria **732**

Legendary founding of Rome **753**

Kingdom of Kush (Nubia) founded **c.900**

Tiglath-Pileser III expands Assyrian Empire **744**

First Olympic Games **776**

United kingdom of Israel and Judah 1050–930

Kingdom of Israel 930–722

Samaria—capital of Israel **c.879**

Jehoahaz **813–798**

Jehoash **798–781**

Jeroboam II **781–753**

Hosea **755–732**

Pekah **740–732**

Hoshea **731–722**

Amos **760**

Assyria Ascendant

Jeroboam I **930–910**

Nadab **910**

Ahab **874–853**

Jonah **760**

Fall of Samaria **722**

Baasha **908**

Elijah **c.870–850**

Zechariah **753–752**

Sargon II **722–705**

Elah **886**

Ahaziah **853–852**

Shallum **752**

Zimri **885**

Joram **852–841**

Menahem **752–742**

Philistines destroy Shiloh **1050**

Tibni **885–880**

Elisha **c.850–790**

Pekahiah **742–740**

Omri **885–874**

Jehu **841–813**

The kingdom divides 930

Saul **1050–1011**

Kingdom of Judah 930–587

David **1011–970**

Rehoboam **931–913**

Joel **c.810–750**

Amaziah **796–767**

Uzziah (Azariah) **767–740**

Solomon **970–930**

Pharaoh Shishak (Sheshonq) invades Palestine **925**

Micah **742–687**

Isaiah **742–700**

Building of the Jerusalem Temple **966–959**

Abijah **913–911**

Asa **911–870**

Jotham **740–732**

Ahaz **732–716**

Hezekiah **716–687**

Jehoshaphat **870–848**

Jehoram **848–841**

Ahaziah **841**

Athaliah **841–835**

Joash **835–796**

Assyria besieges Jerusalem **c.704**

1000

900

800

700

37

A major part of the Judean population is deported to Babylon. The prophet Ezekiel comforts the Israelites in exile. The more tolerant Persians eclipse the Babylonians as the major Middle-Eastern power, and under Cyrus allow the Israelites to return home. The first group, under Sheshbazzar, and the second group, under Zerubbabel and Joshua, begin the rebuilding of the Temple.

Nehemiah is later appointed governor of Judea and oversees the rebuilding of Jerusalem's walls. The priest Ezra reinstitutes the Law, giving the people a new religious identity as Jews. Jews in the diaspora (dispersion) could worship in synagogues; observance of the Law (now known as the Torah), not Temple sacrifice, becomes the mainstay of Judaism. The Old Testament period ends with Ezra and Nehemiah.

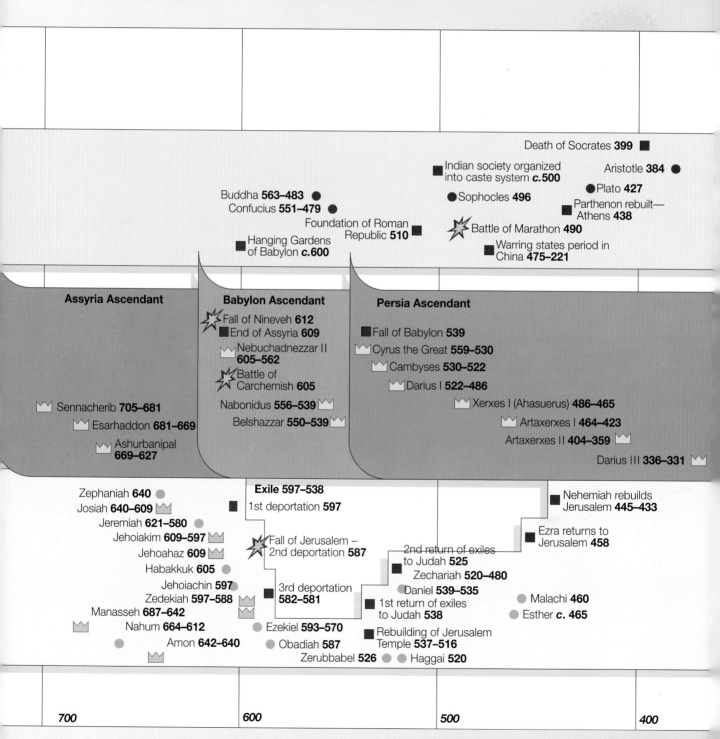

Death of Socrates **399**

Indian society organized into caste system **c.500**

Aristotle **384**

Plato **427**

Buddha **563–483**
Confucius **551–479**

Sophocles **496**

Parthenon rebuilt— Athens **438**

Foundation of Roman Republic **510**

Battle of Marathon **490**

Hanging Gardens of Babylon **c.600**

Warring states period in China **475–221**

Assyria Ascendant

Babylon Ascendant

Fall of Nineveh **612**
End of Assyria **609**
Nebuchadnezzar II **605–562**
Battle of Carchemish **605**
Nabonidus **556–539**
Belshazzar **550–539**

Persia Ascendant

Fall of Babylon **539**
Cyrus the Great **559–530**
Cambyses **530–522**
Darius I **522–486**
Xerxes I (Ahasuerus) **486–465**
Artaxerxes I **464–423**
Artaxerxes II **404–359**
Darius III **336–331**

Sennacherib **705–681**
Esarhaddon **681–669**
Ashurbanipal **669–627**

Zephaniah **640**
Josiah **640–609**
Jeremiah **621–580**
Jehoiakim **609–597**
Jehoahaz **609**
Habakkuk **605**
Jehoiachin **597**
Zedekiah **597–588**
Manasseh **687–642**
Nahum **664–612**
Amon **642–640**

Exile 597–538
1st deportation **597**

Fall of Jerusalem – 2nd deportation **587**

3rd deportation **582–581**

Ezekiel **593–570**
Obadiah **587**
Zerubbabel **526**

2nd return of exiles to Judah **525**
Zechariah **520–480**
Daniel **539–535**
1st return of exiles to Judah **538**
Rebuilding of Jerusalem Temple **537–516**
Haggai **520**

Nehemiah rebuilds Jerusalem **445–433**
Ezra returns to Jerusalem **458**
Malachi **460**
Esther **c. 465**

700

600

500

400

The Maccabees overthrow Seleucid power, and the Jews achieve independence under the Hasmoneans. Apocalyptic literature predicts God's final dramatic entry into human history. The idea is developed of the coming of a messiah, who will liberate the Jews from their oppressors. The Essenes believe the Jews need spiritual reformation to be saved.

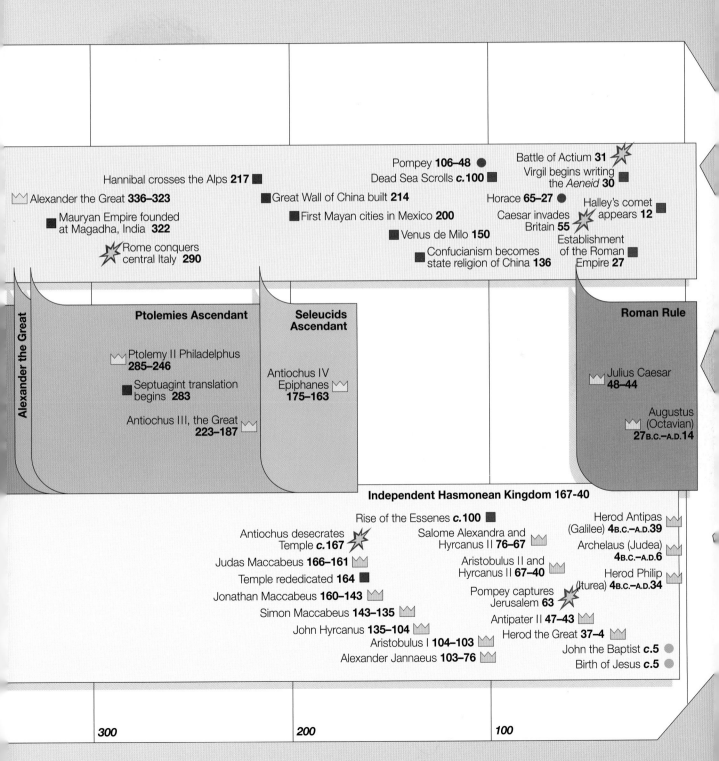

Pompey **106–48** ●
Dead Sea Scrolls *c.***100** ■
Battle of Actium **31**
Virgil begins writing the *Aeneid* **30** ■
Hannibal crosses the Alps **217** ■
Great Wall of China built **214**
Horace **65–27** ●
Halley's comet appears **12** ■
Alexander the Great **336–323**
First Mayan cities in Mexico **200**
Caesar invades Britain **55**
Mauryan Empire founded at Magadha, India **322**
Venus de Milo **150**
Establishment of the Roman Empire **27** ■
Rome conquers central Italy **290**
Confucianism becomes state religion of China **136**

Alexander the Great

Ptolemies Ascendant

Seleucids Ascendant

Roman Rule

Ptolemy II Philadelphus **285–246**
Antiochus IV Epiphanes **175–163**
Julius Caesar **48–44**
Septuagint translation begins **283**
Antiochus III, the Great **223–187**
Augustus (Octavian) **27 B.C.–A.D.14**

Independent Hasmonean Kingdom 167–40

Rise of the Essenes *c.***100** ■
Herod Antipas (Galilee) **4 B.C.–A.D.39**
Antiochus desecrates Temple *c.***167**
Salome Alexandra and Hyrcanus II **76–67**
Archelaus (Judea) **4 B.C.–A.D.6**
Judas Maccabeus **166–161**
Aristobulus II and Hyrcanus II **67–40**
Herod Philip (Iturea) **4 B.C.–A.D.34**
Temple rededicated **164** ■
Jonathan Maccabeus **160–143**
Pompey captures Jerusalem **63**
Simon Maccabeus **143–135**
Antipater II **47–43**
John Hyrcanus **135–104**
Herod the Great **37–4**
Aristobulus I **104–103**
John the Baptist *c.***5** ●
Alexander Jannaeus **103–76**
Birth of Jesus *c.***5** ●

300   *200*   *100*

At the time of Jesus' birth, the Romans control Palestine. John the Baptist heralds the Messiah whom many Jews, especially the Zealot party, think of as a successor to King David who will overthrow the Romans. Jesus' ministry of teaching and healing in Galilee challenges the Jewish

authorities. In time he is seen as a serious political threat, which results in a conspiracy to have him put to death. Jesus is crucified at the festival of Passover and rises from the dead three days later. His gospel is preached by the apostles, whose mission is given divine sanction at the Feast of Pentecost.

A leading Pharisee and Roman citizen named Saul (Paul) receives a blinding vision of the risen Christ while on the road to Damascus. He is converted to Christianity and leads the mission to the Gentiles, undertaking at least three journeys to Greece and Asia Minor. His letters form the basis of

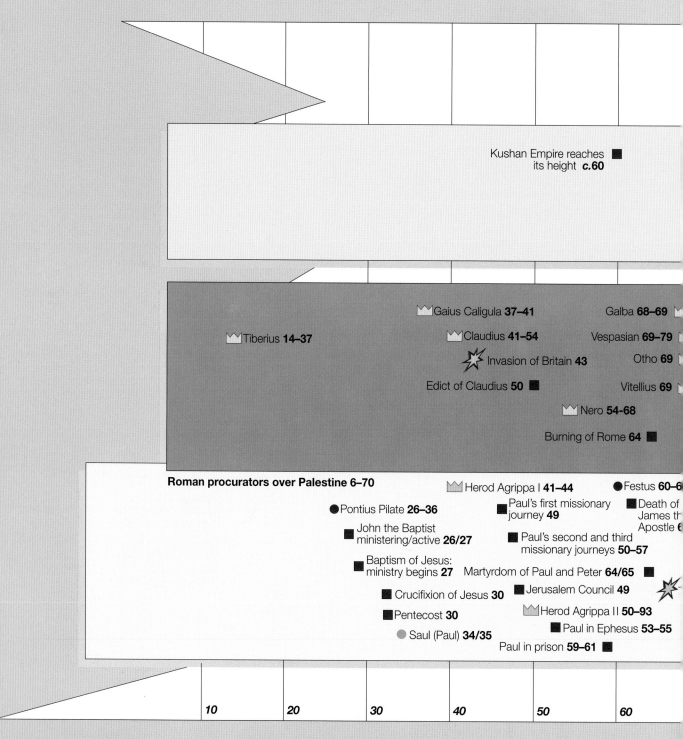

Kushan Empire reaches its height **c.60**

Gaius Caligula **37–41**   Galba **68–69**

Tiberius **14–37**   Claudius **41–54**   Vespasian **69–79**

Invasion of Britain **43**   Otho **69**

Edict of Claudius **50**   Vitellius **69**

Nero **54-68**

Burning of Rome **64**

Roman procurators over Palestine 6–70

Herod Agrippa I **41–44**   Festus **60–6**

Pontius Pilate **26–36**   Paul's first missionary journey **49**   Death of James th Apostle **6**

John the Baptist ministering/active **26/27**   Paul's second and third missionary journeys **50–57**

Baptism of Jesus: ministry begins **27**   Martyrdom of Paul and Peter **64/65**

Crucifixion of Jesus **30**   Jerusalem Council **49**

Pentecost **30**   Herod Agrippa II **50–93**

Saul (Paul) **34/35**   Paul in Ephesus **53–55**

Paul in prison **59–61**

| 10 | 20 | 30 | 40 | 50 | 60 |

early Christian doctrine. Peter leads the mission to the Jews, and James is the head of the Jerusalem church. All three are martyred, and persecution of Christians increases to the end of the century. Jewish revolts against Rome result in the destruction of Jerusalem and the Temple and the mass suicide of Jews at Masada. Many Jews and Christians flee from Palestine.

John, the beloved disciple, is banished to the island of Patmos where he writes the book of Revelation, addressed to seven churches of Asia Minor.

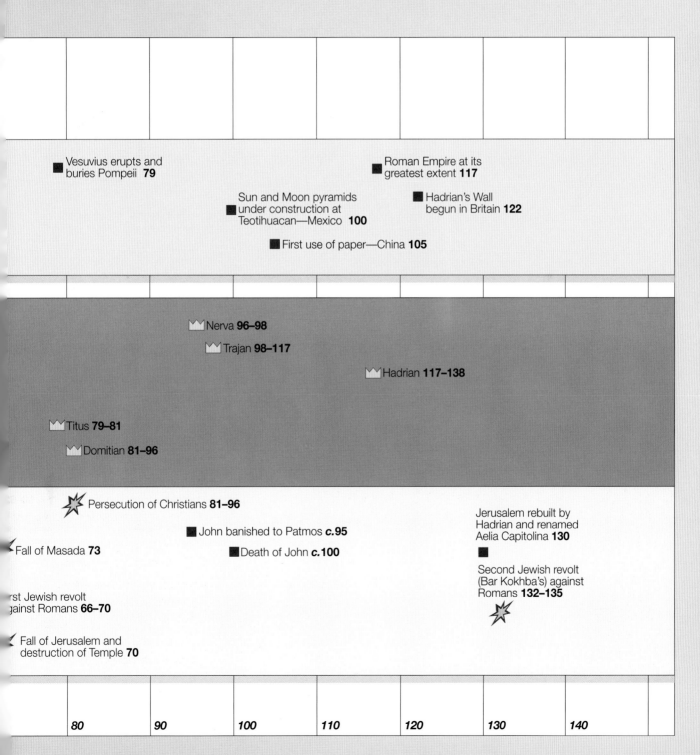

Vesuvius erupts and buries Pompeii **79**

Sun and Moon pyramids under construction at Teotihuacan—Mexico **100**

First use of paper—China **105**

Roman Empire at its greatest extent **117**

Hadrian's Wall begun in Britain **122**

Nerva **96–98**

Trajan **98–117**

Hadrian **117–138**

Titus **79–81**

Domitian **81–96**

Persecution of Christians **81–96**

Fall of Masada **73**

John banished to Patmos *c.***95**

Death of John *c.***100**

Jerusalem rebuilt by Hadrian and renamed Aelia Capitolina **130**

First Jewish revolt against Romans **66–70**

Second Jewish revolt (Bar Kokhba's) against Romans **132–135**

Fall of Jerusalem and destruction of Temple **70**

80   *90*   *100*   *110*   *120*   *130*   *140*

The modern State of Israel

Boundaries as in 1994

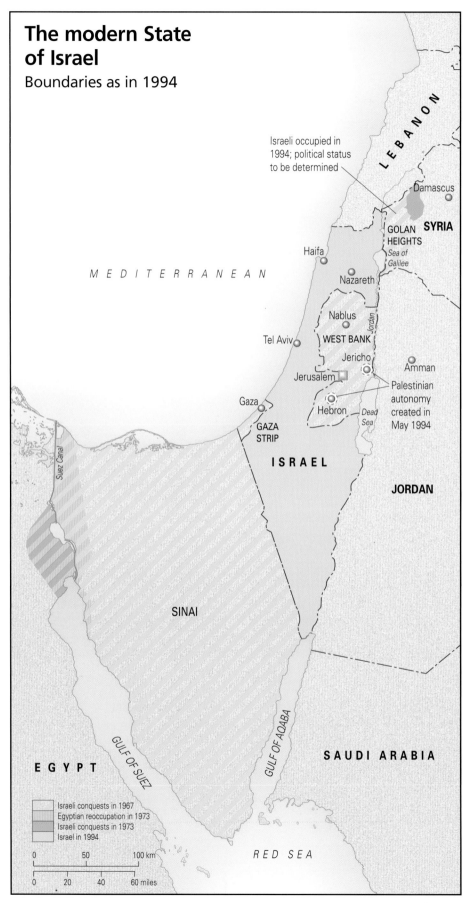

Israeli occupied in 1994; political status to be determined

LEBANON

Damascus

GOLAN HEIGHTS

SYRIA

Sea of Galilee

Haifa

MEDITERRANEAN

Nazareth

Nablus

Jordan

Tel Aviv

WEST BANK

Jericho

Amman

Jerusalem

Palestinian autonomy created in May 1994

Gaza

Hebron

Dead Sea

GAZA STRIP

ISRAEL

JORDAN

SINAI

GULF OF AQABA

Suez Canal

SAUDI ARABIA

GULF OF SUEZ

EGYPT

Israeli conquests in 1967
Egyptian reoccupation in 1973
Israeli conquests in 1973
Israel in 1994

RED SEA

0	50	100 km
0	20	40	60 miles

Tel Aviv, Israel, viewed from the ancient town of Jaffa (Joppa)

Israel today

With the rise of Zionism in the late nineteenth century, many Jewish immigrants came to Palestine from Europe. After the British conquered Palestine during World War I, the League of Nations mandated them to administer the country. The British Balfour Declaration promised a Jewish national homeland in Palestine. However, the aspirations of the Jews and the rise of Arab nationalism led to violent clashes between the Jewish and the Arab populations.

Independence
In 1947, with the British about to leave Palestine, the Arabs attacked the Jews. Israel's War of Independence (1948–49) broke out, ending in the proclamation of the State of Israel. In 1967 the Six-Day War finally brought the whole of Jerusalem into Israeli hands, together with the West Bank territories, which have been in dispute ever since.

Introducing the Old Testament

What is the Old Testament?	44
Old Testament time chart	45
Creation and covenant	46
A chosen family	48
A new nation	50
Into the Promised Land	53
The Judges	55
Kings to lead	56
The kingdom of Saul	58
The united kingdom	59
Solomon's united kingdom	60
The two kingdoms	61
Exile and return	64
Four great empires	66
The methods of the prophets	68
The message of the prophets	71
Poetry and wisdom	72
Between the Testaments	74

What is the Old Testament?

The Old Testament is a history of the nation of Israel. It tells the story of how this particular people was chosen by God, how they constantly rebelled against him, and how they were rescued by him. It describes God's love for them, his patience with them, and his judgment upon them.

The Old Testament is also a library, a collection of 39 different books. It brings together the inspired writings of many different people using many different styles. It includes family stories—detailed accounts of births, marriages, and deaths—and national history—victories, defeats, and tales of good and bad kings. It also includes poetry, law, sermons, and dramas, as well as prophets' predictions, warnings, and encouragement.

The Old Testament is also the handbook for Israel's religion. It gives instructions for Israel's religious rites and celebrations and sets out patterns of behavior. It explains how to worship and describes what religious buildings should be like; it explains how religious taxes are to be paid and what gifts should be offered.

The Old Testament is also a collection of teachings about God. It describes what it means to belong to God—to be his people—and explains who God is and what he does. It shows how God can be worshiped and tells why he deserves worship.

The Old Testament is also communication. It is presented as God's own word to his people—dynamic, and potentially life-changing.

For many people the Old Testament is a closed book. The

An artist's impression of the assault on Lachish by Assyria

following pages give an outline of Old Testament history, a description of Old Testament literature, a summary of the main elements of Old Testament religion, and an account of some Old Testament teachings. An attempt has been made to provide a context in which the Old Testament can be better understood and appreciated.

The Old Testament was never intended to be a closed book; it is hoped you will be encouraged to open it.

An eastern shepherd rests his flock in the shade of a tree.

Old Testament time chart

Abraham
Abraham set out from Mesopotamia on his great journey to the Promised Land.
God promised that through him all peoples would be blessed (Genesis 12:1–25:11). He was given a son, Isaac, in his old age (Genesis 21:1-7; 24:1–28:9).

Jacob
Isaac's son Jacob was forced by famine to go down to Egypt; his people settled there, and, years later, were forced into slavery (Genesis 25:19–35:29; 43:1–50:14).

Moses
Moses led the Hebrew people, Abraham's descendants, out of Egypt (Exodus 1:1–12:51). In the wilderness they were given the Ten Commandments. Eventually, after the death of Moses, the Israelites entered the Promised Land and occupied it (Joshua 1:1–12:24).

Abram leaves Ur

Joseph's family settles in Egypt

Isaac

Jacob and his 12 sons

2000 (B.C.)
1900
1800
1700
1600

Joseph taken to Egypt

1500

Israelites slaves in Egypt

1400

The Exodus

Moses given the Ten Commandments

1300

The Israelites occupy the Promised Land

1200

Temple built

1100

King David

The kingdom divides (981 B.C.)

1000

King Rehoboam

King Jeroboam

900

JUDAH (Southern Kingdom)

ISRAEL (Northern Kingdom)

800

Prophet Daniel in exile

King Hezekiah (716 B.C.)

Samaria destroyed (722 B.C.)

Israel taken captive to Assyria

700

Judah taken captive to Babylon (597, 587 B.C.)

600

Prophet Jeremiah

Second Temple built

500

400

Exile in Babylon

Ezra and Nehemiah return to Jerusalem (458, 445 B.C.)

Walls of Jerusalem repaired

300

Temple desecrated by Antiochus (167 B.C.)

200

Judas Maccabeus, "The Hammer," liberates Jews

100

Herod's Temple started (19 B.C.)

Jesus of Nazareth born

Judges and kings
As the nation of Israel developed, they were led first by judges (Judges 2:16–16:31; 1 Samuel 1:1–8:22) and then by a succession of kings (1 Samuel 9:1–31:13; 2 Samuel 1:1–24:23; 1 Kings 1:1–11:43). After the death of Solomon, the kingdom divided into Israel and Judah (1 Kings 12:1–22:53; 2 Kings 1:1–25:30).

Captivity
When the Assyrian Empire rose to power, Israel was threatened with invasion. Despite God's warnings to his people through the prophets, the northern kingdom (Israel) was taken into captivity by Assyria in 722 B.C., and the southern kingdom (Judah) by Babylon in 587 B.C. (2 Kings 17:1-23; 25:1-30).

Return
The Jews only returned from exile to Palestine by stages, to set about reclaiming their land and rebuilding Jerusalem and the Temple (Ezra 1:1–6:22; Nehemiah 1:1–7:73a). Many of the Jews did not make this journey back to Palestine.

Creation and covenant

Creation

Genesis 1–3, Psalms, Isaiah 40–55, and Job 38–42

It is taken for granted in the Old Testament that God exists—and that he created the world. Most of the writers' earliest thinking about God relates to the Exodus from Egypt or to the covenant. Yet God's creative activity is a vital part of Old Testament teaching.

Two creation stories
There are two creation stories in Genesis 1–2, focusing in different but complementary ways on God's creative activity.

Genesis 1 is a structured account of creation, which is totally God-centered. God sees, creates, speaks, divides, calls, blesses, and makes. We learn that the world is ordered and purposeful; it is made the way that God intended—"God saw that it was good." The climax of this creation is humanity; human beings are created to relate to God and to each other, and to take responsibility for their own actions and the world around them.

God's work in creation is presented in Genesis 1 as finished, yet also continuing. God is the Lord of nature, who rules and maintains creation. He is not merely the initiator of life, but the one who sustains life, enabling the created world and the life it contains to continue.

The Garden of Eden
The Genesis 2 account brings human beings into the spotlight.

It does not recount the creation of the world, but the story of what happened in a garden in one part of God's creation. But the central teaching of both accounts is the same: the world is created by God and belongs to God; human beings relate to God and are responsible to God.

God the Creator
Outside Genesis, when creation and God the Creator are mentioned, the focus of thought usually includes:
• The intricacy and complexity of the creation
• The order and structure of creation
• The beauty and power of creation
• The purpose of creation: it involves God's will
• The uniqueness of the Creator
• The power and sovereignty of the Creator

The consequences of creation
The Old Testament teaching about creation brings meaning to a world of meaninglessness. All life belongs to God; he has the right to make demands on human beings. They are accountable to him and owe him awe and worship as their Creator. God, as the everlasting Creator, also has an ongoing responsibility to his creatures. He knows, understands, comforts, strengthens, and enables his creation. He created the world and subdued chaos, and was also willing to subdue chaos in the lives of his people.

Problems in the world
Yet the Old Testament writers are also aware of the problems in the world. Creation as it exists today is not beautiful in every aspect; alongside its beauty is an ugliness that is not solely the result of human mismanagement. The story of the Fall (Genesis 3) is the first of many reflections on how it is possible to comprehend both the glory and the dreadfulness of the created world as it is.

A flood account on tablet XI of the Assyrian version of the Epic of Gilgamesh. In Genesis God committed himself never again to use a flood to destroy the earth.

Covenant

Genesis 12–25, Exodus, Deuteronomy, 2 Samuel 7, and Jeremiah 31

God created the whole world, but he set up a covenant relationship solely with Israel. Covenants, or treaties—common within the Ancient Near East—were a kind of contract formalizing an alliance between partners. They were not necessarily equal partnerships but called for commitment and responsibility from both sides. The Old Testament develops this concept when it speaks of the relationship between God and his people as a covenant. Covenant is a very significant element of Old Testament teaching.

Contemporary treaties
The covenant between God and Israel is similar to contemporary treaties between imperial powers and vassal states. These so-called "suzerainty" treaties followed a common pattern: they set out the history of the agreement, laid

down rules the vassal must keep, formulated arrangements to keep the covenant document safe and to give periodic public readings, explained the benefits or protection that would be provided, and described the punishment for breaking the rules.

"I will be your God . . ."
In Israel, the covenant is established by God alone; he sets the terms. It is seen as a relationship between God and Israel. The so-called covenant formula "You/they will be my people, and I will be your/their God" is repeated in different forms many times, and it lies at the heart of Israel's understanding of her life and faith.

However, the covenant was not forced upon Israel without her consent. She had the freedom to accept and confirm the relationship. The obligations of the covenant were not arbitrary; they summarized what it meant to be holy and explained how Israel should behave if she were

to enter this relationship with a holy God.

Judgment
If human responsibility is taken seriously, judgment and punishment also become involved, guaranteeing the covenant, and opening up the possibility of repentance, forgiveness, and restoration.

However, the setting aside of the covenant also remains a possibility. The commitment that God makes is unbreakable; yet the covenant ends the moment its obligations are broken. It is clear that, with Israel's constant disobedience and disloyalty, it was only God's grace and mercy that allowed the covenant to continue.

Five covenants are mentioned in the Old Testament
1. *The Noahic covenant*, made between God and the whole creation. This was unconditional, with no human obligations; God committed himself never again to use a flood to destroy the earth.
2. *The Abrahamic covenant*, in which God made promises to Abraham and his family. The obligations on Abraham and his family are not spelled out in detail, but they were called upon to remain in relationship with, and obedient to, God.
3. *The Mosaic,* or *Sinaitic, covenant*, the major covenant with Israel—so called because Moses acted as go-between when it was set up between God and Israel at Sinai.
4. *The Davidic covenant*, in which God made special promises to David about his descendants.
5. *The new covenant.* Jeremiah and Ezekiel speak of a new relationship, in which God's law will be written on people's hearts, and they will know and follow God.

> Now therefore, if you will indeed obey my voice and keep my covenant, you shall be my treasured possession among all peoples.
> Exodus 19:5

A chosen family

Genesis

When we read the Old Testament, we quickly realize that history is *story*. The history of the people of Israel is the story of real people, in real situations, making real decisions, taking real actions, and making real mistakes.

The preface

The first few pages of the Old Testament contain the history of the beginnings of the world, painted in broad brushstrokes. We learn that all people were created by God and were intended to live in ideal circumstances, sharing their everyday lives with God. But people were created able to make choices; they chose to go it alone and hence spoiled things.

The 39 Old Testament books go on to tell how God picked a particular family—the Abraham clan—that grew into a particular nation—Israel. He chose them to be his special people, to show the world what would happen if people lived in obedience to God. Sadly, on many occasions, this family and this nation spoiled their opportunities too by forsaking their Lord.

But, as the story unfolds, we learn about God, his love for these people, his willingness to forgive, and his great sense of justice. We get an idea of how things could have been if the people really had followed God's plans. A sense of hope kept them going.

Abraham's family

We learn initially about four generations of the chosen family. Abraham and Sarah, business people from the great city of Ur, in Mesopotamia, were called by God to leave their home and family and go to live in the land of Canaan. Much of the story revolves around the relationship of Abraham and his family with this God whom they were learning to know.

God promised them that the new land to which they were going would one day belong to their family, although at the outset they lived there as visitors. For many years Abraham and Sarah had no children. Eventually, when they were too old to have children, Isaac, the son God had promised, was born. Isaac's name means "laughter," and everybody seemed to love him.

Jacob the deceiver

Isaac's son, Jacob, was different; his name means "usurper," or perhaps "deceiver," and he lived up to his name. He deceived his brother, his father, and his uncle in his attempts to get his own way. Later he had twelve sons and a daughter, by four different women, and made a favorite of Joseph, one of the boys. Although Jacob matured and learned more about God, his family behaved dysfunctionally.

Joseph's story

Eventually Joseph's brothers grew so jealous of him that they sold him as a slave to traders traveling to Egypt, but told their father that a wild animal had killed him. However, in Egypt, Joseph grew into a godly, gifted leader. Although he was wrongfully jailed, even in prison he was respected. A chain of events led ultimately to his being given

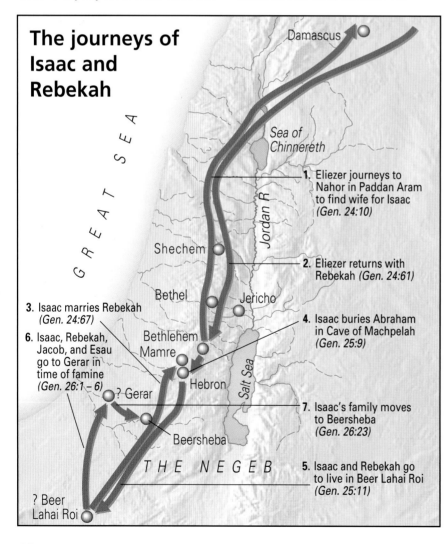

The journeys of Isaac and Rebekah

GREAT SEA

Damascus

Sea of Chinnereth

Jordan R

Shechem

Bethel

Jericho

Bethlehem

Mamre

Hebron

Salt Sea

? Gerar

Beersheba

THE NEGEB

? Beer Lahai Roi

1. Eliezer journeys to Nahor in Paddan Aram to find wife for Isaac (Gen. 24:10)

2. Eliezer returns with Rebekah (Gen. 24:61)

3. Isaac marries Rebekah (Gen. 24:67)

6. Isaac, Rebekah, Jacob, and Esau go to Gerar in time of famine (Gen. 26:1–6)

4. Isaac buries Abraham in Cave of Machpelah (Gen. 25:9)

7. Isaac's family moves to Beersheba (Gen. 26:23)

5. Isaac and Rebekah go to live in Beer Lahai Roi (Gen. 25:11)

Abraham's journey from Ur to the Promised Land

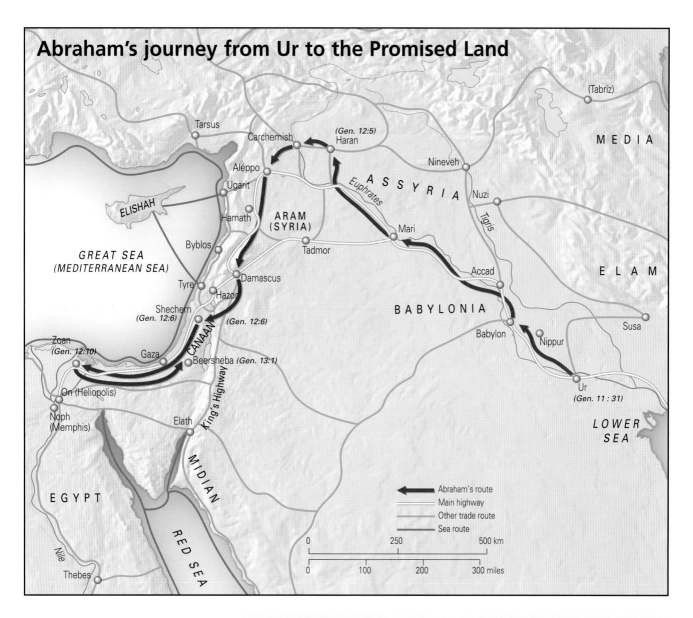

control over the Egyptian economy.

When, years later and in a great famine, Joseph's brothers came to Egypt to try to buy food, they had no idea that Joseph held their fate in his hands. Joseph's family was eventually reconciled with him, and he was able to see that God had intended his circumstances for good, even when some actions, such as those of his brothers, had been intended for bad. The whole family, including Jacob, finally went to live in Egypt.

A chosen people

1. *God chose both parents of the promised son.* Abraham had other sons, but it was only the son of Abraham and Sarah who was to be father of the chosen people.

2. *God chose Abraham and Sarah's family, but this did not mean he was uninterested in other people.* We also learn about God's care for Hagar, the Egyptian slave whom Abraham and Sarah treated badly, and his care for Abraham's nephew Lot, who made some bad decisions.

3. *The people God chose were not perfect;* they made many mistakes. But if they were willing to listen and learn there was always a way forward; God still wanted them to belong to him.

4. *God gave the chosen people the land of Canaan, but that did not mean he could look after them only there.* God was concerned with what was happening in the whole world, including Egypt, and his power was just as real in these other countries.

A new nation

Exodus, Numbers, Joshua, Judges, Ruth

For many years the Abraham clan lived as honored guests of the Egyptians, since they were relatives of Joseph, who had saved Egypt from disaster. (In Egypt they became known as the people of Israel, the name that God gave Jacob.) They prospered in Egypt and did not return to Canaan.

However, after many years, when Joseph had been forgotten, the Egyptians grew jealous of this immigrant community. The Israelites became slaves, used ruthlessly by Pharaoh to construct his magnificent buildings. Eventually, more than 300 years after Joseph's death, the Egyptians murdered a generation of Israelite boys at birth, to avoid any possible future rebellion. At this point God stepped in.

Moses saved from death

A determined mother, her daughter, and a compassionate Egyptian princess were used by God to alter events. Israel was a male-dominated society, but women often played significant roles. These three women ensured that an Israelite baby boy, Moses, was saved from death, brought up in the palace, and given an exclusive education. Later, Moses killed an Egyptian who was mistreating an Israelite. He fled the country and spent 40 years in an isolated desert community.

Moses saves his people

At the age of 80, Moses reluctantly returned to Egypt and eventually became one of Israel's greatest leaders. God used Moses to help his people escape slavery through the Exodus from Egypt, and to set up the legal and religious systems that were to provide the basis of their national life for centuries to come. It seemed that they were now ready to return to the Promised Land—and that Abraham's family could at last fulfill their destiny.

However, at the last moment the Israelites were too timid to go forward, and they ended up wandering around the desert for another 40 years. By the time they entered the land of Canaan, led now by Moses' successor, Joshua, virtually all the adults who had left Egypt with Moses had died.

What were the ten plagues of Egypt?

Exodus 7–12

Moses warned Pharaoh of ten plagues on the land of Egypt. Since the Egyptian gods were thought to be bound up with the forces of nature, each disaster was an attack on their power.

1. Water to blood *Exodus 7:14-24*
The Nile turned to blood. The Nile was essential to the great Egyptian civilization. The first six plagues all seem to emerge from the Nile and demonstrate God's power over it.

2. Frogs *Exodus 8:1-15*
Frogs, a symbol of fertility, overran the land, and when they died, polluted Egypt.

3. Gnats *Exodus 8:16-19*
A small stinging insect, such as the sand flea, is probably meant. Egypt's magicians could not repeat this miracle and told Pharaoh it was the work of God.

4. Flies *Exodus 8:20-32*
Swarms, possibly of biting swamp flies, infested Egypt. The diseases they bear may have been the source of the fifth and sixth plagues.

5. Death of cattle *Exodus 9:1-7*
Many believe that the plague that struck the cattle of Egypt was anthrax. The Israelite cattle were immune, showing that God distinguished between his people and their oppressors.

6. Boils *Exodus 9:8-12*
Probably skin anthrax, carried by the bites of the flies, which fed on the rotting frogs.

7. Hail *Exodus 9:13-35*
The storm ruined the barley and flax but spared the land of Goshen, occupied by the Israelites.

8. Locusts *Exodus 10:1-20*
Locusts stripped the land of any remaining crops. Following the other plagues that devastated the economy of Egypt, this plague was disastrous.

9. Darkness *Exodus 10:21-29*
The sun, representing the Egyptian god Ra, was darkened for three days. Some suggest this was due to a khamsin, a fierce wind that fills the air with dirt. The text, however, indicates a deeper and more terrifying darkness.

10. Death of the firstborn
Exodus 11:1–12:36
This final plague took the firstborn of every Egyptian household but left the Israelites untouched. This caused such terror that Pharaoh finally urged Moses to lead Israel out of his land to freedom. The gods of Egypt were shown to be powerless before the God of the Hebrews.

The Exodus from Egypt

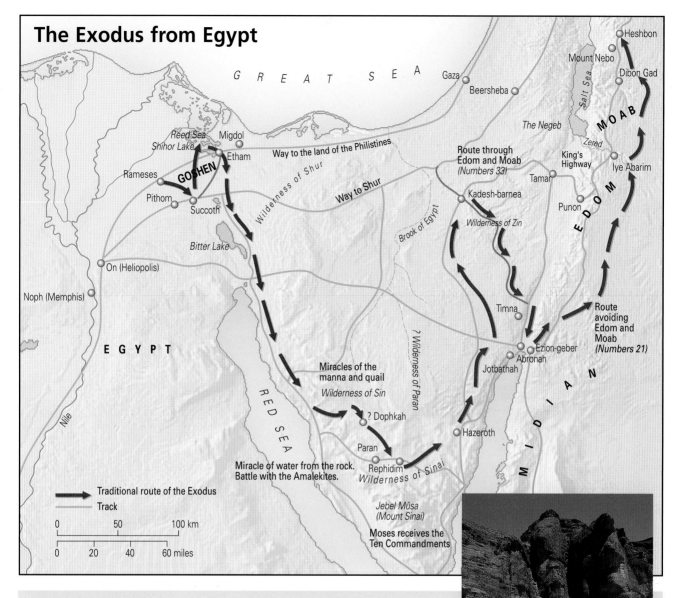

GREAT SEA

Gaza

Heshbon
Mount Nebo
Dibon Gad

Beersheba

The Negeb

MOAB

Salt Sea

Zered

Reed Sea
Shihor Lake
Migdol
Etham

Way to the land of the Philistines

Rameses
GOSHEN

Route through
Edom and Moab
(Numbers 33)

King's
Highway

Iye Abarim

Pithom
Succoth

Wilderness of Shur

Way to Shur

Tamar

Kadesh-barnea

EDOM

Bitter Lake

Wilderness of Zin

Punon

On (Heliopolis)

Brook of Egypt

Noph (Memphis)

? Wilderness of Paran

EGYPT

Timna

Route
avoiding
Edom and
Moab
(Numbers 21)

Nile

Miracles of the
manna and quail

Wilderness of Sin

Ezion-geber
Abronah

Jotbathah

RED SEA

? Dophkah

Paran

Hazeroth

Miracle of water from the rock.
Battle with the Amalekites.

Rephidim

Wilderness of Sinai

MIDIAN

Traditional route of the Exodus

Track

| 0 | 50 | 100 km |
| 0 | 20 | 40 | 60 miles |

Jebel Mûsa
(Mount Sinai)

Moses receives the
Ten Commandments

Cliffs in the Negeb

What happened to the Israelites during the Exodus?

1. The Israelites are told to leave Egypt by Pharaoh Ramses II. The years of slavery are over. *Exodus 12:29-36*

2. They leave Egypt, taking either the route depicted above or a more southerly route leading to the Red Sea. *Exodus 12:37-39; 13:17–14:4*

3. Ramses changes his mind and pursues his escaped slaves. He traps the Israelites at the sea. *Exodus 14:5-12*

4. God tells Moses to hold out his staff over the sea. The waters are driven back, and the people cross on dry land. The Egyptians are drowned as the water returns. *Exodus 14:13-31*

5. After three days they arrive at Marah—but the water is too bitter to drink. *Exodus 15:22-26*

6. God first provides manna and quail to eat. *Exodus 16*

7. God provides water from a rock. The Amalekites attack and are defeated. Moses' father-in-law advises Moses. *Exodus 17–18*

8. Israel receives the Law from God at Mount Sinai. *Exodus 19–32*

9. Miriam becomes leprous for her jealousy and rebellion against Moses. *Numbers 12:1-16*

10. Eleven days after leaving Mount Sinai, Moses sends twelve spies into Canaan. *Numbers 13:1-24*

11. The spies return. Ten bring bad reports, leading the people to rebellion. They want a new leader to take them back to Egypt. *Numbers 13:5–14:10*

12. As punishment, God sends them to wander in the desert 40 years before entering Canaan. *Numbers 14:11-38*

From this Orthodox monastery can be seen the traditional site of the Israelite camp near Mount Sinai.

The giving of the Law

The most important event of the wilderness period took place at the foot of Mount Sinai, where Israel accepted a God-given code of Law and undertook to worship Yahweh (the more accurate form of the name "Jehovah") and no other god. Moses played the leading role in this event, a key milestone in Israel's monotheistic faith—a faith virtually unique in the ancient world—even though for some centuries idolatry continued to plague Israelite society. (See also "The people of the Law," pages 166–167.)

The golden calf

While Moses was on Mount Sinai, the Israelites created and began to worship a golden calf. The calf symbolized fertility and strength in Canaanite culture, and Canaanite gods were often depicted standing on the back of a bull or calf. The Israelite worship of a calf violated the second commandment, forbidding the worship of idols.

Quail to eat

The Israelites were provided with quail to eat in the desert. The quail, a small, plump migrating bird, often flies in swarms across Sinai en route to Europe from Sudan. They usually fly with the wind and get driven to the ground if they encounter a cross-wind. As they become exhausted by their exertions, the quail are easy to catch. Observers in Sinai have on occasion seen them cover the ground.

Manna
The Israelites' other main food in the desert was manna, which they found on the ground each morning. It was white, looked like coriander, and tasted of honey. Its nature has been much debated, but its provision was ultimately miraculous. It taught the Israelites how important it was that they trust God.
Exodus 16:13ff., Deuteronomy 8:3,16.

Into the Promised Land

The new nation was now in the Promised Land, but life was still not easy. Joshua was a good leader and achieved great successes, such as the defeat of the city strongholds of Jericho and Ai. The Israelites annexed large tracts of land throughout Canaan and recommitted themselves to serving God and living as his covenant people.

However, Joshua died before the new nation was fully established in its new land, and no national leader replaced him. The Israelites were not completely committed to serving God, and enemies within and outside the supposedly conquered territories posed major problems for them. The Israelite tribes were very conscious of their individual identities, but less confident about their allegiance to the nation, resulting in much intertribal conflict.

Highs and lows

The book of Judges records the highs and lows of these years, until the setting up of a monarchy eventually united the nation. The judges were regional rather than national leaders, and though they sometimes acted as legal advisers, they were normally military leaders.

The book of Judges is no collection of hero stories. Its narratives concern a varied group of men and women used by God to prevent Israel from becoming absorbed into surrounding nations. The accounts make no attempt to hide the decline in standards since Moses and Joshua, or to justify the behavior of the nation and its leaders.

Judges records, but does not praise, Jephthah's thoughtless vow, which led to the death of his daughter, and Samson's immoral lifestyle. Judges amounts to a sorry story of syncretism, disobedience, and disloyalty, alongside a number of high points. In this book, the women come out slightly better than the men, and Deborah is the only major judge who did not fall from grace.

Ruth

Ruth was a Moabite woman living in the time of the judges, and the main protagonist of the book of the same name. She married an Israelite who moved to Moab with his father and brother and his mother, Naomi. When Naomi's two sons both died, she decided to return to Israel, and Ruth went with her. In Bethlehem, Ruth claimed the protection of Naomi's relative Boaz, who married her after she gleaned in his fields. Ruth is important in the history of Israel because she was the great-grandmother of David.

By tradition the book of Ruth was written by Samuel, and it is set in the period of the judges. Its story of Ruth's faithfulness in helping her mother-in-law, and God's faithfulness in preserving a family line that led ultimately to Jesus, is a welcome respite from the violence and unfaithfulness of much of the book of Judges.

Invasion of Canaan

Ajalon
Beth-horon
Bethel
Gezer
Ai
Jericho
? Gilgal
Plains of Moab
Abel-shittim
Gibeon
Kiriath-Jearim
Jebus (Jerusalem)
Azekah
Jarmuth
Bethlehem
? Libnah
Lachish
Hebron
Eglon
Salt Sea
Debir

Dividing the land

Once the Israelites had entered Canaan, each tribe was given an area in which to settle, mostly west of the River Jordan. The tribe of Levi was given no land, but was allocated certain towns to live in. Six "cities of refuge" were also named.

After the death of Joshua, judges such as Ehud, Gideon, and Samson led the Israelites against the Philistines and other enemies.
Joshua 8:13-21; Judges

The six cities of refuge
Moses was told to set up six cities of refuge (Numbers 35:6-15), spread throughout the land. Three were located east of the River Jordan, at Bezer, Ramoth-gilead, and Golan; and three west of the Jordan at Kedesh, Shechem, and Kiriath-arba (Hebron).

A city of refuge provided a safe place to which a person who had killed someone could flee and obtain asylum until a trial could be held. If subsequently found innocent, the fugitive was allowed to remain in the city of refuge, safe from the revenge of the victim's family and friends.

Altars

From earliest times, altars were set up where people could worship God. They were usually simple piles of stones, set up to remind them of God's presence, or a kind of table where sacrifices could be offered. Before the priestly system originated, apparently anyone could build his or her own altar; but later the system became regulated and worship was centralized.

In Israel, altars were made of stone, with no carving on them, and they were not usually cut to shape. This was to show that God was in control and could not be manipulated by human artistry. Later, altars became more complex and were sometimes overlaid with metal.

GREAT SEA

Tyre
DAN
Dan (Laish)
Kedesh
ASHER
NAPHTALI
Golan
ZEBULUN
Sea of Chinnereth
Shimron
Endor
MANASS
Megiddo
ISSACHAR
Ramoth-gil
MANASSEH
Jordan
Shechem
Succoth
Beth-dagon
EPHRAIM
Shiloh
GAD
DAN
Bethel
BENJAMIN
Gibeah
Jericho
Jebus (Jerusalem)
Heshbon
Be
JUDAH
REUBEN
Salt Sea
Hebron
Gaza
MOAB
Beersheba
SIMEON
E D O M

| 0 | 25 | 50 kr |
| 0 | 10 | 20 | 30 mil |

Probable boundary of tribe of Israel
Migration of the tribe of Dan
City of refuge

54

The judges

The twelve tribes of Israel

Reuben	Gad
Judah	Joseph
Dan	Levi
Naphtali	Issachar
Simeon	Asher
Zebulun	Benjamin

Worship site at Dan

Who were the judges of Israel and their adversaries?

Judge *Oppressor*	Actions	Years the judge led Israel *Years of oppression*	Reference in book of Judges
Cushan, king of Aram		*8*	*3:8*
Othniel	Freed Israel from Mesopotamian oppressors	40	*3:7-11*
Eglon, king of Moab		*18*	*3:14*
Ehud	Freed Israel from Moabite oppressors	80	*3:12-30*
Shamgar	Freed Israel from Philistine oppressors	10	*3:31*
Jabin, king of Canaan		*20*	*4:3*
Deborah	Deborah the only woman judge With Barak, freed Israel from Canaanite oppressors	40	*4:4–5:31*
Midianites		*7*	*6:1*
Gideon	Sought a sign from God Freed Israel from Midianite oppressors	40	*6:11–8:35*
Abimelech	*Terrorized the people as self-proclaimed king of Israel*	*3*	*9*
Tola		23	*10:1-2*
Jair		22	*10:3-5*
Ammonites		*18*	*10:7-9*
Jephthah	Freed Israel from Ammonite oppressors	6	*10:6–12:7*
Ibzan		7	*12:8-10*
Elon		10	*12:11-12*
Abdon		8	*12:13-15*
Philistines		*40*	*13:1*
Samson	Famous for his remarkable strength	20	*13–16*
Eli	High priest and judge	40	*1 Samuel 1:1–4:18*
Samuel	High priest and judge	21	*1 Samuel 1:11–13:15*
Joel/Abijah			*1 Samuel 8:1-2*

Kings to lead

1 & 2 Samuel, 1 & 2 Kings, 1 & 2 Chronicles

Samuel—prophet and judge—initiated the monarchy to maintain Israel's national identity and hold the country together. For about a hundred years the country functioned successfully as a united kingdom, but King Solomon's ruthless efficiency was detested by the northern tribes, and after his reign they broke away.

For the next 200 years two kingdoms, Israel in the north and Judah in the south, coexisted. They were sometimes at war, sometimes in alliance; sometimes seeking to live as God's covenant people, more often turning away from God and ignoring the demands of the Law and the covenant. In 722 B.C. the northern capital, Samaria, fell to the Assyrians, Israel was exiled, and the northern kingdom ceased to exist.

Beyond this outline, the story revolves around people, their interrelationships, and their relationship with God. We learn about the lives of ordinary people, particularly in accounts of the work of Elijah and Elisha and in the writings of the prophets Amos, Hosea, and Micah. However, most of the records focus on the rulers and how they used and abused their power.

Samuel
Samuel can be seen as either the last of the judges or the first genuine national leader since Joshua. He was a prophet, priest, and king-maker, who succeeded in holding the people together and making them think about God. He did not cling to power himself but handed over authority, first to Saul and then to David.

Saul
Saul, the first king of Israel, was chosen and called, but not faithful. He was little different from the judges, except that his leadership was officially recognized and more permanent. But Saul became more interested in his kingly status than in the task God gave him; he began to assume that he could overrule God's commands—and was therefore replaced.

David
Although David never sought the crown during Saul's lifetime, when Saul died in battle he was pleased to take it. After initial skirmishes with Saul's son Ish-bosheth, David took over the entire kingdom. Though a good soldier and diplomat, a committed believer and an able poet, he had a number of serious failings. He controlled the kingdom but did not always control himself or his own family, and he experienced major problems with his sons.

Solomon
Solomon was in many ways the most gifted king of Israel. He inherited his father David's poetic skills, was a gifted scholar, and brought prosperity to the nation. However, he led a life alien to God's pattern of kingship in Israel. Deuteronomy 17 states that kings should avoid stock-piling wealth, dependence on military strength, idolatry, polygamy, and oppressive rule; but Solomon's reign was characterized by all of these.

Rehoboam
Solomon's son Rehoboam did not inherit his father's gifts, but followed his father's harsh treatment of the people. It is not surprising that the northern tribes rejected his kingship.

The world at large
In addition to the regular feuding between northern Israel and southern Judah, Israel's relationships with surrounding nations were often strained.

In the northwest, Tyre (in modern Lebanon) was normally friendly toward Israel. In the north, Syria was growing more powerful, sometimes acting as an ally but more often as an enemy, devastating farms in border raids. East of Israel, Ammon, Moab, and Edom caused the Jews problems, although after Solomon's reign

David defeated the Jebusite inhabitants and made Jerusalem his capital city.

they were weaker than Israel and Judah, and easily contained. To the south, Egypt was declining in power, while Greece, to the west, was growing in influence: Homer was writing at this time, and the first Olympic Games took place at the time when the northern kingdom of Israel was disappearing. However, Greek influence had not yet reached so far east.

Assyria, to the northeast, beyond Ammon and Syria, was emerging as the dominant power in the region. The Assyrian Empire initiated magnificent architectural schemes, but was famously cruel, with military power the key to status.

Israel and Judah were situated on important trade routes between Egypt and Assyria and particularly in the late ninth and early eighth centuries B.C. had great opportunities for economic growth. Assyria first dominated then destroyed Syria, and for a time Israel was left to her own devices. But this period of prosperity proved to be illusory, and Israel was in turn destroyed.

Israel: the northern kingdom

There were 19 kings of Israel, starting with Jeroboam. Although his reign began well, Jeroboam soon became more concerned with maintaining power than obeying God. In the books of Kings, all 19 northern

kings are described as "evil."

Nevertheless, despite the ministry of such prophets as Elijah, Elisha, Amos, and Hosea, and the existence of many true believers, Israel eventually ceased to be part of God's covenant people. 2 Kings 17 serves as an epitaph for the northern kingdom, making it clear that their demise was totally deserved.

Judah: the southern kingdom

During this same period there were twelve rulers in Judah—eleven kings and the notorious Queen Athaliah, who killed her own grandchildren to retain her throne. Seven kings, six of whom reigned for 25 years or more, are described as "doing what was right in the eyes of the Lord"—though this does not mean their reigns were perfect, as the writings of the prophets Micah and Isaiah make clear.

Corruption, injustice, and idolatry do not seem to have been much less common than in Israel. However, the "good" kings did make some attempt to lead the people within the requirements of the covenant. Possibly this led God to be merciful to Judah, so that the kingdom lasted for a further hundred years before being conquered by Babylon.

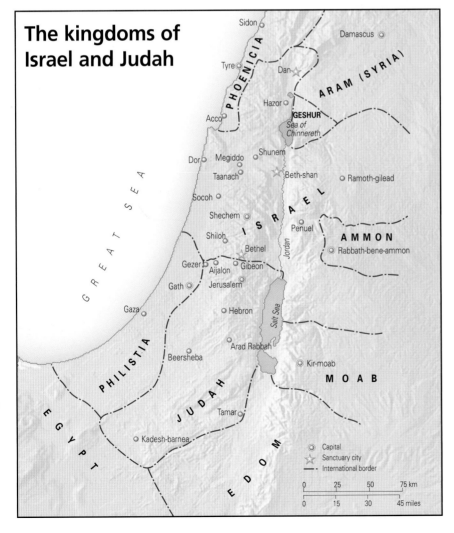

The kingdoms of Israel and Judah

The kingdom of Saul

Since the Philistines posed a
constant threat, the Israelites
demanded a king to lead them,
like the nations around them.
The last judge, Samuel, anointed
Saul their king. Saul, a fine
warrior, held back challenges
from the Ammonites to the east
and the Philistines in the west.
Saul's jealousy of his
successor David marks
the turn in Saul's fortunes.
He was defeated and
killed by the Philistines
at Mount Gilboa.
1 Samuel 9–31

PHOENICIA

ARAM
(SYRIA)

Damascus

Tyre

Dan

Kedesh

*Sea of
Chinnereth*

Endor

Valley of Jezreel

Megiddo

Beth-shan

7. Death of Saul
on Mount Gilboa

△ *Mount Gilboa*

Ibleam

Jabesh-gilead

Bezek

1. Rescue of besieged
Jabesh-gilead

Shechem

Jordan

Aphek

AMMON

4. Campaign against the
Ammonites

G R E A T   S E A

Rabbath-bene-ammon

Ophrah

Ramah   Bethel

Gezer

Mizpah

Gilgal

Aijalon

2. Battle of Michmash

Ekron

Gibeah

Nob

Ashdod

Azekah

Jebus (Jerusalem)

Gath

Socoh

Bethlehem

3. Campaign against
the Philistines

Ashkelon

Salt Sea

5. Campaign against
the Moabites

Gaza

Hebron

Ziklag

M
O
A
B

6. Campaign against the
Edomites and Amalekites

Kir-hareseth

P H I L I S T I A

A M A L E K

E D O M

◎ Capital
→ Philistine incursions
— Saul's campaigns

0   25   50 km

0   10   20   30 mile

58

The united kingdom

Under King David and his son Solomon the kingdom prospered. David pushed the frontiers of Israel to their farthest extent, conquering the Philistines, Moab, Edom, and Ammon, and leaving Solomon a peaceful and secure inheritance. David's empire stretched to the Euphrates in the north and Ezion-geber on the Gulf of Aqaba in the south, while the peoples of Edom, Moab, Ammon, and Aram became his vassal states and were forced to pay tribute. But David's most lasting achievement was his conversion of the newly captured Jerusalem into the state capital and national center of worship.
2 Samuel, 1 Kings

Jerusalem in the time of David and Solomon

Suggested extension of Jerusalem during Solomon's reign extension of Jerusalem during Solomon's reign

N

Temple

?Mount Moriah

Palace

Valley Gate

Tyropoeon Valley

Ophel

City of David

Gate

Gihon Spring

Kidron Valley

Suggested line of city wall

Kidron Brook

Hinnom Valley

HAMATH

Cun
Lebo-hamath

Berothah

G R E A T   S E A

P H O E N I C I A

A R A M
(S Y R I A)

Damascus

Sidon

Ijon (Jaan)

Tyre
Usu

Dan

Kedesh

Acco

Chinnereth

GESHUR

Sea of Chinnereth

Dor

Megiddo

Ramoth-gilead

Taanach

Beth-shan

I
S
R
A
E
L

Shechem

Jordan

Joppa

Jazer

A M M O N

Gezer

Rabbath-bene-ammon

Ashdod

Jerusalem

Ashkelon

Gath

Medeba

Gaza

Hebron

Salt Sea

Aroer

J
U
D
A
H

Beersheba

King's Highway

M
O
A
B

Zoar

Brook of Egypt

Tamar

Kadesh-barnea

E
D
O
M

	Territory of Judah and Israel
	Vassal territory
	Conquered territory

0   25   50   75 km

0   15   30   45 miles

Ezion-geber

59

Solomon's united kingdom

Solomon reigned for some 40 years (c. 970–930 B.C.). The era of prosperity begun by David continued through his reign, during which Israel reached a peak of magnificence. Solomon's strengths were in administration, public works, and diplomacy, and his reputation for wisdom became legendary.

Solomon divided his kingdom into twelve administrative districts, which facilitated a nation-wide building program. Solomon developed a trade monopoly and exploited the natural resources of his empire, and also founded Israel's navy.
1 Kings, 2 Chronicles

Solomon's Temple
Solomon's most famous achievement was the building of the Jerusalem Temple, of which nothing now remains.
(See pages 180–183.)

The Queen of Sheba
Solomon's wisdom is celebrated by the story of the visit of the Queen of Sheba (2 Chronicles 9:1-12), who came to sample his learning. Sheba is often identified with modern Yemen, in the southwest corner of the Arabian peninsula. Since Solomon's new trading post at Ezion-geber may have threatened Sheba's trade, the queen's visit might also have been intended to build good relations with the emerging nation.

Boundary of Solomon's empire
Boundary of administrative district
Solomonic fortification or building project
United kingdom of Israel and Judah
Vassal kingdoms

0   25   50 km
0   10   20   30 mile

The two kingdoms

1 & 2 Kings, 1 & 2 Chronicles

When the kingdom split into two, Solomon's son Rehoboam held on to Judah, plus Benjamin; this proved to be a small but stable political unit, called the kingdom of Judah. The northern part of Israel, which kept the name Israel, was bigger but never achieved political stability. After the first king, Jeroboam, scarcely any king or any dynasty was safe for long. Jeroboam's first tasks were to replace Jerusalem as capital and worship center and to construct a new administration. The ancient shrines of Bethel and Dan were given new prominence. The first capital was Shechem, but later Samaria became the chief city.

During David's reign many Canaanites were absorbed into Israel and Judah, with the result that Canaanite religion, especially Baal-worship, became widely practiced. Some of the prophets vigorously condemned this trend. It affected both kingdoms, but especially the northern one. In the ninth century, King Ahab's queen, Jezebel, tried to promote Baal-worship and persecuted those prophets who opposed her plans. Elijah successfully opposed her (1 Kings 17–18). Ahab's dynasty was overthrown; the new king, Jehu, fiercely attacked Baal-worship, but it still continued. Hosea, in the eighth century, saw it as the chief religious problem of his day.

The ninth century also saw the rise of two military threats to Israel. One came from the neighboring Aramean kingdom of Damascus, the other threat from the powerful kingdom of Assyria to the northeast. As early as Ahab's reign, in 853 B.C., several Palestinian states, including Israel and Damascus, formed an alliance to fight an invading Assyrian army. In the end Assyria destroyed the kingdom of Damascus, thus removing one threat to Israel, and

for a time allowing Israel some peace and prosperity.

734 B.C. was a crisis year for Judah. The kings of Israel and Damascus joined forces and attacked Judah, besieging Jerusalem. The king of Judah, Ahaz, was advised by the prophet Isaiah to stand firm and take no action. Ahaz, however, took the unnecessary step of asking the Assyrians for help; that made Judah a vassal of Assyria and liable to pay a heavy annual tribute.

The end came for the kingdom of Israel in 722 B.C. Under her last king, Hoshea, Israel had foolishly rebelled against Assyria, after earlier submission, and the Assyrian armies devastated Israel and besieged Samaria, which fell after three years. Many citizens of Israel died, and many others were taken into exile (2 Kings 17). The traditional Israelite faith was not abandoned, but the large numbers of immigrants resulted in a mixed population, and the "Samaritans," as they came to be called, were often despised and disliked by the Jews.

Judah: from Hezekiah to Zedekiah

Judah was not threatened by Assyria as early as Israel. But after King Ahaz became subject to the Assyrians (see above), the next king of Judah, Hezekiah, tried to reassert his independence. He can be praised for his religious reforms, but this political objective was impossible.

In consequence, in 701 B.C. Jerusalem suffered another siege, this time by the king of Assyria, Sennacherib. Hezekiah's kingdom was reduced by Sennacherib to less than half its previous size. Against all probabilities the city of Jerusalem was spared and Hezekiah retained his throne, though he had to submit again to Assyrian

domination.

Thus Judah entered the seventh century B.C. alone (for Israel was now part of the Assyrian Empire) and subject to Assyria. It was during this period that Judah became increasingly idolatrous, and the long reign of Manasseh is denounced (2 Kings 21) for its evil practices.

The situation changed during the reign of Josiah (640–609 B.C.), whose reform program resulted from the discovery of a "book of the Law" in the Temple. During his reign the Assyrian Empire collapsed under attacks from the Medes and Babylonians. The Assyrian capital Nineveh fell in 612 B.C., an event hailed with joy by Nahum.

For ten years before Nineveh's fall, Josiah had been independent, able to carry out his own religious and political wishes. The prophet Jeremiah had nothing but praise for him (Jeremiah 22:15-16). However, his reign ended in tragedy. Judah had no hope of maintaining independence; the fall of Assyria meant that either Egypt or Babylon was certain to dominate Palestine. Egypt sent an army through Palestine in 609 B.C., which Josiah tried to prevent, only to die in battle (2 Kings 23:29-30).

Before long the Babylonians took control of the whole Palestinian area, led by Nebuchadnezzar, their most famous king (605–562 B.C.). The last kings of Judah never came to terms with Babylonian control. Jehoiachin rebelled, and the Babylonian army swiftly besieged Jerusalem in 597 B.C. Jehoiachin capitulated and was taken into exile in Babylon. His successor, Zedekiah, rebelled some years later, and Jerusalem suffered a longer and more disastrous siege. This ended in 587/86 B.C. with the destruction of the city and its Temple and the deportation of all its leading citizens to Babylonia. Judah was no longer a kingdom and was partly depopulated. Many fled to Egypt, among them a reluctant Jeremiah, who throughout a long ministry had repeatedly warned against the political follies of Judah's kings.

Who were the kings and prophets of Judah and Israel?

| Judah | | Date B.C. | Israel | | Assyria |
King	Prophet		King	Prophet	
Rehoboam	Shemaiah	931	Jeroboam I	Ahijah	
Egypt invades Jerusalem					
Abijah	Iddo	913	*War with Judah*		
Asa	Azariah	911			
	Hanani	910	Nadab		
		909	Baasha	Jehu	
Allies with Syria against Baasha					
		886	Elah		
		885	Zimri		
		885	Tibni		
		885	Omri		883-859 Ashurnasirpal II
			Samaria becomes capital		
		874	Ahab	Elijah, Micaiah	
Jehoshaphat	Jehu	870	*Allies with Judah against Syria*		
	Jahaziel	853	Ahaziah	Elisha	858-824 Shalmaneser III
	Eliezer	852	Jehoram Joram		
Jehoram Joram		848			
Ahaziah		841	Jehu		
Athaliah		841			
Jehoash Joash	Joel	835			
	Zechariah	814	Jehoahaz		
		798	Jehoash Joash		
Amaziah		796	*Fights Amaziah*		
		782	Jeroboam II	Jonah	782-773 Shalmaneser IV
Uzziah Azariah		767		Amos	
	Isaiah	753	Zechariah	Hosea	
Jotham regent		752	Shallum		
		752	Menahem		744-727 Tiglath-Pileser III
		742	Pekahiah		
			Pays tribute to Assyria		
Jotham		740	Pekah	Oded	
			Fights Assyria		
			Many deported		
Ahaz	Micah	732	Hoshea		
Tribute to Assyria			*Tribute to Assyria*		726-722 Shalmaneser V
		722	*Fall of Samaria*		721-705 Sargon II
Hezekiah		715			704-681 Sennacherib
Sennacherib invades		701			
Manasseh		687			680-669 Esarhaddon
Amon		642			
Josiah	Nahum	640			
Religious reform	Zephaniah				
	Habakkuk	612			*Nineveh falls*
Jehoahaz	Jeremiah	609			
Jehoiakim	Uriah	609			
		605			*Egypt loses battle of Carchemish*
Tribute to Egypt					
Jehoiachin		598			
Many deported to Babylon					
Zedekiah		597			
Fall of Jerusalem		587/86			

Israel and Judah during the reigns of Jeroboam II and Uzziah

Israel and Judah became powerful and wealthy nations during the reigns of Jeroboam II and Uzziah in the eighth century. Once again Israel and Judah gained control of the commercial highways in the region. Jeroboam reigned in Israel from *c.* 782 B.C. He recovered lands taken earlier by the Arameans of Damascus now that their power had been broken by the Assyrians. He established control over a large area of Aram (2 Kings 14:25). The prophets Amos and Hosea condemned the internal moral and religious corruption and materialistic lifestyle.

Uzziah reigned in Judah from *c.* 767 B.C. He pushed back the frontier with the Philistines and recovered the territory of Edom, which King David had conquered. The port of Ezion-geber was rebuilt, giving a renewed outlet to the Red Sea.

ARAM (SYRIA)

Lebo-hamath (Hamath)

PHOENICIA

Sidon

Damascus

ISRAEL

Tyre

Dan

Hazor

Sea of Chinnereth

Megiddo

Ramoth-gilead

Jordan R.

Samaria

Rabbath-ammon

AMMON

Ashdod

Jerusalem

Ashkelon

Gath

Gaza

PHILISTIA

Salt Sea (Sea of the Arabah)

Beersheba

JUDAH

MOAB

EDOM

Ezion-geber (Elath)

GREAT SEA

0   50   100 km

0   20   40   60 miles

Exile and return

2 Kings, 2 Chronicles, Jeremiah, Ezra, Nehemiah, and Ezekiel

The Exile started with key workers and students being taken to Babylon on a scheme probably considered to benefit a poorer subsidiary nation. Then, as Judah continued to trouble Babylon, a large group, including the prophet Ezekiel, was exiled in 597 B.C., and a second large group followed after the destruction of Jerusalem in 587 B.C.

However, life was not all bad for the exiles in Babylon. They could practice trade, plant crops, mingle with the local population, and even work in the Babylonian civil service. They were also allowed to maintain their own community and follow their own religion.

Ezekiel spent his first years as a prophet in Babylon trying to convince the people—who still hoped to return to Jerusalem—that exile was a deserved punishment from God. Once Jerusalem had been destroyed and they had lost hope, Ezekiel's message changed to one of encouragement and hope for the future. The Jews' God was a God of grace, who would show mercy to a penitent people and one day bring them back to their own land.

Babylon falls
Then, in a remarkably quick turnabout, Babylon was defeated by the Medo-Persians from the south. Persian influence rapidly stretched from Greece and Egypt in the west to India in the east, making it one of the world's most extensive empires.

The return
Almost immediately after coming to power in Babylon, the Persian ruler Cyrus instituted a policy of encouraging exiled communities to return home, taking with them their confiscated religious treasures and generous resettlement grants. Many of the exiles from Judah decided to remain in Babylon, but a committed group decided to return, and in 538 B.C. they began to restore the nation.

Rebuilding the Temple
The returnees started well, rebuilding the altar in Jerusalem and laying foundations for the Temple; but the work was harder than they had expected. The land had been neglected, the people who had moved into the territory in the Jews' absence were hostile, and for several years harvests were poor. The Temple was eventually finished 17 years later, after the people had been challenged by the prophets Haggai and Zechariah. Although the community survived and

Babylonian infantryman

sought to live as God's covenant people, it was weak both economically and spiritually.

Rebuilding Jerusalem
Some 60 years later Ezra and Nehemiah, encouraged by later emperors, returned, giving the people new hope, and rebuilding the walls of Jerusalem. The capital city was restored, the economic system revived, and religion renewed. It may not have been the triumphant return expected in Isaiah and elsewhere, but was nevertheless a remarkable achievement.

Sadly, fifth-century B.C. Judah proved no better than her predecessors at taking advantage of new opportunities. Oppression of the poor and religious syncretism soon became rife. While religion became strong, it also became legalistic and introspective; ritual became more important than justice and mercy. It is perhaps not surprising that prophecy, which had formerly played such an important part in Israel's life, disappeared for four centuries—until John the Baptist emerged.

Glimmers of light
Old Testament history is seldom uplifting. However, through its pictures of human failure and disobedience we see glimmers of light. We read of faithful believers and see a clear picture of the Creator God, who has made a covenant with his people: always there, always faithful, always just and with a plan that can bring human beings back into a relationship with himself.

The scene is set for the coming of Jesus.

The three Jewish returns from exile

	First return	Second return	Third return	
Scripture	Ezra 1	Ezra 2–6	Ezra 7–10	Nehemiah 1–2
Date	538 B.C.	525 B.C.	458 B.C.	445 B.C.
King of Persia	Cyrus the Great 559-530 B.C.	Cambyses 530-522 Darius 522-486	Artaxerxes I 465–425	Artaxerxes I
Leader of return		Zerubbabel	Ezra	Nehemiah
Leader's role		Governor	Priest	Governor
Number of returnees		49,897	1,774	Armed escort
Other leaders at the time		Joshua the priest Haggai, Zechariah	Nehemiah, Malachi	Ezra, Malachi
Result	Temple foundations laid Work stops	Work finished in 516	Law taught	Jerusalem's people separated from non-Jews Jerusalem's walls rebuilt

Rulers of the Persian Empire

Cyrus II "the Great" 550–530
The conqueror of Babylon, Cyrus II, reversed previous policy and returned exiled peoples to their homelands. By his decree, the Jews returned to Judea.
2 Chronicles 36:22, 23; Ezra 1–6; Isaiah 44:28; 45:1; Daniel 10:1

Cambyses II 530–522

Darius I 530–486
Darius I, a strong ruler, confirmed the decree of Cyrus II and ordered the Jerusalem Temple to be completed at Persian expense.
Ezra 5:3–6:15; Nehemiah 12:22; Haggai 1:1; Zechariah 1:1

Xerxes I 486–465
Xerxes I, probably Ahasuerus in the book of Esther, failed in two attempts to invade Greece.
Esther

Artaxerxes I 464–423
Nehemiah was cupbearer to Artaxerxes I, who made him governor of Judea. During his rule the walls of Jerusalem were rebuilt.
Ezra 7:1, 21-26; Nehemiah 2:1-8

Xerxes II 425–424

Darius II 423–404

Artaxerxes II 404–359

Artaxerxes III 359–338

Arses 338–336

Darius III 336–331

All dates are approximate and B.C.

Relief of head of Darius I

Four great empires

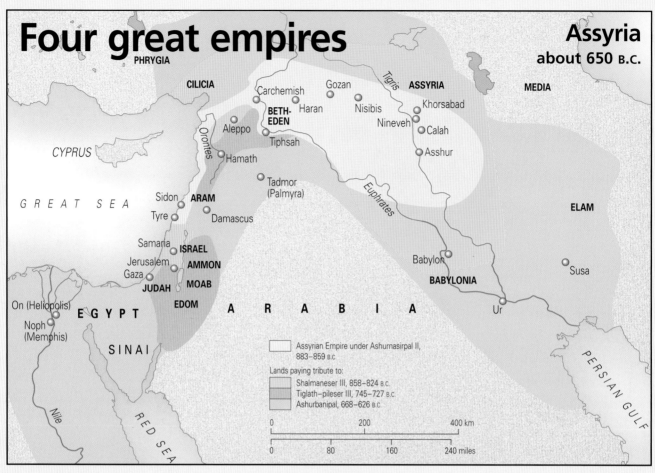

Assyria
about 650 B.C.

PHRYGIA

CILICIA

CYPRUS

MEDIA

ASSYRIA

Carchemish
Gozan
Khorsabad
BETH-EDEN
Haran
Nisibis
Nineveh
Calah
Aleppo
Tiphsah
Asshur
Hamath
Orontes
Tigris

GREAT SEA

Tadmor (Palmyra)

Sidon
ARAM
Tyre
Damascus
Euphrates
ELAM

Samaria
ISRAEL
Jerusalem
AMMON
Gaza
JUDAH
MOAB
EDOM

Babylon
BABYLONIA
Susa
Ur

On (Heliopolis)
E G Y P T
A R A B I A

Noph (Memphis)

SINAI

PERSIAN GULF

Nile

RED SEA

Assyrian Empire under Ashurnasirpal II, 883–859 B.C.

Lands paying tribute to:
Shalmaneser III, 858–824 B.C.
Tiglath–pileser III, 745–727 B.C.
Ashurbanipal, 668–626 B.C.

0	200	400 km
0	80	160	240 miles

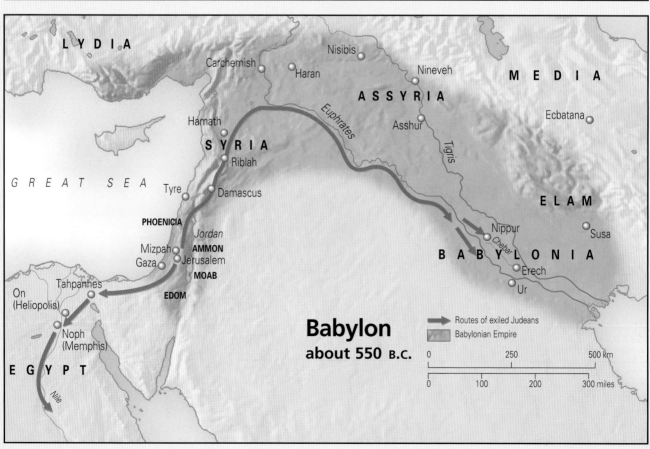

L Y D I A

Nisibis
Carchemish
Haran
Nineveh
M E D I A

A S S Y R I A
Ecbatana

Hamath
Euphrates
Asshur
Tigris

S Y R I A
Riblah

GREAT SEA

Tyre
Damascus

E L A M

PHOENICIA
Jordan
Nippur
Susa
Mizpah
AMMON
Chebar
Gaza
Jerusalem
B A B Y L O N I A
MOAB
Erech

Tahpanhes
EDOM
Ur

On (Heliopolis)

Noph (Memphis)

E G Y P T

Nile

Babylon
about 550 B.C.

Routes of exiled Judeans
Babylonian Empire

0	250	500 km
0	100	200	300 miles

66

Persia
about 450 B.C.

THRACE
Byzantium
BLACK SEA
LYDIA
Pteria
Halys
URARTU (ARMENIA)
Sardis
PHRYGIA
Ephesus
CILICIA
Haran
Nineveh
PARTHIA
BACTRIA
GANDHARA
CRETE
Carchemish
ASSYRIA
MEDIA
GREAT SEA
CYPRUS
Asshur
Ecbatana
INDIA
Sidon
ABAR-NAHARA
Euphrates
Tigris
Susa
Tyre
Damascus
Jerusalem
Babylon
Nippur
ELAM
(SUSIANA)
LIBYA
BABYLONIA
PERSIS
(PERSIA)
Memphis
PERSIAN GULF
Persepolis
EGYPT
RED SEA
ARABIA
Thebes
Nile
HYRCANIAN SEA (CASPIAN SEA)
Oxus
Indus

Royal Road
Persian homeland
Annexed land of the Medes, 550 B.C.
Annexed land of the Babylonians, 539 B.C.
Maximum extent of the Persian Empire

The Greek Empire
about 323 B.C.

GREECE
Delphi
Pergamum
Sardis
Sicyon
Piraeus
Ephesus
CAPPADOCIA
Corinth
Side
Tarsus
PARTHIA
BACTRIA
Sparta
Halicarnassus
Antioch
Dura-Europus
Ecbatana
RHODES
Phaselis
Aradus
Euphrates
Tigris
CRETE
CYPRUS
Sidon
Palmyra
Ctesiphon
MEDITERRANEAN SEA
Tyre
Damascus
Pumbeditha
Samaria
Antioch (Jerash)
Nehardea
Seleucia
Alexandria
Joppa
Philadelphia (Amman)
Babylon
Nippur
Susa
Gaza
Jerusalem
BABYLONIA
Heliopolis
Petra
Uruk
Memphis
Heracleopolis
Oxyrhynchus
EGYPT
GEDROSIA
Panopolis
Nile
Thebes
Elephantine

City with Jewish population
Ptolemaic Empire
Seleucid Empire

The **Assyrian Empire** reached its peak of power between 880 B.C. and 612 B.C. In 722 B.C. Assyria destroyed the northern kingdom, Israel, deporting its people, and subdued Judah, the southern kingdom.

The **Babylonians** took Nineveh, the Assyrian capital, in 612 B.C. and beat the Egyptians at Carchemish in 605 B.C.

In 586 B.C. Nebuchadnezzar destroyed Jerusalem and deported most of the people of Judah. So ended the kingdom of Judah.

In 539 B.C. Cyrus of **Persia** captured Babylon and took over the empire. Cyrus II encouraged his subject peoples to retain their religion and culture; in 538 B.C. the Jews were allowed to return

to Judah to restore Jerusalem and rebuild the Temple.

Between 513 B.C. and 333 B.C. the Persians and Greeks struggled for supremacy in the Middle East. Finally Alexander the Great swept into Persia, conquering all in his path. At his death in 323 B.C. the huge **Greek Empire** was broken up; Palestine was now ruled by the Seleucid kings.

The methods of the prophets

even the main role of the Old Testament prophets. In general the prophet's role was to help people understand what it meant to be the people of God in their particular circumstances. The prophets' messages were as varied as the circumstances in which their listeners found themselves, but the pattern is similar.

One of the most important ways in which God spoke to Israel was through the prophets. These people—usually but not always men—had received a special calling from God. Some worked alone and some in groups; some were government officials and advisers of the king; others were critics of the government. Some were not concerned with government, but brought messages to ordinary people. Some spoke in very down-to-earth language; others used visions and obscure imagery.

Fortune-tellers?

We often think of prophets as those who told what was going to happen in the future—but that was not the only role or

A variety of methods

Prophets could speak in parables and visions, hymns, calls to battle, oracles of woe, triumphant proclamations, and laments. However, although the prophets' methods varied, there were five main elements in their ministry:

1. Analyzing the current situation. This could originate from thoughtful observation as well as from direct divine inspiration. The people needed to have a realistic picture of what was going on—and the prophet's role was to "tell it like it is." Often they denounced immorality, idolatry, injustice, and oppression, while the people still regarded themselves as good and religious. In contrast, sometimes the people felt their position was so hopeless that the prophet's task was to help them to know the reality of God's sovereignty.

2. Telling the people how God viewed their situation. How did God regard their despair and disappointment? What did God think of their injustice and corruption? Did God share their joys? More often than not the people disobeyed God, rejecting his plans for them, and the prophets pronounced God's judgment on them.

3. Initiating change. The prophets wanted to change peoples' attitudes and behavior. Having shown God's attitude toward a situation, the next step was to explain what God wanted the people to do about it: to repent, turn back to God, act against a particular enemy, or let justice enter their lives. These and similar

The non-writing prophets

Sixteen prophets left books, and their writings make up almost one-third of the Old Testament. However, these were not the only people God used to prophesy. Many other prophets are mentioned in the Old Testament historical writings, and they too were ordinary people with strengths and weaknesses, joys and sorrows.

Non-writing prophets include:

• **Nathan,** who played a significant role in the life of King David. He explained to David what God thought about the building of a Temple in Jerusalem and set out the possibilities for David's dynasty, if his descendants acted with integrity. Nathan challenged David with God's view of his adultery, and later intervened to ensure that David was succeeded by Solomon rather than another of his sons.
• **Elijah** worked as a prophet in the northern kingdom of Israel for about 50 years, challenging paganism during Ahab's

Miracles of Elijah and Elisha

Elijah

Fed by ravens
(1 Kings 17:1-7)

Meal and oil for the widow of Zarephath
(1 Kings 17:16)

Fire on the altar
(1 Kings 17:38)

Taken in a whirlwind
(2 Kings 2)

Elisha

River Jordan purified
(2 Kings 2:19-22)

Mockers killed by bears (2 Kings 2:24)

Widow's oil multiplied
(2 Kings 4:1-7)

Widow's son raised from dead (2 Kings 4:32-36)

Naaman's leprosy cured
(2 Kings 5:10-14)

Axe-head restored
(2 Kings 6:1-7)

Arameans struck with blindness
(2 Kings 6:8-23)

Syrian army put to flight (2 Kings 7:6-7)

Sennacherib's army destroyed
(2 Kings 19:35)

Hezekiah healed
(2 Kings 20:1-7)

reign, proclaiming God's sovereignty over the false god Baal and his prophets, and encouraging those who continued to serve God in difficult times.

• **Elisha** succeeded Elijah, beginning as the latter's personal servant, but ending up influencing the life of Israel and surrounding nations. Elisha was one of the few prophets whose ministry involved events regarded as miraculous.

• **Huldah** is one of the few women prophets we hear of. When King Josiah discovered the book of the Law, as he was restoring the Temple, he asked Huldah God's will in the matter.
• **Miriam,** the sister of Moses, was also considered a prophet. She led the Israelite women in a victory song after the Exodus from Egypt.

Elijah's successor as prophet of Israel, Elisha was renowned for his miracle-working ministry.

messages played a major part in the prophets' oracles.

4. Foretelling the future. If the people heeded the prophets' message and followed God's path, then the future would be wonderful. The Old Testament includes many pictures of a glorious future when Israel, enjoying prosperity and hope, stands as a model to the nations. However, if the Jews failed to heed the prophets' words, the future would be bleak; the Old Testament also has many pictures of the disaster and devastation that awaited them. The prophets referred to the future in order to influence behavior in the present. Which of the possible futures lay ahead for Israel depended on how, and how far, they responded to the messages of God sent through the prophets.

5. Telling the people what God was like. What was supremely important was God—and the people's relationship with him. God was real, God cared for them, they mattered to God. God would judge them—but he still loved them, and they were still his people.

The flight of Elijah

Mount Carmel
Jezreel

Beersheba

Salt Sea

To Damascus

Mount Horeb
(Mount Sinai)

Elijah hears a
whisper in a cave
in Sinai
(1 Kings 19:4–18)

RED SEA

GREAT SEA

Sidon

Zarephath

Elijah raises the
widow's son to
life (1 Kings 17:9)

Damascus

Tyre

PHOENICIA

ARAM

Elisha anoints
Hazael king of
Syria
(2 Kings 8:7–15)

Elisha raises child
of the Shunammite
woman to life
(1 Kings 4)

Sea of
Chinnereth

Mount Carmel

Kishon

Shunem

Elijah defeats the
prophets of Baal
(1 Kings 18:30–40)

Jezreel

Birthplace of Elijah
(1 Kings 17:1)

Ramoth-gilead (853 B.C.)

Elijah flees from Jezebel
(1 Kings 18:41–46)

Dothan

Cherith

Abel-
meholah

Tishbe

Elijah is fed by
ravens during
drought
(1 Kings 17:3–5)

Elisha prophesies
lifting of the siege of
Samaria (2 Kings 6–7)

Samaria
(855 B.C.)

I S R A E L

Jordan

Elisha cures
Naaman of
leprosy
(2 Kings 5:8–14)

Elisha picks up the
mantle of Elijah
(2 Kings 2:1–9)

Elisha purifies
poisoned food
(2 Kings 4:38–41)

AMMON

Bethel

Gilgal

Elijah ascends to heaven
(2 Kings 2:1–11)

Jerusalem

Jericho

Elisha purifies water
(2 Kings 2:23)

Salt Sea

PHILISTIA

JUDAH

M O A B

Beersheba

The Negeb

Elijah and Elisha

Prophets such as Elijah played a
significant role in Israel and Judah
during the period of the divided
kingdom. Elijah denounced Ahab
for his religious defection and the
oppression of his subjects. Elisha
succeeded Elijah and continued his
policies. Other prophets followed,
condemning social evils, faulty
foreign policy, and the worship of
pagan gods.

E D O M

— ·· — Borders of Israel and Judah during
the reigns of Omri and Jehoshaphat

| 0 | 25 | 50 | 75 km |

| 0 | 15 | 30 | 45 miles |

Ezion-
geber

The message of the prophets

Isaiah—Malachi

Eighth century B.C.

Amos and Hosea, the only writing prophets from the northern kingdom, worked at this time, as did Isaiah and Micah in the southern kingdom. Isaiah addresses three separate situations, which we will look at separately.

Amos

Situation: Great prosperity and great corruption in the northern kingdom.
Message: God's judgment on injustice must be taken seriously.

Hosea

Situation: Great prosperity and great corruption in the northern kingdom.
Message: God loves the people deeply and is angry about their idolatry and corruption. Because he takes them seriously, they will be judged.

Isaiah 1–39

Situation: The country was prosperous, profiting from problems in surrounding countries and enemies being occupied elsewhere. A big gap had opened up between rich and poor, and the judicial system benefited the rich at the expense of the poor.
Message: God is great and will judge injustice and oppression.

Isaiah 40–55

Situation: The Exile is assumed to have happened, judgment has fallen, and Israel can now look ahead to a new future.
Message: God is great and will save. This section includes some of the greatest proclamations about God's nature in the Old Testament, looking forward to the coming of the Servant of God, the Messiah.

Isaiah 56–66

Situation: This looks further ahead to the situation after the return from exile, when the nation was reestablished. But there was disappointment that hopes for the future had not worked out as the people expected.
Message: God is great, even when life does not appear to be so great.

Micah

Situation: Great prosperity and great corruption in the southern kingdom.
Message: God will judge the people for their injustice and immorality; but for those who repent there is a great future and hope.

Up to the Exile

Four prophets—Nahum, Zephaniah, Habakkuk, and Jeremiah—began work during the seventh century B.C. The dating for Obadiah, Jonah, and Joel is less clear.

Nahum

Situation: Cruelty and sin in Nineveh, Assyria's capital.
Message: Judgment upon Nineveh.

Zephaniah

Situation: Sin and irreligion in Judah.
Message: Repent while there is still time.

Habakkuk

Situation: Corruption in Judah and the wickedness of her enemies.
Message: Amidst confusion and doubt, the reality of God remains.

Jeremiah

Situation: Babylon was attacking, and Judah was about to be conquered.
Message: Be realistic about the situation. This is a well-deserved judgment from God, who will not intervene to save his people. Transform your lifestyle, accept punishment, and wait in hope for God to bring salvation.

Obadiah

Situation: Trouble from enemies.
Message: Watch out, Edom! Israel's God is sovereign.

Jonah

Situation: Cruelty and sin in Nineveh, Assyria's capital city.
Message: Repent—or face destruction. God cares about the nations. Repentance is followed by mercy.

Joel

Situation: Life—and sin— continues.
Message: God will act. Calamity follows disobedience, and blessing follows righteousness.

The Exile—and beyond

Ezekiel

Situation: In Babylon during the Exile.
Message: Accept your punishment, love God, and hope for the future.

Haggai

Situation: Returned from exile, the Temple has not been rebuilt.
Message: Put God first if you are to prosper.

Zechariah

Situation: Back from the Exile; but where was the glory?
Message: Visions, and God's coming Day.

Daniel

Situation: In Babylon.
Message: Stories of honor and resistance, dreams and visions of the future.

Malachi

Situation: The ongoing struggle in Judah. The people believed but were uncommitted.
Message: Get your act together! If you do, you will be overwhelmed by blessings; if you don't, you will be overwhelmed by judgment.

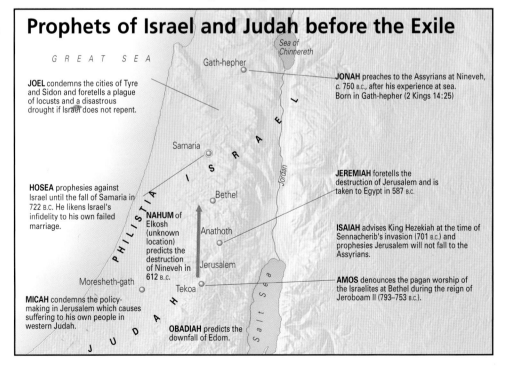

Prophets of Israel and Judah before the Exile

JOEL condemns the cities of Tyre and Sidon and foretells a plague of locusts and a disastrous drought if Israel does not repent.

JONAH preaches to the Assyrians at Nineveh, c. 750 B.C., after his experience at sea. Born in Gath-hepher (2 Kings 14:25)

HOSEA prophesies against Israel until the fall of Samaria in 722 B.C. He likens Israel's infidelity to his own failed marriage.

NAHUM of Elkosh (unknown location) predicts the destruction of Nineveh in 612 B.C.

JEREMIAH foretells the destruction of Jerusalem and is taken to Egypt in 587 B.C.

ISAIAH advises King Hezekiah at the time of Sennacherib's invasion (701 B.C.) and prophesies Jerusalem will not fall to the Assyrians.

AMOS denounces the pagan worship of the Israelites at Bethel during the reign of Jeroboam II (793–753 B.C.).

MICAH condemns the policy-making in Jerusalem which causes suffering to his own people in western Judah.

OBADIAH predicts the downfall of Edom.

Poetry and Wisdom

Job, Psalms, Proverbs, Ecclesiastes, and Song of Solomon

Poetry is not confined to one part of the Old Testament. Ceremonial poems and hymns are found in the historical books, while many of the prophets were also gifted poets, with songs and poems scattered throughout their writings. However, poetic material is most heavily concentrated in the book of Psalms.

Psalms contains an unclassified collection of 150 poems, originally on five separate scrolls. They include collections of psalms written by individuals, notably David; collections linked to specific places; psalms of a particular type, such as marching songs, used on annual trips to Jerusalem for the great feasts; and psalms that defy classification. The psalms appear to have been collected over a number of years, in much the same way as a church hymn-book might be put together today. The result is a fascinating collection of songs for every season, occasion, and mood.

It is interesting to consider the situations in which the psalms were originally composed and used. Note that the categories on the opposite page overlap, and that a few psalms do not fit neatly into any category.

Replica of a *kinnor*, or lyre, which would have accompanied singing of the psalms

Wisdom literature

Some psalms are known as wisdom poems, and are similar in content to such books as Proverbs, Ecclesiastes, and Job. Old Testament wisdom literature is essentially a collection of commonsense observations about life. The wisdom thinker is not seeking to display his cleverness, but to work out what life is about.

Proverbs
The search for knowledge
Collections of "have you noticed this" statements about how life *is* lived, aimed at working out how it *should be* lived. Proverbs reflects on hard work and laziness, pride and humility, friendship, discipline, speech, money, and family life.

Job
The search for answers
Job is of course about suffering— but the underlying question is not so much, "Why does suffering happen?" but, "How should I react when suffering happens?"

Ecclesiastes
The search for meaning
How do we make sense of a world that at times appears meaningless?

1. Psalms of praise and thanksgiving
Some of these are clearly written for public worship and are intended to be sung by a congregation. Others are written in the light of some circumstance or incident, by or on behalf of a particular person or family.

Some psalms reflect on God and praise him for his majesty, compassion, justice, or love, while others reflect on the wonder of creation and the created world. There are also harvest hymns, hymns for other festivals, and hymns recounting Israel's history and how God has constantly acted on the nation's behalf.
"I will bless the LORD at all times; his praise shall continually be in my mouth" Psalm 34:1.

2. Psalms of lament or complaint
The book of Psalms is often seen as the hymnbook of ancient Israel, yet although praise psalms form a large group, the largest group is psalms of lament. Like the praise psalms, some relate to the whole community and were probably sung or recited when the people came together, while others are linked to individual circumstances. These psalms make it clear the writer is not happy—with his or her circumstances, his or her self, or often with God. They express, in vivid and emotive language, grief, confusion, misery, and anger.

The psalmist may be persecuted, reflecting sadly on his own sin, depressed, or simply perplexed. The lament psalms have in common a desire to express to God how the psalmist is feeling. There is no hint that the psalmists felt there were things too awful to talk about in God's presence.
"O my God, I cry by day, but you do not answer, and by night, but I find no rest" Psalm 22:2.

The previous two categories overlap. Some psalms begin with despair and, as the writer thinks about God or comes into the Temple to meet fellow Israelites, gradually he comes to terms with it and introduces a note of hope. Other psalms begin with hope and decline into despair. There was always a psalm that helped the Israelites express how they were feeling. Faith in Israel's God did not have to include pretense. *"My heart is in anguish within me; the terrors of death have fallen upon me. . . . But I call to God, and the LORD will save me"* Psalm 55:4, 16.

3. Other psalms
Smaller groups of psalms include:

Royal psalms—written by a kind of national poet, celebrating such occasions as the enthronement of a new king or a royal marriage.

Teaching psalms—where lessons about faith and belief are expressed in poetic form.

Nationalistic psalms—to encourage the people in the face of danger from enemies.

Psalms of intercession—asking God's help for the nation or for individuals.

Philosophical psalms—reflecting on difficult questions, such as why the wicked prosper and why the righteous suffer.

Jews visiting Jerusalem for the festivals would have this view from the Mount of Olives.

Between the Testaments

From the Persians to the Greeks

The Old Testament historical story ends with Ezra and Nehemiah. We know very little in detail about Jewish affairs until about 200 B.C. The best information we have is the outline of history presented in Daniel 11.

The major event of this period was the fall of the Persian Empire to Alexander the Great (336–323 B.C.), whose home was Macedon (northern Greece), and who inaugurated an era of Greek rule throughout the eastern Mediterranean region and far beyond. He created an enormous empire, which embraced most of the diaspora Jews as well as those in Judea. Both Egypt and the former Babylonia came under his control, as well as the whole of Palestine.

Greek culture very soon became dominant throughout the eastern Mediterranean—the fact that the whole of the New Testament is written in Greek demonstrates this clearly. Greek ideas, philosophy, and customs were soon widespread. (This process is known as Hellenization.) Many Greek ways of thinking were absorbed by subject peoples such as the Jews.

After Alexander's death in 323 B.C., his empire broke up into several smaller empires. The Greek general who became king of Egypt was named Ptolemy, and it was his Ptolemaic Empire that governed Judea for the next century. After the Exile the high priesthood had become the most important political position in Judea, subject to the foreign governor.

The neighboring Greek Empire to the north centered on Syria; it is known as the Seleucid kingdom, after its first ruler, Seleucus. They quarreled over the ownership of Palestine, and a Seleucid king, Antiochus III, defeated the armies of Egypt in 198 B.C. and took possession of Palestine.

The Maccabean revolt

When Antiochus III conquered Judea in 198 B.C., the high priest was Simon II, who is praised in Ecclesiasticus 50; he gained important privileges for the Jews from the Seleucid authorities. A generation later, the Seleucid king Antiochus IV saw no reason why he should not make his own appointments to the high priesthood, which he considered primarily a political office, and so brought to an abrupt end eight centuries of Zadokite high priests.

Devout Jews were outraged at this interference in their religious affairs, but worse was to follow. In 168 B.C., angered by unrest in Jerusalem and frustrated in an attempt to invade Egypt, Antiochus made a violent attack on Jewish practices. He plundered the Temple, erected an altar there to a pagan god, and banned Jewish customs. The pagan altar was called by the Jews the "abomination that makes desolate" (Daniel 11:31). Many devout Jews died for their faith (1 Maccabees 1).

A Jewish family known as Hasmonean or Maccabean now sprang to prominence. An elderly priest named Mattathias sparked a revolt. He had five sons, one of whom, Judas Maccabeus, soon became the leader of the rebels (1 Maccabees 2). He died in battle in 160 B.C., but his able brothers Jonathan (till 142 B.C.) and Simon (till 135 B.C.) continued the struggle. The Seleucid Empire was weakened by internal divisions, and eventually the Jews gained virtual independence. As early as 164 B.C. they were able to cleanse and rededicate the Temple.

Not all Jews were devout, and an influential party had hoped to encourage Hellenization, opposed by those known as the Hasidim, "the Devout." The latter supported Judas in his fight to cleanse the Temple and to regain their right to practice their ancestral religion, but they were not ambitious for political independence. There were thus various groupings among the Jews, which presently gave rise to the parties and sects well known by New Testament times—Pharisees, Sadducees, and others.

Judas Maccabeus never held an official position, but his brother Jonathan was made high priest in 152 B.C. by a Seleucid king. Jonathan's family was priestly but not Zadokite, and this breach of sacred tradition scandalized some Jews.

Simon not only held on to the high priesthood but made sure that it would remain in his family (see 1 Maccabees 14:41). His successors went on to add the title of king to that of high priest. By now Judea was independent of the Seleucids, whose own kingdom was increasingly divided; the power of the future belonged to the Romans. Meanwhile the Hasmonean rulers were able to enlarge their realm at others' expense, taking control of such regions as Idumea to the south and Galilee to the north.

If the early Hasmoneans were patriots, their successors were worldly and violent men, especially Alexander Jannaeus (103–76 B.C.), who quarreled with the pious Pharisees and executed hundreds of them. The period ended in civil war, with two Hasmonean brothers fighting for supremacy. The Romans stepped in and in 63 B.C. took control of the whole region; from now on they would organize affairs in Judea as they saw fit. The Roman general who marched into Judea was Pompey the Great.

Palestine under the Maccabees

The Seleucid kings were hated by the Jews for imposing Greek ("Hellenistic") culture and religion. Led first by Judas Maccabeus (166–160 B.C.), the Jews drove the Greeks out of Jerusalem and founded a new dynasty, the Hasmoneans. Probably the most triumphant moment came in 164 B.C. when, after its defilement by the Seleucids, the Temple was purified and restored, and sacrifices began to be offered again, inaugurating the Jewish festival of Hanukkah, or Dedication (see John 10:22). Alexander Jannaeus (103–76 B.C.) completed the conquest of almost the whole of Israel.
1 and 2 Maccabees

Tyre

PHOENICIA

Antiochia

Ptolemais

Gischala

Seleucia

Sea of Galilee

Gabara

Sepphoris

Hippos

Dium

Geba

Mount Tabor △

Philoteria

Abila

Dora

GALILEE

Gadara

Strato's Tower

Scythopolis

GILEAD

Pella

SAMARIA

Samaria

Shechem

Gerasa

Mount Gerizim

Apollonia

Joppa

Arimathea

PEREA

Philadelphia

Lydda

JUDEA

Jamnia

Jericho

Samaga

Emmaus

Jerusalem

Azotus

Medeba

Ascalon

PARALIA

Anthedon

Beth-zur

Gaza

Marisa

Hebron

Orda

Gerar

IDUMEA

En-gedi

Dead Sea

MOAB

Raphia

Beersheba

Malatha

Rhinocorura

NABATEA

Zoar

Jordan

MEDITERRANEAN SEA

Independent Judea after Jonathan's campaigns, 142 B.C.
Land conquered by Simon, 142-135 B.C.
John Hyrcanus I, 128-104 B.C.
Aristobulus I, 104-103 B.C.
Alexander Jannaeus, 103-76 B.C.
Boundary of Hasmonean kingdom, 76 B.C.
Hellenistic city

0   25   50 km

0   10   20   30 miles

What does the Old Testament Apocrypha consist of?

The Apocrypha is a collection of books and additions to Old Testament books written after 300 B.C. These books were not accepted by the Jews as part of the Hebrew Scriptures. They were, however, included in the Septuagint (the Greek translation of the Hebrew Bible). The books of the Apocrypha are interesting, and valuable as historical documents, and range from narrative history to pious fiction. Most Protestants acknowledge the literary value and historical significance of the Apocrypha, but do not view it as possessing spiritual authority. Roman Catholics and some Eastern Orthodox Churches recognize most of the Apocryphal writings as Scripture (see page 11).

1 Esdras
A historical account, paralleling Chronicles, Ezra, and Nehemiah, of the return of the Jews from Babylonian captivity.

2 Esdras (4 Ezra)
Visions and revelations of early Jewish rabbis.

Tobit
A didactic fiction about Tobit's trials in eighth-century B.C. Nineveh.

Judith
The fictional exploits of a Jewish heroine, Judith, who assassinated the Assyrian general Holofernes.

Additions to Esther (also known as The Rest of Esther)
Five additions that give a more religious emphasis to the book of Esther.

The Wisdom of Solomon
A first-century B.C. exhortation to wisdom.

Ecclesiasticus (also known as the Wisdom of Sirach/Ben Sira)
A collection of the writings of Joshua ben-Sira (c. 180 B.C.) giving his advice for a successful life—combining personal piety with practical wisdom.

Baruch
This book was allegedly written by Baruch, a friend of Jeremiah, and was meant as an encouragement to Jews in the Babylonian Exile of 597 B.C.

The Letter of Jeremiah
An attack on idolatry in the form of a letter from Jeremiah, often added to the book of Baruch.

The Song of the Three Holy Children
A hymn of praise sung by Shadrach, Meshach, and Abednego in the fiery furnace described in Daniel.

The Story of Susanna
The story of a virtuous woman who was falsely accused of adultery and defended by Daniel.

Bel and the Dragon
A folkloric story written to ridicule idolatry.

The Prayer of Manasseh
The prayer of the idolatrous king Manasseh, begging for forgiveness, as referred to in 2 Chronicles 33:11-19.

1 Maccabees
The struggle of Jews against Hellenistic rulers (175–134 B.C.), particularly the battle with Antiochus Epiphanes.

2 Maccabees
A narrative of the Maccabean revolt.

3 Maccabees
An account of Jewish life under Ptolemy IV (221–204 B.C.).

4 Maccabees
A tract about the rule of reason over passion.

Psalm 151

Assyrian relief showing a defeated city being pillaged

Part of a Greek text of the Bible

Introducing the New Testament

Jesus—the reason for it all	78
Jesus' life	80
The political background of Jesus' life	82
The Roman Empire	84
The Gospels	86
Four Gospels . . . one life	88
Matthew	90
Jesus' words and deeds	92
Who was Jesus of Nazareth?	94
Luke	96
Jesus in Galilee	98
Palestine	99
John	100
Jesus' last week	102
Jerusalem—Jesus' last week	103
Jesus' resurrection appearances	104
The good news travels	105
The Acts of the Apostles	106
Paul's early letters	108
Paul and Corinth	110
Paul and Rome	112
Paul's later letters	114
Hebrews	116
Peter and John	118
Extent of the Church in A.D. 100	120
James, Jude, and 2 Peter	122
Revelation	124

Jesus—the reason for it all

The New Testament exists only because of Jesus of Nazareth. Though he wrote nothing himself, he caused the New Testament—a collection of writings of such extraordinary quality that they have shaped world history and continue deeply to affect the lives of those who read them.

Yet, strangely, less than half of the New Testament (47 percent) is directly concerned with the life and teaching of Jesus. The rest is taken up with descriptions of his effect on people after his death. Although the Gospels record his powerful impact on some individuals, his life ended in apparent failure.

But after his death, that all changed. Suddenly there were thousands of disciples, and within a few years even the opponents of this new Jesus movement recognized that it had "turned the world upside down" (Acts 17:6).

The resurrection
Why this sudden change? The New Testament hinges around it, focusing the reason for it on Jesus' resurrection from death. This is central to the literary phenomenon we call "the New Testament." For Jesus became both the content of the message and the source of it. Unlike other disciples of great teachers, the first Christian apostles, who wrote the New Testament, did not just think of themselves as passers-on of tradition—the stories of Christ's life and records of his teaching. Instead, they were proclaimers of the Savior, who by his death and resurrection had opened heaven to all.

It was not that the memories of Jesus' life were unimportant: the very presence of the Gospels in the New Testament shows how vital they were for the first

A typical artist's impression of Jesus of Nazareth. But who was Jesus? What was he really like?

Christians. But the remaining 53 percent of the New Testament, beginning with Acts, arises primarily from this conviction about his resurrection and its significance. The early confessions of faith in (for instance) Philippians 2:6-11 or 1 Timothy 3:16, summarize the message beautifully.

So who was Jesus?
For years scholars have searched for the "historical Jesus"—whom they separate from the "Jesus of faith." They imagine that we need to peel back the layers to discover who Jesus really was. But such an attempt has always been misguided. Frequently when these scholars finally unveil their

"Jesus of history," he looks a lot like the scholars themselves! No, Jesus cannot be recast into our own image. While the Gospels are more than history, they are not less. The authors of the Gospels heard Jesus with their own ears, saw him with their own eyes, and touched him with their own hands (1 John 1:1). The so-called "Jesus of faith" is one and the same with the "Jesus of history."

In 1 Corinthians 15:3-4, Paul says, "Christ died for our sins in accordance with the Scriptures . . . he was buried . . . he was raised on the third day." This past-tense statement is the basis for Paul's present-tense claim that "Jesus is Lord" (1 Corinthians 12:3) and the future-tense claim that Jesus will come again (1 Thessalonians 5:2). These statements cannot be separated from each other. Without the historical, miraculous birth, life, death, and resurrection of Jesus, there can be no lordship of Jesus. In fact, if he has not been raised, Paul says, we remain in our sins and misrepresent God, having a futile faith and a pitiable life (1 Corinthians 15:14-19).

Jesus told Peter that there were many views about Jesus' identity. "But who," Jesus asked, "do you say that I am?" Peter answered correctly: "You are the Christ, the Son of the living God" (Matthew 16:16). All of us must answer that same question. Who do you say that he is?

Why did Jesus come?
To discover why Jesus was sent by God to become man, we need to look at his "I have come" statements. Jesus tells us that he did not come to call the righteous but to call sinners to forgiveness and fellowship (Mark 2:17). He did not come to bring peace but

A rabbi from Bible times. Jesus was not a typical rabbi.

A tomb with a roll-away stone. The New Testament hinges on Jesus' resurrection.

a sword—dividing even families over their ultimate allegiance (Matthew 10:34-35). He came to seek and to save the lost (Luke 19:10). He came to be a friend of sinners (Matthew 11:19). He came not to abolish but to fulfill the law (Matthew 5:17). He came not to be served but to serve and to give his life as a ransom for many (Mark 10:45). In short, he came to live in order that he might die, so that sinners might be saved and his Father might be praised.

Who *is* Jesus?

In terms of who he was as a person, the historic Christian view is that Jesus was both God and man.

1. *Jesus is a man.* He had a human body that became tired (John 4:6), thirsty (John 19:28), and hungry (Matthew 4:2), and that eventually died. Jesus grew in wisdom (Luke 2:52) and obedience (Hebrews 5:8). He also experienced emotion, for he marveled (Matthew 8:10), wept (John 11:35), and had reverence (Hebrews 5:7).

2. *Jesus is God.* The New Testament explicitly refers to Jesus as God (John 1:1; 1:18; 20:28; Romans 9:5; Titus 2:13; Hebrews 1:8; 2 Peter 1:1). Jesus also referred to himself as "Lord," "I am," and "Son of Man." Furthermore, he is described as the Creator and Sustainer of the universe (Colossians 1:15-17), as well as the one who forgives sins.

If the New Testament teaches that Jesus is 100 percent God and 100 percent man, what then does it teach about the roles he fulfills as our Lord and Savior?

Comparative lengths of New Testament books

- Matthew
- Mark
- Luke
- John
- Acts
- Romans
- 1 & 2 Corinthians
- Galatians
- Ephesians
- Philippians
- Colossians
- 1 & 2 Thessalonians
- 1 & 2 Timothy
- Titus
- Philemon
- Hebrews
- James
- 1 & 2 Peter
- 1, 2, & 3 John
- Jude
- Revelation

1. *Jesus is a prophet.* In the Old Testament God spoke in various ways through his prophets, but in the latter days, he has spoken through his Son, the prophet par excellence (Hebrews 1:1-2). His words are the words of eternal life (John 6:68).

2. *Jesus is a priest.* In the Old Testament the priests offered sacrifices for sins, but they also had to offer a sacrifice for their own sins. Jesus, on the other hand, is not only our great high priest but is himself the spotless sacrifice for our sins (Hebrews 5:1-10).

3. *Jesus is a king.* When Jesus was crucified he was mocked as the "King of the Jews" (John 19:3). This was wrong, not because it claimed too much, but because it claimed too little! Jesus is not only "King of the Jews," he is also "King of kings" (Revelation 17:14)!

"He was manifested in the flesh, vindicated by the Spirit, seen by angels, proclaimed among the nations, believed on in the world, taken up in glory.
1 Timothy 3:16

Jesus' life

Jesus was born in Bethlehem, in Judea, probably in about 4 to 6 B.C. He lived most of his life in Galilee, became an itinerant preacher and healer in his mid-thirties, but soon was executed on false charges of political sedition. He left no writings, just a small group of about 120 followers.

Hardly the stuff of religious revolution. How did this beginning produce such a world-changing result? We need to explore his life and teaching by interrogating all the New Testament witnesses. We start by thinking about the basic facts.

Three crowded years

Jesus lived in obscurity in Nazareth, a village in Galilee, until he began his public ministry in about A.D. 27. The story really begins in the previous year, as dated by Luke (Luke 3:1-2), when Jesus' cousin John the Baptist started a brief career as a prophet. Huge crowds flocked to hear him (Matthew 3:5), among them Jesus, whose baptism by John in the Jordan river marks the beginning of his ministry in all four Gospels.

The most likely broad chronology of Jesus' ministry is provided by John's Gospel, in which three Passovers are mentioned (including the Passover at which he was executed). The date of his death can fairly securely be fixed in April A.D. 30: so from sometime in mid-A.D. 27 until then, he traveled around Galilee, Samaria, and Judea (then under Roman rule). Occasionally he ventured outside traditional Jewish territory (Matthew 15:21; 16:13), but basically he confined himself to "the lost sheep of the house of Israel," as he put it (Matthew 10:6). He had remarkable powers of healing, which created a huge response. But all the Gospels agree that it was his teaching which captivated people, conveying a powerful sense of the majesty and significance of his own person.

Jesus' message

According to Matthew, Jesus' proclamation was the same as

A quiet stretch of the River Jordan, near the Sea of Galilee

John the Baptist's: "Repent, for the kingdom of heaven is at hand" (Matthew 3:2; 4:17). But in fact Jesus approached it from a unique perspective. "The kingdom of God" (or "of heaven") was a potent idea for Jews, expressing their sense that their real king was God, and fueling their expectation that one day God himself would come to deliver them from alien rule and establish them again as his chosen people. So "The kingdom of God is at hand" could have been a message loaded with political freight—and revolutionary fervor.

Both John and Jesus tried to dampen down political excitement. John emphasized the personal response of repentance, and he kept away from Jerusalem where all messianic revolution-aries would press their cause. In addition, he pointed people away from himself to one "coming after me" (Matthew 3:11), with whom the kingdom would really arrive. Similarly, Jesus told his followers not to reveal, just yet, that he was the Messiah, and he avoided political arguments. Asked whether he supported Roman taxation (the

Cave beneath the modern Chapel of the Annunciation, Nazareth

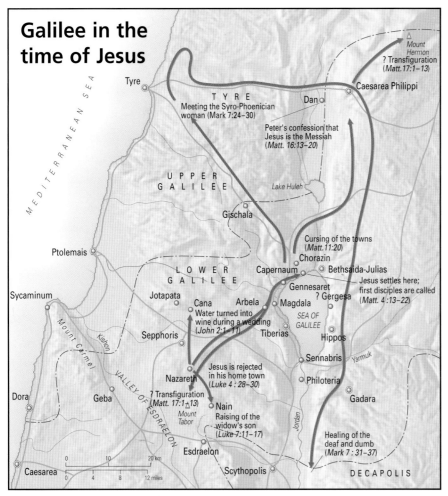

Galilee in the time of Jesus

Mediterranean Sea

Tyre

TYRE
Meeting the Syro-Phoenician woman (Mark 7:24–30)

Dan

Mount Hermon
? Transfiguration (Matt.17:1–13)

Caesarea Philippi

Peter's confession that Jesus is the Messiah (Matt. 16:13–20)

UPPER GALILEE

Lake Huleh

Gischala

Ptolemais

Cursing of the towns (Matt.11:20)

Chorazin

LOWER GALILEE

Capernaum

Bethsaida-Julias

Jesus settles here; first disciples are called (Matt. 4:13–22)

Gennesaret
? Gergesa

Sycaminum

Jotapata

Cana Arbela Magdala

Water turned into wine during a wedding (John 2:1–11)

SEA OF GALILEE

Sepphoris

Tiberias

Hippos

Mount Carmel

Kishon

VALLEY OF ESDRAELON

Nazareth

Jesus is rejected in his home town (Luke 4:28–30)

Sennabris Yarmuk

Philoteria

Dora Geba

? Transfiguration (Matt. 17:1–13)

Mount Tabor

Nain

Raising of the widow's son (Luke 7:11–17)

Gadara

Jordan

Healing of the deaf and dumb (Mark 7:31–37)

Esdraelon

Caesarea

Scythopolis

DECAPOLIS

0 10 20 km
0 4 8 12 miles

Star of Bethlehem

One candidate for the famous "star of Bethlehem" described in Matthew 2 is a comet, recorded by Chinese astronomers, which appeared in the eastern sky in March, 5 B.C., and remained visible for about 70 days, moving slowly toward the south. (Research by Prof. Colin Humphreys of Cambridge University: *Tyndale Bulletin* 43, 1992, 31-56)

Death and resurrection

In this increasingly tense situation, Jesus began to predict his own death—but the Gospels are united in recording that he also predicted his resurrection, and that he spoke of his death as being "for others," "a ransom for many" (Mark 10:45; John 6:51; Luke 18:31-34). Is this just later Christian thinking, read back onto his lips? In the search for the origin of the Christian view that Jesus' death was planned by God as a means of salvation, the best answer is that Jesus himself began to speak of his death in this way—and expected his own resurrection, in fulfillment of the same Scriptures that had already been fulfilled in part through his ministry.

He demanded, and received, a tremendous response from his disciples (Mark 10:28-31). And when the conviction of his resurrection grew, this response became the heart—as we shall see—of all authentic Christian worship and living.

hottest issue of all), he rerouted the question toward duty to God (Luke 20:21-26). He broke religious taboos in reaching out to the outcasts and "untouchables," and proclaimed a kingdom in which the poor are blessed and the self-righteous condemned.

More than a prophet

But there came a moment when an excited Passover crowd wanted to make Jesus king (John 6:15). Jesus refused to precipitate an uprising. For he preached a kingdom of God which in one sense had come already (see e.g. Luke 17:20-21). And this is where we must consider that majestic quality that set Jesus apart from John and all other prophets—a quality that people found very hard to define, but which led the first Christians to know for certain that in Jesus they had met God in a unique way. Whereas John told his disciples to fast in order to

prepare for the kingdom, Jesus and his disciples feasted in celebration of its arrival (Mark 2:18-20). The sick were healed in fulfillment of Scriptures that promised God's presence with his people (Matthew 11:2-6; Isaiah 35:4-6). Jesus forgave sins with divine authority (Mark 2:1-12; Luke 7:36-50). He taught with authority, not like the teachers of the law (Matthew 7:29).

What gave Jesus these qualities? Was it simply the power of a unique personality? Or—the view that began to appeal to the religious authorities—was he able to exert demonic control over people (Luke 11:15; John 8:48)? In addition, the authorities began to feel threatened as Jesus began criticizing them directly in the last year of his ministry (see Matthew 23; John 8:42-47).

The political background of Jesus' life

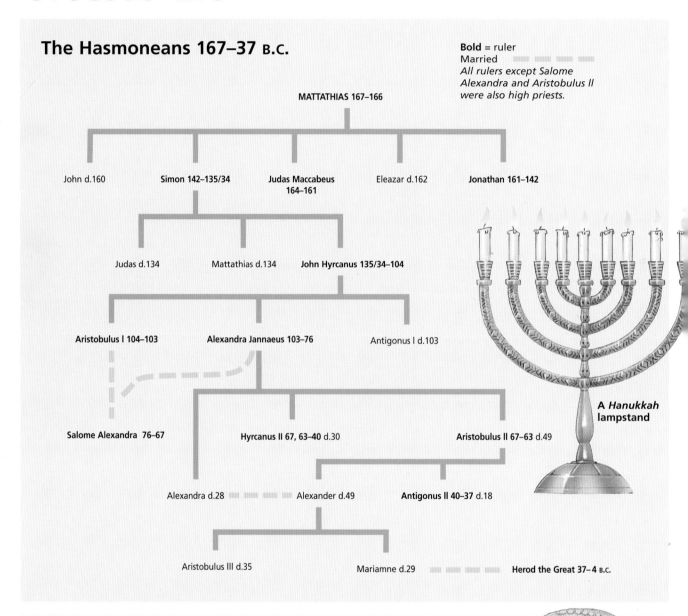

The Hasmoneans 167–37 B.C.

Bold = ruler
Married ▬ ▬ ▬ ▬
All rulers except Salome Alexandra and Aristobulus II were also high priests.

MATTATHIAS 167–166

John d.160   **Simon 142–135/34**   **Judas Maccabeus 164–161**   Eleazar d.162   **Jonathan 161–142**

Judas d.134   Mattathias d.134   **John Hyrcanus 135/34–104**

Aristobulus I 104–103   **Alexandra Jannaeus 103–76**   Antigonus I d.103

Salome Alexandra 76–67   **Hyrcanus II 67, 63–40 d.30**   **Aristobulus II 67–63 d.49**

Alexandra d.28 ▬ Alexander d.49   **Antigonus II 40–37 d.18**

Aristobulus III d.35   Mariamne d.29 ▬ ▬ **Herod the Great 37–4 B.C.**

A *Hanukkah* lampstand

Roman official posts in New Testament times

Caesar	Family name of Julius Caesar, taken by Augustus and used as a title for the emperor from that time. *Luke 2:1; 3:1*
Proconsul	Governor of a province administered by the Roman Senate. *Acts 13:7; 18:12*
Procurator	Imperial financial agent in a Senate province, or governor of a minor province under an imperial legate. *Matthew 27:11; Acts 23:24; 24:27*
Tribune	High-ranking military officer in charge of up to 1,000 men. *Acts 21:31*
Centurion	Officer in charge of 100 men. *Mark 15:39; Acts 10:1*

Roman coin of Tiberius

Who were the Roman emperors of Bible times?

Name	Reign	Christian events	Bible reference
Julius	49–44 B.C.		
Augustus	27 B.C.–A.D.14	Birth of Jesus	*Luke 2:1*
Tiberius	A.D.14–37	Ministry and death of Jesus	*Luke 3:1*
Caligula	A.D. 37–41		
Claudius	A.D. 41–54	Jews expelled from Rome	*Acts 11:28; 18:2*
Nero	A.D. 54–68	Trial of Paul Persecution at Rome	*Acts 25:10–12; 27:24*
Galba	A.D. 68–69		
Otho	A.D. 69		
Vitellius	A.D. 69		
Vespasian	A.D. 69–79	Jerusalem destroyed	
Titus	A.D. 79–81		
Domitian	A.D. 81–96	?Persecution	
Nerva	A.D. 96–98		
Trajan	A.D. 98–117		
Hadrian	A.D. 117–138		

Dating

The first Christian calendar, dividing history into B.C. (before Christ) and A.D. (*anno domini*, "in the year of our Lord"), was worked out by a monk in the sixth century A.D. But it has now been discovered that he was about five years off in his calculations, so Jesus was born about 4 to 6 B.C.—not A.D. 1—toward the end of the reign of Herod the Great.

Star in the grotto in the Church of the Nativity, in Bethlehem

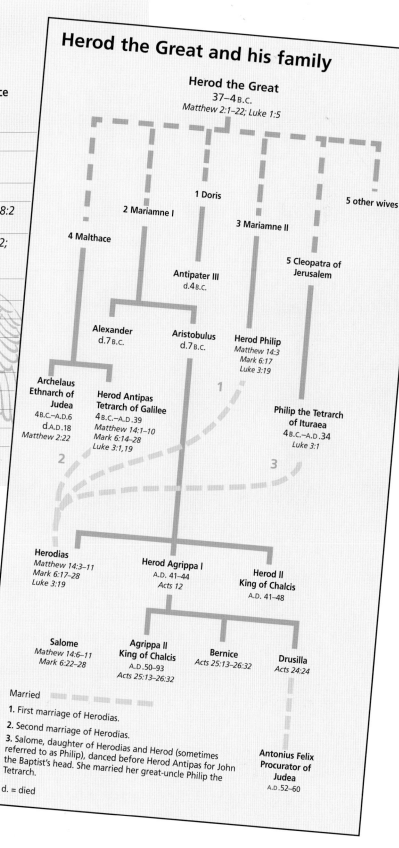

Herod the Great and his family

Herod the Great
37–4 B.C.
Matthew 2:1–22; Luke 1:5

1 Doris

2 Mariamne I

3 Mariamne II

4 Malthace

5 Cleopatra of Jerusalem

5 other wives

Antipater III
d.4 B.C.

Alexander
d.7 B.C.

Aristobulus
d.7 B.C.

Herod Philip
Matthew 14:3
Mark 6:17
Luke 3:19

Archelaus Ethnarch of Judea
4 B.C.–A.D.6
d.A.D.18
Matthew 2:22

Herod Antipas Tetrarch of Galilee
4 B.C.–A.D.39
Matthew 14:1–10
Mark 6:14–28
Luke 3:1,19

Philip the Tetrarch of Ituraea
4 B.C.–A.D.34
Luke 3:1

Herodias
Matthew 14:3–11
Mark 6:17–28
Luke 3:19

Herod Agrippa I
A.D. 41–44
Acts 12

Herod II King of Chalcis
A.D. 41–48

Salome
Matthew 14:6–11
Mark 6:22–28

Agrippa II King of Chalcis
A.D. 50–93
Acts 25:13–26:32

Bernice
Acts 25:13–26:32

Drusilla
Acts 24:24

Antonius Felix Procurator of Judea
A.D. 52–60

Married ▬ ▬ ▬ ▬

1. First marriage of Herodias.

2. Second marriage of Herodias.

3. Salome, daughter of Herodias and Herod (sometimes referred to as Philip), danced before Herod Antipas for John the Baptist's head. She married her great-uncle Philip the Tetrarch.

d. = died

ATLANTIC
OCEAN

BRITANNIA

GERMANIA
INFERIOR

Rhine

BELGICA

LUGDUNENSIS

Danube

RAETIA

GERMANIA
SUPERIOR

NORICUM

AQUITANIA

PANNONIA

NARBONENSIS

ALPES POENINAE

DALMATI

○ Salon

ALPES
COTTIAE

ALPES
MARITIMAE

LUSITANIA

TARRACONENSIS

Rome ○

CORSICA

ITALIA

BAETICA

SARDINIA

EPIR

MAURETANIA

Carthage ○

SICILIA

Syracuse ○

AFRICA

M E D I

☐ Roman Empire in A.D. 14

☐ Client state

–·– Boundary of province

—— Roman Empire at its greatest extent in A.D. 116

—— Roman road

0   250   500 km

0   100   200   300 miles

The Gospels

The four Gospels are the centerpiece of the New Testament—indeed, of the Christian faith. Without them Christianity could not have developed as it did, for as a religion it depends absolutely on the historical claim that Jesus of Nazareth lived, taught, acted, died, and rose from death at a particular time and place, and that these events show him to be Son of God and Savior.

So Christianity exposes itself to the fundamental challenge:

• *Are the Gospels reliable?* They clearly purport to be historical accounts of the life of Jesus, but does the claim stand critical scrutiny? This question quickly involves another:

• *What exactly are the Gospels?* We need to judge them on their own terms, and not ask them to conform to our requirements. And this in turn makes us ask:

• *Why are there four Gospels— and how should we understand the relationship between them?* At first sight, both the overlaps and differences between them set a question mark against their reliability.

What are the Gospels?

Upon first reading the Gospel accounts of the life of Christ, two things stand out. First, these Gospel accounts are intended to convey real history. Luke explicitly tells us in the opening to his Gospel that he is writing an "orderly account" based upon eyewitness testimony (Luke 1:1-4). The second thing is that the Gospels are not biographies in the modern sense of the word. Contemporary biographies attempt to collect information about a person and tell about the entire life on a timeline. But in the case of the

Gospels, there is very little information about the first 30 years of Jesus' life. In fact, over half of Mark's Gospel is devoted to the events surrounding Christ's death and resurrection. It was a common practice in that time to paint a person's life in broad-brush strokes, focusing only on the most significant events. Therefore, it should not be surprising that the Gospels are in a similar genre.

Are they reliable?

The Gospel writers, as noted above, claim to record historical events and to do so accurately. As other historical writings of that time period have been studied and as archaeological discoveries of political inscriptions and dates have

been uncovered, there continues to be greater confirmation of the historical reliability of the Gospel accounts. Non-Christian writers like Pliny, Tacitus, and Josephus confirm that Jesus was executed between 26 and A.D. 36 in Judea, that he was worshiped, and that by A.D. 50 (or earlier) Christianity had spread to Rome and elsewhere. This shows that the historical framework of the Gospels is correct. In addition, early church leaders like Clement, Ignatius, and Polycarp wrote in the late first and early second centuries, quoting extensively from virtually every New Testament scroll, which validates a first-century date of composition for the Gospels.

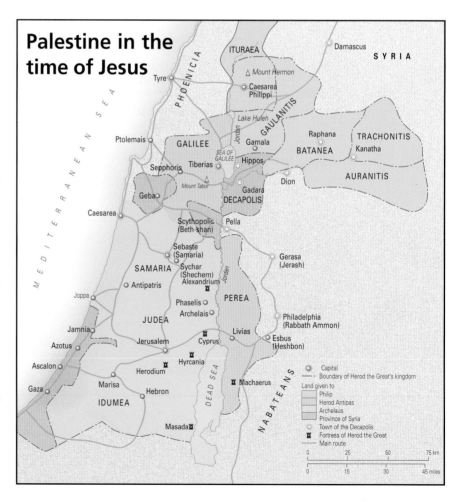

Palestine in the time of Jesus

SYRIA
ITURAEA
Damascus
PHOENICIA
Tyre
Mount Hermon
Caesarea Philippi
GAULANITIS
Lake Huleh
Jordan
Raphana
TRACHONITIS
Ptolemais
GALILEE
Gamala
BATANEA
Kanatha
SEA OF GALILEE
Sepphoris
Tiberias
Hippos
AURANITIS
Mount Tabor
Dion
Geba
Gadara
DECAPOLIS
Caesarea
Scythopolis (Beth-shan)
Pella
Sebaste (Samaria)
Gerasa (Jerash)
SAMARIA
Sychar (Shechem)
Alexandrium
Antipatris
Jordan
Joppa
Phaselis
PEREA
Philadelphia (Rabbath Ammon)
Archelais
JUDEA
Jamnia
Livias
Esbus (Heshbon)
Azotus
Jerusalem
Cyprus
Ascalon
Hyrcania
Herodium
DEAD SEA
Marisa
Machaerus
Gaza
Hebron
NABATEANS
IDUMEA
Masada
MEDITERRANEAN SEA

Capital
Boundary of Herod the Great's kingdom
Land given to
Philip
Herod Antipas
Archelaus
Province of Syria
Town of the Decapolis
Fortress of Herod the Great
Main route

0   25   50   75 km
0   15   30   45 miles

Why four Gospels?

The existence of four Gospels—Matthew, Mark, Luke, and John—allows us to look at Jesus' life from multiple angles. Matthew, Mark, and Luke are called the "Synoptic" Gospels (from the Greek word synopsis, which means "seeing together"), because of their similarity. These three authors did not work in complete isolation from one another. Most scholars believe that Mark—the shortest of the three books—was written first. Matthew and Luke, when recording the same event, usually write the same thing as Mark. But when they write about something that Mark didn't record, they write about it in different ways. The theory is that both Matthew and Luke had access to Mark and relied on his manuscript, but worked independently in expanding upon what he wrote.

John's Gospel is usually considered to be in a different category from the three Synoptic Gospels. It has a different style and has more theological explanations. It was also written later than the other three. Although there are differences between John's account and the Synoptic accounts, the differences are complementary, not contradictory. In short, God inspired four accounts—not just one—so that we might look upon Jesus' life, teachings, and work from multiple angles to see its richness, complexity, and beauty.

Mark

An early tradition connects Mark's Gospel with Peter (see 1 Peter 5:13), and it is likely that Mark represents the collection of stories and traditions which Peter used in his long ministry. But Mark has woven them together into a crisp and vivid presentation of Jesus, emphasizing his power as a healer, his preaching (although Mark doesn't record much of it), the opposition he provoked, the puzzlement he caused even among his disciples, and their difficulty in deciding who or what he was. Mark emphasizes Jesus' expectation of his own death, his call to sacrificial discipleship embracing suffering like his, and his pronouncement of judgment on the Temple and the leaders of Israel. He tells the story of Jesus' last week in great detail.

Outline of Mark

1:1-15	The scene is set
1:16–3:6	Jesus' initial ministry in Galilee
3:7–4:34	Jesus the teacher
4:35–6:6	Jesus the healer
6:7–9:1	On a wider stage: Jesus the Messiah
9:2–10:45	The heart of discipleship: Jesus the leader
10:46–13:37	Jesus the Son of David, the Master of the House
14:1–15:47	Jesus the new covenant sacrifice
16:1-8	The new start

The Church of the Holy Sepulchre, Jerusalem, probable site of Jesus' death and burial

> "If anyone would come after me, let him deny himself and take up his cross and follow me. For whoever would save his life will lose it, but whoever loses his life for my sake and the gospel's will save it."
>
> Mark 8:34-35

Four Gospels . . .
one life

Jesus' life
A simple harmonization of the Gospels

	Matthew	Mark	Luke	John
Jesus' birth and childhood				
Jesus' genealogy	1:1-17		3:23-38	
Jesus' birth is foretold	1:18-25		1:26-38	
Jesus is born	2:1-12		2:1-39	
Jesus' childhood and visit to Temple			2:40-52	
Jesus prepares for his public ministry				
Jesus is baptized	3:13-17	1:9-11	3:21-22	
Jesus is tempted in the wilderness	4:1-11	1:12-13	4:1-13	
Jesus' ministry begins				
John points to Jesus				1:19-34
John's disciples attracted				1:35-51
The first miracle: water into wine				2:1-11
"You must be born again"				3:1-21
Jesus in Galilee				
Jesus arrives in Galilee	4:12-17	1:14	4:14	4:43-45
Jesus calls the first of the Twelve	4:18-22	1:16-20	5:1-11	
Many miracles	8:1-17	1:40–2:12	5:12-26	
The Sermon on the Mount	5:1–7:29		6:20-49	
Jesus speaks in parables	13:1-53	4:1-34	8:4-18	
A series of miracles	8:23–9:8, 18-26	4:35–5:43	8:22-56	
Jesus affirmed as Christ and Son of God	16:13-26	8:27–9:1	9:18-27	
Jesus is transfigured	16:27–17:13	9:2-13	9:28-36	
Jesus predicts his death and resurrection	17:22-23	9:31-32	9:43-45	
Jesus' last Galilean ministry	17:24–18:35	9:33-50	9:46-50	7:1-9
Jesus in Judea and Perea				
Jesus' journey to Jerusalem	19:1-2	10:1	9:51-62	7:10
Jesus claims deity				8:12-59
Jesus the good Shepherd				10:1-21
Parable of the good Samaritan			10:25-37	
Jesus in Mary and Martha's home			10:38-42	
Jesus teaches a prayer			11:1-13	
Jesus raises Lazarus				11:1-44
Jesus travels towards Jerusalem				
The rich young ruler	19:16-30	10:17-31	18:18-30	
Jesus predicts his death	20:17-19	10:32-34	18:31-34	
Jesus arrives at Bethany				11:55–12:11

Jesus' last week, death, and resurrection–see pages 102-104

Who wrote the New Testament?

Name	Nationality	Occupation	Writings	How he died
Matthew	Jewish	Tax collector	Gospel of Matthew	By tradition martyred in Ethiopia
Mark	Jewish		Gospel of Mark	By tradition martyred
Luke	Greek	Physician	Gospel of Luke Acts	By tradition martyred in Greece
John	Jewish	Fisherman	Gospel of John 1, 2, & 3 John Revelation	Banished to Patmos; natural death
Paul	Jewish	Pharisee/ Tentmaker	Romans 1 & 2 Corinthians Galatians Ephesians Philippians Colossians 1 & 2 Thessalonians 1 & 2 Timothy, Titus Philemon	By tradition martyred in Rome by Nero
James	Jewish		James	By tradition martyred
Peter	Jewish	Fisherman	1 & 2 Peter	By tradition crucified upside down in Rome by Nero
Jude	Jewish		Jude	By tradition martyred
Author unknown	Jewish		Hebrews	

Who are the Marys of the New Testament?

Mary, mother of Jesus
The Jewish woman from Nazareth whom God chose to give birth to his Son. Married to Joseph, she was a descendant of David. Mary stood at the foot of the cross as Jesus died.
Matthew 1:18-25; Luke 1:26-45; John 19:25-27; Acts 1:14

Mary of Bethany
With her sister Martha and brother Lazarus, a close friend of Jesus, whose feet she anointed with perfume.
Luke 10:38-42; John 11:1-45; 12:1-3; compare Matthew 26:7; Mark 14:3

Mary, mother of James and Joseph (Joses)
A Galilean woman who, after being healed, followed Jesus and supported his ministry financially.
Matthew 27:56; 28:1; Mark 15:40, 41, 47

Mary Magdalene
Another Galilean woman whom Jesus healed, and who helped to support Jesus' ministry.
Matthew 27:56, 61; 28:1; Mark 15:40, 47; 16:1, 9; Luke 8:2; John 20:1, 2, 11-18

Mary, mother of John Mark
A relative of Barnabas; her home was a gathering place for the Jerusalem church.
Acts 12:12, 13; Colossians 4:10

Mary of Rome
A woman commended by Paul.
Romans 16:6

New Testament Apocrypha

A number of books, dating from the second century to the Middle Ages, were not accepted into the canon of Scripture, and are known as New Testament apocrypha. These books are similar in style but differ markedly in content from the canonical books: for instance, the apocryphal Gospels focus on parts of Jesus' life (for instance, his infancy) and have little interest in his adult ministry. Some are bizarre or offensive, some heretical, and some offer "secret knowledge." Although the apocryphal New Testament books may contain some genuine words of Jesus, it is almost impossible to distinguish these words from the added and worthless material.

Examples of New Testament Apocrypha include:

Gospel of Hebrews: which records Jesus' resurrection appearance to James

Gospel of Peter: which heightens the miraculous in the accounts of the death and resurrection of Jesus

Gospel of Thomas: which has many sayings similar to those in the Synoptic Gospels, but with an added Gnostic flavor

Acts of Peter: which tells how Peter defeated Simon Magus (Acts 8) and how Paul founded the Roman church

Matthew

Matthew's Gospel is very different from Mark's, although he incorporates nearly the whole of Mark (about 92 percent). When he uses Mark's material, he usually condenses it, telling the stories with less detail (and thus less vividly). His Gospel is about 60 percent longer than Mark, with a wealth of new material.

Who wrote the first Gospel—and when?
The ascription to Matthew, one of Jesus' disciples (also called "Levi": Matthew 9:9; 10:3; Mark 2:14) goes back to the early second century, and there is little reason to doubt it.

The second question is harder to answer. Jesus' prediction in chapter 24 of the destruction of the Temple drops no hints that it has already happened. Furthermore, the Gospel of Matthew contains repeated warnings about the Sadducees, a sect that went out of existence after A.D. 70. So in all likelihood Matthew's Gospel was published before A.D. 70.

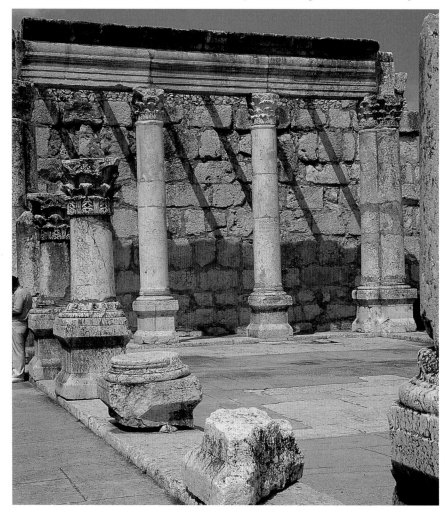

This early synagogue at Capernaum stands over the synagogue that Jesus knew. Jesus made the lakeside town of Capernaum his headquarters during his Galilean ministry.

Why was Matthew written?
Matthew's Jewishness (his interest in the fulfillment of Scripture, for instance—see below) has suggested to some that he was writing for Jewish Christians, perhaps for a specific group troubled by a difficult relationship with the synagogue. At first, most Jewish Christians continued to worship in their local synagogue. But as the first century progressed, relationships became increasingly strained, especially as the number of Gentile Christians multiplied, and Jewish Christians felt more and more pressure to live in fellowship with them. If they did so, they could no longer obey the traditional Jewish food and purity laws.

So in many places there came a "parting of the ways," to use the understated phrase by which scholars describe a painful severing of relationships between Jews and Christians. For instance, the ways parted in Jerusalem when the Jewish Christians there obeyed Jesus' command in Matthew 24:15-16 and fled across the Jordan when the Romans advanced to attack. They did not stay to defend Jerusalem alongside their fellow Jews.

Some suggest that the trauma surrounding this parting of the ways prompted Matthew to write for his group of churches. He wanted to show how Jesus fulfills the Law (e.g., 5:17), how he too was rejected by his fellow Jews, how he criticized the Jewish leadership and especially accused them of wrongly interpreting the Law (chapters 5 and 23), and how he called his followers to respond with love toward their enemies (5:43ff.) and to reach out positively to the Gentile world in his name (10:18; 28:18-20).

Matthew's special emphases
Here is a summary of the four emphases that distinguish Matthew from the other Gospels:

• *The fulfillment of the Old Testament.* On twelve occasions

A Pharisee at prayer, with prayer shawl and phylacteries

Outline of Matthew

1:1-17	Prologue: Jesus the bearer of Israel's promise
1:18–2:23	His birth, in fulfillment of prophecy
3:1–9:35	**Introducing the Son of God**
3:1–4:25	Attested, tested, and into action
5:1–7:29	The authority of his word in his teaching
8:1–9:35	The authority of his word in his healing
9:36–12:50	Following the Son of God: issues of discipleship
13:1–16:12	The King, the kingdom, and the rulers of Israel
16:13–20:34	Confessing the Son of God: issues of self-giving and suffering
21:1–23:39	The Son of God and the past: issues of Scripture, people, and interpretation
24:1–25:46	The Son of God and the future: issues of judgment and salvation
26:1–28:20	The Son of God, crucified, risen, and Lord of all

Matthew notes that this or that took place "in order to fulfill what was written by the prophet…" In addition, he records Jesus' saying that he did "not come to abolish" the law and the prophets, "but to fulfill them" (5:17). The genealogy with which he begins emphasizes Jesus' position as "Son of David"—the Messiah who comes laden with Old Testament promise.

• *Jesus as teacher.* Matthew includes five solid blocks of teaching from Jesus, most notably the "Sermon on the Mount" (chapters 5–7; also chapters 10, 13, 18 and 23–25). This probably reflects a concern with teaching and discipling new converts. Matthew has written his Gospel so that the story has a kind of topical structure—see the outline alongside.

• *Outreach to the Gentile world.* The appearance in chapter 2 of the "wise men" from the East signals Matthew's conviction that this "King of the Jews" is set to rule the whole world. This conviction is given concrete shape at the other end of the Gospel, when Jesus claims authority over heaven and earth and commissions his disciples to "make disciples of all nations" (28:18-19). In between we meet significant individuals such as the Roman centurion whose faith is greater than any Jew's (8:5-13), we see "the Son of Man" sitting on the throne to judge all nations (25:31ff.), and we hear Jesus' famous "mission discourse" (chapter 10).

• *Issues of church peace and discipline.* Matthew's emphasis on practical discipleship shades over into a concern with conflict management and discipline within the Church. This appears especially in chapter 18 (where he uses the word "church," 18:17, compare 16:18), but we can discern this interest in other passages also, like 5:21-26 and 7:1-5.

> "Therefore every scribe who has been trained for the kingdom of heaven is like a master of a house, who brings out of his treasure what is new and what is old."
> Matthew 13:51-52

Matthew's interest in the Old Testament

A survey of Matthew's "fulfillment" passages conveys the strength of his concern to show how the Old Testament was fulfilled through Jesus.
Matthew 1:22; 2:15; 2:17; 2:23; 4:14; 8:17; 12:17; 13:14; 13:35; 21:4; 26:56; 27:9

Jesus' words and deeds

Miracles of Jesus

Healing of individuals

Healing of individuals	Matthew	Mark	Luke	John
Son of government official				4:46-54
Sick man at a pool				5:1-15
Man in synagogue		1:21-28	4:31-37	
Man with skin disease	8:1-4	1:40-45	5:12-14	
Roman officer's servant	8:5-13		7:1-10	
Dead son of a widow			7:11-15	
Peter's mother-in-law	8:14-15	1:29-31	4:38-39	
An uncontrollable man	8:28-34	5:1-20	8:26-39	
Paralyzed man	9:1-7	2:1-12	5:17-26	
Woman with severe bleeding	9:20-22	5:25-34	8:43-48	
Dead girl	9:18-26	5:21-43	8:40-56	
Mute man	9:32-34			
Man with a paralyzed hand	12:9-14	3:1-6	6:6-11	
Blind and mute man	12:22		11:14	
Canaanite woman's daughter	15:21-28	7:24-30		
Deaf and mute man		7:31-37		
Blind man at Bethsaida		8:22-26		
Boy with epilepsy	17:14-18	9:14-29	9:37-43	
Blind Bartimaeus	20:29-34	10:46-52	18:35-43	
Woman with a bad back			13:10-17	
Sick man			14:1-6	
Man born blind				9:1-41
Dead friend named Lazarus				11:1-44
Slave's ear			22:47-51	

Healing of groups

Healing of groups	Matthew	Mark	Luke	John
Crowd in Capernaum	8:16-17	1:32-34	4:40-41	
Two blind men	9:27-31			
Crowd by Lake Galilee		3:7-12		
Crowd on the hillside by Lake Galilee	15:29-31			
Ten men			17:11-19	

Control over laws of nature

Control over laws of nature	Matthew	Mark	Luke	John
Water changed into wine				2:1-11
Catch of fish			5:1-11	
Jesus calms a storm	8:23-27	4:35-41	8:22-25	
Crowds: over 5,000 people fed	14:13-21	6:32-44	9:10-17	6:1-13
Jesus walks on the water	14:22-33	6:45-52		6:16-21
Crowds: over 4,000 people fed	15:32-38	8:1-10		
A fish and the payment of taxes	17:24-27			
Fig tree withers away	21:18-22	11:12-14, 20-24		
Another catch of fish				21:1-11

Where do we find miracles in the Bible?

Most of the miracles in the Bible are clustered around a few people and events:

- **Moses** and the beginnings of the people of Israel

- **Elijah** and **Elisha** and the beginnings of the line of prophets who recalled their people to their covenant (agreement) with God

- **Jesus** and the beginning of the new Israel

- The **apostles** and the founding of the Christian Church

People raised from the dead

Zarephath widow's son
1 Kings 17:17-24

Shunammite woman's son
2 Kings 4:32-37

Man whose body touched Elisha's bones
2 Kings 13:20-21

People at Jesus' death
Matthew 27:52-53

Son of the widow of Nain
Luke 7:11-15

Jairus's daughter
Luke 8:41-42, 49-55

Lazarus
John 11:1-44

Dorcas
Acts 9:36-42

Eutychus
Acts 20:9-10

Parables and illustrations of Jesus

	Matthew	Mark	Luke	John
About nature and farm life				
Birds and flowers	6:25-34	12:22-31		
A tree and its fruit	7:15-20		6:43-45	
The sower	13:1-9, 18-23	4:1-9, 13-20	8:4-8, 11-15	
Growing seed		4:26-29		
Unfruitful fig tree			13:6-9	
Weeds	13:24-30, 36-43			
Mustard seed	13:31-32	4:30-32	13:18-19	
Lost sheep	18:10-14		15:1-7	
Workers in the vineyard	20:1-16			
Tenants in the vineyard	21:33-46	12:1-12	20:9-19	
Fig tree	24:32-35	13:28-31	21:29-33	
Sheep and goats	25:31-46			
Harvest time				4:35-38
The shepherd				10:1-18
Grain of wheat				12:20-26
The vine				15:1-17
About familiar things in Bible times				
Water				4:5-14
				7:37-39
Salt	5:13			
Light	5:14-16	4:21, 22	8:16-18	12:35-36
Bread				6:25-35
House builders	7:24-27		6:46-49	
Patching clothes	9:16	2:21	5:36	
New wine	9:17	2:22	5:37-39	
Yeast	13:33		13:20-21	
The pearl	13:45-46			
The fishing net	13:47-50			
Lost coin			15:8-10	
About everyday life				
Unwilling children	11:16-19		7:31-35	
New truths and old	13:51-52			
Forgiveness	18:21-35			
Two sons	21:28-32			
The wedding feast	22:1-14		14:15-24	
Ten girls at a wedding	25:1-13			
Servants	25:14-30		19:11-27	
Debts and debtors			7:41-47	
Good Samaritan			10:25-37	
Friend in need			11:5-13	
Rich fool			12:16-21	
Watchful servants		13:33-37	12:35-40	
Humility and hospitality			14:7-14	
Cost of discipleship			14:25-33	
Lost son			15:11-32	
Shrewd manager			16:1-13	
Rich man and Lazarus			16:19-31	
A servant's duty			17:7-10	
The persistent widow			18:1-8	
Pharisee and tax-collector			18:9-14	

Parables

Parables are stories based on everyday life. They teach a particular truth.
There are different types of parables:

• **short sayings,** for example: "You are the light of the world" *Matthew 5:14*.
• **longer sayings,** for example: "No one sews a piece of unshrunk cloth on an old garment. If he does, the patch tears away from it, the new from the old, and a worse tear is made" *Mark 2:21*.
• **complete stories,** for example: the man sowing seed *Luke 8:4-8*.

Jesus' parables divided the listeners into two groups: those who wanted to understand and those who were unwilling or uninterested. To those who wanted understanding they were a means of learning more.

There are no parables in John's Gospel, but John does record Jesus using common things and everyday life to point to truths about God and God's world.

Jesus met the Samaritan woman at the well.

Who was Jesus of Nazareth?

Who did Jesus think he was?
Who did those around him think he was?
Who *was* Jesus of Nazareth?
To answer these questions, let us look at four titles that have been applied to him.

A wandering rabbi?

In many respects Jesus was very much like the rabbis of his period, who roamed around, accompanied by disciples, dispensing advice and debating interpretations of the Law. But they tended to come from one of the recognized rabbinic schools, and to be sought out by disciples who would attach themselves to them. By contrast, in spite of Jesus' ability to speak with authority (Mark 1:22 and parallels), he appears to have had no such formal training, and is the one who took the initiative to gather his inner circle of twelve disciples around him.

Messiah/Christ

By the time that the apostle Paul was writing, 20 or so years after Jesus' life, he was using the term *Christos* (which is simply the Greek word for *Messiah*) as a title for Jesus. But at the time of Jesus, *Messiah* would have called forth Jewish hopes and expectations regarding the arrival of a Messiah which were complex and varied. There was a significant stream of thought that hoped for the arrival of a great leader from the line of King David, who would come and deliver military victory over the occupying Roman powers and herald a new age of freedom and prosperity for Israel.

Jesus fulfilled some, but not all, of these expectations. He came from David's line, he restored many to wholeness, he chose twelve disciples in a clear allusion to the twelve tribes of Israel, and

Relief of Jesus praying in Gethsemane

The Church of the Transfiguration, Mount Tabor

he entered Jerusalem riding on a donkey in fulfillment of Zechariah 9:9. Yet, he had no intention of bringing about a military uprising, and, when one of his disciples acknowledged him as Messiah, he instructed him to tell no one (Mark 8:30 and parallels).

Some scholars claim that Jesus had no Messianic pretensions at all, and that all references to his being Messiah are later inventions of the early Church. But it would make no sense for the Church to give him that title if he hadn't made some reference to it himself; for, by not bringing about military victory and by dying an ignominious death, he had ultimately failed to meet the popular expectation of a Messiah.

So why did Jesus sometimes tell others to be silent about his Messiahship? This could be for a number of reasons:

1. There would be great political danger in making such a claim openly, for the occupying powers would be very sensitive to someone making claims to be a savior of the nation. It is surely no coincidence that it is when Jesus is under arrest and knows that he is about to die that he is most open about his identity.

2. Because Jesus' idea of a suffering Messiah was so different from popular conceptions, it would have led to misunderstanding.

3. Jesus knew that he would be fully revealed as Messiah only after his death and resurrection. And then he would be fully revealed not just as Israel's Messiah but as the Savior of all from every nation who believe in him.

Son of God

At the time, the term *son of God* was sometimes used to refer to particularly special people or heavenly beings. Paul and other later New Testament writers spoke of *the* Son of God to refer to Jesus in a special relationship to God. Jesus never used the term himself, but the Gospels clearly record many references to Jesus' unique sonship.

Most significantly, on two occasions a voice from heaven described him to be "my beloved son." The first was at the beginning of his ministry, at his baptism (Mark 1:11 and parallels), and the second was at the extraordinary event known as the Transfiguration (Mark 9:7 and parallels). At this event, the disciples who were with Jesus saw his clothes become dazzling white, as he appeared to be joined by Moses and Elijah before being enveloped by a cloud. Jesus was also pleased to talk about God as "my Father" (e.g., Matthew 11:27), and even referred to him by the familiar term, *abba*, whose closest translation is *dad* or *daddy*.

Son of Man

This was Jesus' favored way of talking about himself. Some scholars see it as just another way of saying "I" or "a man like me." While there may be some truth in this in some instances, there must be more, given the heavenly associations of the term in Daniel 7 and some of the inter-testamental writings. Whatever its origins, it certainly helped Jesus to identify himself with humankind.

Artist's impression of rabbi displaying the Torah in a synagogue. Notice the woman in the separate gallery.

Luke

Luke's Gospel is the longest of the four—in fact, the longest single work in the New Testament. It forms a two-volume work with the Acts of the Apostles, ascribed to Paul's traveling companion Luke from the earliest years of the Church.

Luke contains material found also in Mark's Gospel, but less than Matthew—about 55 percent of it, contributing about 30 percent of his material. But unlike Matthew, Luke has "bunched" the material he has in common with Mark: it appears (broadly) in chapters 5–6, 8–9, 18, and 19–22. In the middle of Luke's Gospel is a long section (9:51–18:14) which has no parallels in Mark, and not many in Matthew. It has been called Luke's Travel Narrative, for at the start of this section Jesus "set his face to go to Jerusalem" (9:51), and from then onward is on the move, gradually traveling south from Galilee for the final showdown in Judea.

Luke's purpose
Luke himself refers to "many" who had produced written accounts of Jesus before him (1:1). In comparison with these "many," Luke sets out to produce "an orderly account" based on his own careful research (1:3), for someone he calls "Theophilus." He wanted to provide a definitive account of the life and message of Jesus (1:4).

Theophilus
Some have argued that Theophilus is an imaginary figure, and they point to the meaning of his name, "lover of God." But in all likelihood he was real, perhaps a wealthy, newly converted (and confused?) Christian who supported Luke through his period of research. Maybe he lived in Caesarea Philippi, for it appears that Luke was with Paul for at least part of his two-year imprisonment there (Acts 27:1), and this would have been an excellent base from which to research the Gospel.

Luke with Acts
It is important to read the Gospel and Acts together, for they have many themes in common and an overarching structure that unites them. For instance, Luke's birth narrative (unique to him) contains the figure of Simeon, an old Jew "waiting for the consolation of Israel" (Luke 2:25), who recognizes the baby Jesus as the Messiah and prophesies that he will bring salvation to "all peoples, a light for revelation to the Gentiles, and for glory to your people Israel" (2:31–32). This prophecy looks forward to the end of the book of Acts, where

Birth, childhood, and baptism of Jesus

SEA OF GALILEE

GALILEE

Nazareth
Home town of Joseph, Mary and Jesus

Scythopolis

4. Joseph, Mary and Jesus return to Nazareth

Salim Aenon
Site of John baptising (John 3 : 23)

1. Joseph and Mary go to Bethlehem for Roman census (Luke 2:4)

SAMARIA

DECAPOLIS

Sebaste (Samaria)

Testing of Jesus for 40 days in the wilderness (Matt. 4:1–11)

PEREA

5. At age 12, Jesus goes to Jerusalem for Passover Feast (Luke 2:42)

3. Jesus is presented in Temple (Luke 2:21)

JUDEA
Jerusalem
Bethlehem

Jericho

Bethabara
Probable site of John's baptism of Jesus (Matt. 3:13–17)

2. Jesus is born (Luke 2:7)

MEDITERRANEAN SEA

Jordan R

WILDERNESS OF JUDEA

DEAD SEA

IDUMEA

Journeys of the nativity and childhood
Journey to be baptized

0   25   50 km
0   10   20   30 miles

"Lord, now you are letting your servant depart in peace, according to your word; for my eyes have seen your salvation that you have prepared in the presence of all peoples, a light for revelation to the Gentiles, and for glory to your people Israel."

Luke 2:29-32

Luke's themes and interests

There are many, including:

• *The Holy Spirit.* Luke emphasizes the rebirth of prophecy at the time of Jesus' birth (e.g., 1:41; 1:67), and the power of the Spirit resting on Jesus (1:35; 3:22; 4:14), and this anticipates his great interest in the Spirit in Acts.

• *Poverty and riches.* Much material signals Luke's interest in the deceptiveness of wealth, and the blessings of poverty, especially the voluntary poverty to which Jesus calls his disciples (e.g., 1:53; 6:20-26; 12:13-21; 14:33; 16:19-31; 19:1-10, etc.). This theme, too, is developed in Acts.

• *Women.* The prominent role played by women in the Acts story is anticipated in the Gospel as we see Jesus treating women very differently from the norm in Jewish culture: (e.g., 7:36-50; 8:1-3. And Luke follows this through by emphasizing women: Mary, Elizabeth, Anna (2:36-38), the widow of Nain (7:11-17), Martha and Mary (10:38-42), and the "daughter of Abraham" bound by Satan (13:10-17—the only known occasion on which this female equivalent of "son of Abraham" is used).

• *Social outcasts.* Jesus' ministry to social outcasts is a feature in all the Gospels, but Luke takes special delight in it. Whether it's poor shepherds (2:8 ff.), a rich tax collector (19:1-10; 18:9-14), a prodigal (15:11-32), unclean Samaritans (17:11-19; 10:29-37), a prostitute (7:36-50), or a crucified criminal (23:39-43), Luke loves to show the doors of the kingdom being thrown wide for them.

• *Prayer.* Where his story runs parallel to Matthew and Mark, Luke adds a reference to prayer on no fewer than eleven occasions. He emphasizes Jesus' private prayer (5:16; 6:12; 9:18), especially at vital moments (3:21; 9:28), and makes his example inspiring (11:1), not to say awesome (22:40-46).

the gospel has reached Rome, the center of the empire, and we hear Paul's comment that "this salvation of God has been sent to the Gentiles" (Acts 28:28). Luke's message is that Israel finds her salvation and "glory" in and through the salvation of the Gentiles by faith in Christ, and not in rivalry or separation. Luke probably wrote primarily for Gentile readers such as Theophilus. His Greek is cultured and vivid, although he deliberately employs the style of Septuagint (Old Testament) Greek in his opening chapters, likely to underline the Jewishness of the start of this powerful, well-told story.

Outline of Luke

1:1-4	Literary preface
1:5–2:52	The story begins: two wonderful births
3:1–4:13	The turning point in history, the birth of the New Age
4:14–9:50	Jesus' Galilean ministry, in fulfillment of Isaiah 61:1-2 (*see 4:18-19*)
9:51–19:28	Jesus en route to Jerusalem: the new lifestyle of the kingdom
19:29–21:38	In Jerusalem, ministry in the Temple
22:1–24:53	Trial, death, resurrection, and ascension

Luke stresses Jesus' ministry to outcasts such as poor shepherds.

He unrolled the scroll and found the place where it was written,
"The Spirit of the Lord is upon me . . ."
Luke 4:17-18

Jesus in Galilee

Jesus spent much of his ministry preaching and healing in Galilee. Although this Roman province was largely Jewish, many non-Jews also settled there. The Galileans, with a dialect of their own, were despised by many Jews from Jerusalem.

• In Jesus' time, many towns clustered around the **Sea of Galilee**. It was while sailing across the lake that Jesus calmed a sudden storm (Mark 4:35-41).

• Jesus came to live in **Capernaum** (Matthew 4:13) and cured a Roman officer's slave (Matthew 8:5-13), a leper (Matthew 8:2-4), Peter's mother-in-law (Matthew 8:14-15), a man with an evil spirit (Mark 1:21-26), and a paralyzed man (Mark 2:1-12). Jesus preached in the Capernaum synagogue (Mark 1:21), called Matthew (Matthew 9:9), paid the Temple tax here (Matthew 17:24), and denounced the town for its lack of faith (Matthew 11:23).

• In **Chorazin**, Jesus performed miracles and later denounced the people for their lack of faith (Matthew 11:21).

• Jesus also visited **Bethsaida,** where he restored the sight of a blind man (Mark 8:22), and withdrew for a time of rest (Luke 9:10).

• At **Magdala**, Jesus was dining with Simon the Pharisee, when Mary anointed him (Luke 7:36-8:2).

• **Tabgha** may be the place where the risen Christ met the disciples and ate with them (John 21:1-14).

• The **Mount of Beatitudes** is the hill where, by tradition, Jesus taught the Sermon on the Mount (Matthew 5:1–7:29).

Above: The Sea of Galilee from near the site of Gergesa

Palestine

Palestine consists of a backbone of hill country, broken by the Valley of Jezreel, bordered on the west by the coastal plain and on the east by the deep Jordan Valley. East of the Jordan is a high plateau cut by four rivers. To the south lies the desert of the Negeb; to the north the mountains of Hermon and Lebanon. In the Jordan Valley, part of a deep rift valley stretching far into Africa, lies the Dead Sea, well below sea level and with no outlet.

Tyre

PLAIN OF PHOENICIA

Mt. Hermon
(9,232ft / 2,184m)

Caesarea Philippi

Lake Huleh

SYRIAN DESERT

Hazor

Ptolemais

Capernaum

SEA OF CHINNERETH
(SEA OF GALILEE)

Mt. Carmel
(1,732ft / 528m)

Tiberias

Nazareth

Mt. Tabor
(1,929ft / 588m)

Yarmuk

PLAIN OF SHARON

VALLEY OF JEZREEL

Megiddo

Scythopolis

Mt. Gilboa
(1,630ft / 497m)

Pella

Caesarea

Samaria

Mt. Ebal
(3,083ft / 940m)

Shechem

Mt. Gerizim
(2,889ft / 881m)

Jabbok

HILLS OF EPHRAIM

Jordan

THE ARABAH

GREAT SEA

(MEDITERRANEAN SEA)

Joppa

Shiloh

Lod

Bethel

Gibeon

Jericho

Gezer

Mt. of Olives
(2,723ft / 830m)

Jerusalem

Ashkelon

PLAIN OF PHILISTIA

SHEPHELAH

Bethlehem

Mt. Nebo
(2,630ft / 802m)

HILLS OF JUDEA

WILDERNESS OF JUDEA

SALT SEA (DEAD SEA)

Lachish

Hebron

Machaerus

Gaza

Arnon

Beersheba

THE NEGEB

THE ARABAH

Zered

meters	feet
1,000	3,281
500	1,640
200	656
0	0
below sea level	below sea level

0   25   50 km

0   10   20   30 miles

John

"John last of all, conscious that the 'bodily' facts had been made clear in the [Synoptic] Gospels, was urged by his companions and, divinely moved by the Spirit, composed a 'spiritual' Gospel." These words come from the end of the second century, from the pen of Clement of Alexandria. And in modern scholarship Clement's description of John as "a spiritual Gospel" has seemed to summarize John's apparent interest in the meaning of Jesus' life, rather than just in the facts of it. For instance, John includes long "discourses," unparalleled in the Synoptics, in which Jesus makes powerful and dramatic claims for himself (e.g., 5:19-47; 6:35-58; 10:1-39). Whereas in the Synoptics Jesus seems reluctant to call himself "Messiah" or "Son of God" in public (e.g., Mark 8:29-30), he does not hesitate to do so in the Gospel of John!

John's aim
But even a quick reading reveals that John is not unaware of a distinction between "the facts"

and "the meaning." He includes hosts of narrative details, for instance, of time and place, and it is he who gives us the tradition that Jesus' ministry lasted for over two years, including at least three Passovers. The Gospel presents itself as eyewitness testimony to the incarnation of the Word (1:14). In this respect, John is no different from the Synoptics: his Gospel aims to present the historical facts about Jesus so that readers may understand and worship him.

John and the Synoptics
Why then is John so different from the Synoptics? The earliest answer was given by second-century Gnostic Christians, who fell in love with John because it seemed to contain special, secret traditions of Jesus which supported their mystical approach to the faith. They believed that John had drawn on separate traditions, unknown or unused by the other evangelists.

This view of John was revived in the twentieth century by some who argued that John wrote independently of the Synoptic Gospels, drawing on traditions about Jesus associated with Judea rather than with Galilee. This proposal, however, is inadequate, for in John, even when Jesus is in

Coin of the Roman emperor Augustus (31 B.C. –A.D. 14), who was emperor at the time of the birth of Jesus of Nazareth (Luke 3:1).

Galilee, the stories barely coincide. John gives us the wedding at Cana (2:1-11), to which there is no Synoptic parallel; the royal official (4:46-54), which has some elements in common with the centurion story in Luke 7:1-10, is a different story altogether; and the feeding of the 5,000 followed by the stilling of the storm, which occur together in Matthew and Mark as in John (Mark 6:34-52; John 6:1-21), but which John expands with the "Bread of Life" discourse (6:22-59). John is aware of a wider ministry in Galilee (7:1) but did not depend on the Synoptic materials.

Deliberately? We agree with those scholars who have suggested

A tiled café sign in modern Cana. John gives us the wedding at Cana (2:1–11), to which there is no Synoptic parallel.

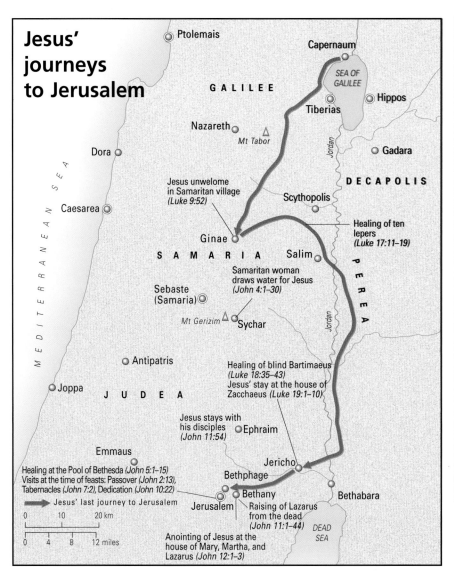

Jesus' journeys to Jerusalem

Ptolemais

Capernaum

SEA OF GALILEE

GALILEE

Tiberias

Hippos

Nazareth

Mt Tabor

Dora

Gadara

Jesus unwelome in Samaritan village (Luke 9:52)

DECAPOLIS

Caesarea

Scythopolis

Healing of ten lepers (Luke 17:11–19)

Ginae

Salim

S A M A R I A

Samaritan woman draws water for Jesus (John 4:1–30)

P E R E A

Sebaste (Samaria)

Mt Gerizim

Sychar

Antipatris

Healing of blind Bartimaeus (Luke 18:35–43)
Jesus' stay at the house of Zacchaeus (Luke 19:1–10)

Joppa

J U D E A

Jesus stays with his disciples (John 11:54)

Ephraim

Emmaus

Jericho

Healing at the Pool of Bethesda (John 5:1–15)
Visits at the time of feasts: Passover (John 2:13),
Tabernacles (John 7:2), Dedication (John 10:22)

Bethphage

Bethany

Bethabara

Jesus' last journey to Jerusalem

Jerusalem

Raising of Lazarus from the dead (John 11:1–44)

DEAD SEA

0   10   20 km

0   4   8   12 miles

Anointing of Jesus at the house of Mary, Martha, and Lazarus (John 12:1–3)

Outline of John

1:1-18	The Prologue: the Word of God becomes flesh
1:19–2:12	The Word revealed to Israel in the testimony of others
2:13–4:54	The Word revealed as Savior of Israel, Samaria—and the world (Passover)
5:1–6:71	The Word as the Giver of Life (Tabernacles, Passover)
7:1–10:21	The Word and human reaction: faith and dispute (Tabernacles)
10:22–11:54	The Word as the Restorer of Israel (Dedication)
11:55–13:30	The Word prepares for Passover, to lay down his life
13:31–17:26	The Word looks forward to the life of the Church
18:1–20:31	The death and resurrection of the Word
21:1-25	The Word commissions the Church

that the Synoptic Gospels present the meaning of Christ and his ministry in seed form, and that the Gospel of John represents a further flowering of that understanding. It is not that the two are in contradiction to each other. They are of one organic whole. The other three Gospels often describe the event or recount the teaching and then quickly move on to the next action in the plot. But John often takes his time, offering explanatory asides to give the readers more information and more insight about what was happening. In this way, our understanding of the divine drama is deepened and widened.

John's readership
What governed John's choice? Recent scholarship has underlined his Jewishness—revealed in his interest in the Temple and the Jewish festivals (around which he structures the Gospel), in the Old Testament and its right interpretation, and in his use of "wisdom" ideas, of material about Moses, of the "I am he" sayings in Isaiah 40–55, and of the imagery of light, water, bread, and sheep associated with the Law and with Israel. While clearly directed at a wide audience—for instance, explaining Jewish customs and terms for Gentile readers—it could well be that John wrote especially for Jews in the aftermath of the destruction of the Temple and Jerusalem in A.D. 70, wanting to present Jesus as the answer to their loss and their need.

Many recent writers have underlined the literary artistry of John's Gospel, its quality and power as a story. It retains this power across time and culture, one of the great classics of world literature.

Now Jesus did many other signs in the presence of the disciples, which are not written in this book; but these are written so that you may believe that Jesus is the Christ, the Son of God, and that by believing you may have life in his name.
John 20:30-31

Jesus' last week

	Matthew	Mark	Luke	John
Sunday (Palm Sunday)				
Jesus enters Jerusalem in triumph	21:1-9	11:1-10	19:28-44	12:12-19
Jesus visits Temple and returns to Bethany	21:10-17	11:11	19:45-46	
Monday				
Jesus curses an unfruitful fig tree	21:18-19	11:12-14		
Jesus cleanses the Temple court		11:15-19	19:45-48	
Tuesday				
Jesus explains the withered fig tree	21:20-22	11:20-26		
Jesus' authority is questioned	21:23-27	11:27-33	20:1-8	
Jesus teaches in the Temple	21:28–22:45	12:1-37	20:9-44	
Jesus condemns the scribes and Pharisees	23:1-36	12:37-40	20:45-47	
Jesus points out the widow's gift		12:41-44	21:1-4	
Jesus predicts the destruction of the Temple and the end of the world	24:1-44	13:1-37	21:5-36	
Wednesday				
Jewish leaders conspire against Jesus	26:1-5	14:1-2	22:1-2	
Jesus anointed at Bethany	26:6-13	14:3-9		
Judas agrees to betray Jesus	26:14-16	14:10-11	22:3-6	
Thursday (Maundy Thursday)				
Jesus prepares to celebrate Passover	26:17-19	14:12-16	22:7-13	
The Last Supper	26:20-29	14:17-25	22:14-38	13:1-38
Jesus and disciples withdraw to Gethsemane	26:30-46	14:26-42	22:39-46	18:1
Jesus betrayed and arrested	26:47-56	14:43-52	22:47-53	18:2-12
Jesus tried before Annas				18:12-14, 19-23
Jesus before Caiaphas and the Sanhedrin; Peter's denial	26:57-75	14:53-72	22:54-71	18:15-18, 24-27
Friday (Good Friday)				
Jesus tried before Pilate; Judas's suicide	27:1-10	15:1-5	23:1-5	18:28-38
Jesus sent to Herod			23:6-16	
Pilate imposes sentence of death	27:15-26	15:6-15	23:17-25	18:39–19:16
Jesus scourged and led to Golgotha	27:27-32	15:15-21		19:16, 17
Jesus' crucifixion and death	27:33-56	15:22-41	23:33-49	19:18-30
Jesus is buried	27:57-61	15:42-47	23:50-56	19:31-42
Saturday				
The tomb is guarded	27:62-66			
Sunday (Easter)				
The empty tomb and the risen Christ	28:1-20	16:1-8	24:1-53	20:1–21:25

Jerusalem—Jesus' last week

Garden of Gethsemane

N

Kidron Valley

Sheep Pool
(Pool of
Bethesda)

Tower Gate

1. Triumphal entry
of Jesus

Fish

Antonia
Fortress

Israel Pool

3. Return to
Bethany

Sheep
Gate

Golden
Gate

Tyropoeon Valley

Temple

Mount of
Olives

Golgotha

Beautiful
Gate

Garden of
Gethsemane

8. Crucifixion
and burial

Warren's
Gate

2. Cleansing
of the Temple

5. Arrest of Jesus

Barclay's
Gate

Court
of the
Gentiles

Ophel

Gennat

Pinnacle of
the Temple

? Palace of
Herod Antipas

Huldah
Gates

Herod's
Palace

7. Trial by
Pontius Pilate

Aqueduct

Valley
Gate

Gihon
Spring

6. Night hearing
before the high
priest

UPPER CITY

Tyropoeon Valley

Kidron

Hezekiah's
Tunnel

From Bethany

? House of
Caiaphas

Upper
Room

4. Last Supper

Pool of
Solomon

ESSENE QUARTER LOWER

Gate of the
Essenes

Pool of
Siloam

Aqueduct

Water
Gate

Aqueduct

Valley of Hinnom

Area of the city at the time of Jesus

Modern city wall

Route of Jesus' last days

0   250   500 metres

0   250   500 yards

Jesus' resurrection appearances

The Gospels do not describe the resurrection itself, but they recount the meetings of many different people with the risen Christ. Many reliable witnesses claimed to have seen Jesus alive after his death (1 Corinthians 15:3-8).

Mary Magdalene

The following people all met the risen Christ:

1. Mary Magdalene (John 20:11-18).

2. Simon Peter (Luke 24:34).

3. The two disciples on the road to Emmaus (Luke 24:13-22).

4. The disciples—apart from Thomas (John 20:19-23).

5. The disciples—including Thomas (John 20:24-29).

6. Mary Magdalene and "the other Mary" (Matthew 28:1-10).

7. The apostles in Galilee (Matthew 28:16-17).

8. Seven disciples by the Sea of Tiberias (John 21:1-14).

9. More than 500 of his followers (1 Corinthians 15:6).

10. James (1 Corinthians 15:7).

11. His disciples (Acts 1:4-9).

12. Paul (Acts 9:1-9).

The Garden Tomb, in Jerusalem, is probably similar to the tomb in which Jesus was buried.

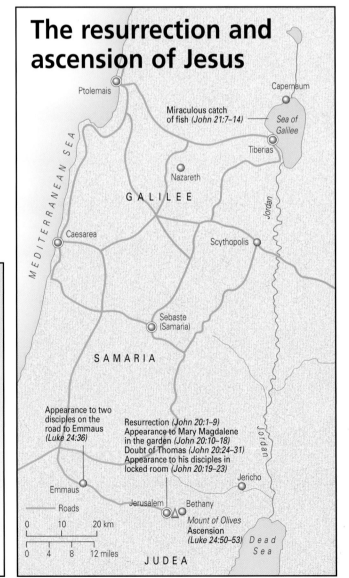

The resurrection and ascension of Jesus

Ptolemais

Capernaum

Miraculous catch of fish (John 21:7–14)

Sea of Galilee

MEDITERRANEAN SEA

Tiberias

Nazareth

GALILEE

Jordan

Caesarea

Scythopolis

Sebaste (Samaria)

SAMARIA

Appearance to two disciples on the road to Emmaus (Luke 24:36)

Resurrection (John 20:1–9)
Appearance to Mary Magdalene in the garden (John 20:10–18)
Doubt of Thomas (John 20:24–31)
Appearance to his disciples in locked room (John 20:19–23)

Jericho

Jordan

Emmaus

Jerusalem

Bethany

Roads

Mount of Olives
Ascension (Luke 24:50–53)

0   10   20 km

0   4   8   12 miles

JUDEA

Dead Sea

Jesus ascends to heaven

40 days after his resurrection Jesus ascended to heaven. In the period since his resurrection, Jesus had appeared many times to his disciples, teaching them and preparing them for his departure.

As his disciples watched, Jesus rose bodily from the Mount of Olives until he was hidden by a cloud (Mark 16:19; Luke 24:50-51; Acts 1:9-11).

The ascension of Jesus
• symbolizes his raising to "[God's] right hand in the heavenly places" (Ephesians 1:20-22)
• signifies Christ's completed work of redemption (Hebrews 10:11-14)
• is linked with the sending of the Holy Spirit (John 15:26–16:16)
• promises Christ's bodily return (Acts 1:11)

The good news travels

After the coming of the Holy Spirit on the Day of Pentecost, the believers in Jerusalem began to preach boldly and increased in numbers daily (Acts 2:1-47). The Jewish leaders tried to stop them, but in fact helped the young movement to spread (Acts 4:1-31).

Stephen, a leader of the church in Jerusalem, was accused of blasphemy, and the Jews had him stoned to death (Acts 6:1–8:2). Believers in Jerusalem were persecuted, and many fled—south into Judea, north to Samaria, and west to the coast and even as far as Cyprus (Acts 8:1-3; 11:19). Many of the apostles also left Jerusalem and preached elsewhere—even in Samaria (Acts 8), a "no-go" area for religious (or "strict") Jews.

Philip set out for Gaza, baptizing an official from Ethiopia, before moving on to preach in the coastal towns (Acts 8:26-40).

Peter traveled to Caesarea, after having been shown in a vision that he should take the gospel to the Gentiles (Acts 10:1-48). As the persecution of Christians by Jews in Jerusalem became more evident, Jewish Christians dispersed northward. They had reached as far as Antioch, third largest city in the Roman Empire, by the time Paul embarked on his missionary journeys (Acts 13).

Paul's journey to Damascus

Some time after Stephen's death, while Paul (then called Saul) was still a Pharisee, he got permission from the Temple authorities to go to Damascus to search out Christians (Acts 9:1-2). It was on the way there that he received his blinding vision of the risen Christ. After regaining his sight in Damascus with the help of Ananias in Straight Street, Paul became a Christian and was himself forced to flee for his life back to Jerusalem (Acts 9:23-26). He was soon in danger again, from Hellenist Jews, and departed for his hometown of Tarsus via Caesarea.

The spread of Christianity before Paul

Believers disperse from Jerusalem

MEDITERRANEAN SEA

CYPRUS

Antioch

Sidon

Tyre

Damascus

Jerusalem

0   25 km

0   5   10   15 miles

MEDITERRANEAN SEA

Plain of Sharon

7. Peter at the house of Cornelius (Acts 10)

Caesarea

4. Philip preaches from Azotus to Caesarea (Acts 8:40)

SAMARIA

Sebaste (Samaria)

Jordan

6. Peter raises Dorcas from the dead (Acts 9:36–43)

Peter's vision (Acts 10:1–10)

Joppa

Antipatris

Lydda

Jamnia

5. Peter heals Aeneas (Acts 9:32–35)

1. Philip preaches in Samaria (Acts 8:5)

2. Baptism of Simon Magus; Peter and John preach in villages of Samaria (Acts 8:9–25)

JUDEA

Azotus

Jerusalem

Ascalon

3. Philip converts Ethiopian eunuch (Acts 8:26–39)

DEAD SEA

Gaza

The eunuch returns to Ethiopia

→ Route of Peter
→ Route of Philip
→ Return journey of the Ethiopian eunuch

35°

The Acts of the Apostles

Relief on a Roman gravestone, Philippi, scene of Paul's imprisonment (Acts 17)

Luke's second volume, Acts, is the second longest document in the New Testament. Like his Gospel, it is structured around a journey. Parallel to Jesus' journey to Jerusalem is Paul's journey to Rome.

Paul's commission
At Paul's conversion, the Lord appoints him as "a chosen instrument . . . to carry my name before the Gentiles and kings and the children of Israel" (9:15). He becomes the center of the story from chapter 13 onward, as we see the gospel spreading westward through Paul's ministry, until he reaches Rome (as a prisoner) in chapter 28. But Israel is never forgotten—throughout the story Paul's priority is to proclaim the gospel to Jews first. But Luke's great passion is to display the universal relevance and power of the gospel, as foreshadowed at the start of the story in Acts 1:8.

Luke's participation
Luke himself becomes a participant in the second half of the book. In 16:10, in the middle of Paul's second missionary journey, a "we" suddenly appears in the narrative, and the author apparently accompanies Paul on the following journey to Philippi. The "we" ceases when Paul leaves Philippi (16:40), only to reappear when Paul returns there in 20:5. The author then accompanies Paul to Jerusalem (21:17), disappears during the events related in chapters 22–26, but reappears for Paul's final journey to Rome (27:1–28:16).

The author thus subtly gives us confidence in the reliability of the narrative. It is clear, for instance, that he took great pains to note the details of the sea journey and shipwreck in Acts 27 (one of the "we" passages). Because this fits so well with his comment in Luke 1:3 about careful research, we gain confidence in the whole story.

Luke's purpose
But Luke was writing as an ancient, not a modern, historian. So he does not provide answers to some of the questions that interest us. What, for instance, happened to the other apostles listed in Acts 1:13? How many of the 3,000 converted at Pentecost were from the places listed in 2:9? Did they then establish churches "back home"? How did the gospel spread east from Jerusalem? What in fact were the dates of the landmark events— Paul's conversion, the murder of James, the Apostolic Council (Acts 15)? Asking questions like these reveals that Luke's purpose was not to provide a detailed survey of the first three decades of church history, but to give a demonstration of the power and potential of the gospel in action, and of its growth from Jewish infant to worldwide adolescent.

Built into the story—and arising from this purpose—are various theological issues, discussion of which Luke skillfully weaves into his narrative. We pick out three:

• *Church growth and the plan of God.* Luke wanted to show God at work through the story, because he believed that the gospel was God's means of salvation for all (4:12). But at the same time he had a very human story to tell, including many mistakes, disagreements, and setbacks. On the one hand, God had already appointed the "times and seasons" by which the kingdom would come (1:7), so that the growth of the Church was inevitable and irresistible (5:38-39). But on the other hand, the gospel encountered strong opposition, and that opposition was actually

All Pharisees respected labor and hard work and they had to have a trade. Tentmaking was Paul's trade.

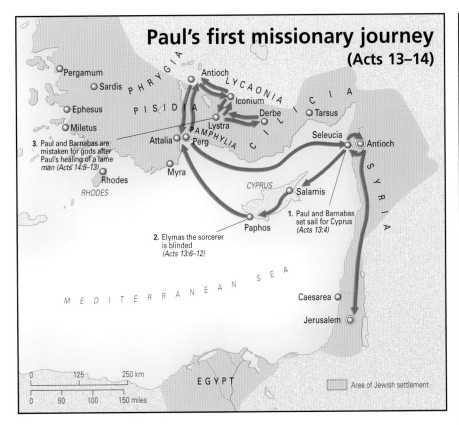

Paul's first missionary journey
(Acts 13–14)

Pergamum

Sardis

Ephesus

Miletus

PHRYGIA

PISIDIA

Antioch

LYCAONIA

Iconium

Derbe

Tarsus

Lystra

PAMPHYLIA

Attalia

Perg

Seleucia

Antioch

Myra

CYPRUS

SYRIA

3. Paul and Barnabas are mistaken for gods after Paul's healing of a lame man (Acts 14:8–13)

Rhodes

RHODES

Salamis

Paphos

1. Paul and Barnabas set sail for Cyprus (Acts 13:4)

2. Elymas the sorcerer is blinded (Acts 13:6–12)

M E D I T E R R A N E A N   S E A

Caesarea

Jerusalem

0   125   250 km
0   50   100   150 miles

E G Y P T

Area of Jewish settlement

Outline of Acts

1:1–2:47	The story begins: all God's people receive the Spirit
3:1–4:37	The Spirit-filled life: power, boldness, prayer, fellowship
5:1–8:3	Opposition in Jerusalem: the Empire strikes back
8:4–11:18	Victory through defeat: the secret of church growth
11:19–14:28	Bursting out: the Antioch church moves into mission
15:1-35	Fightings within: Jews and Gentiles in the Church
15:36–18:22	Paul's second mission from Antioch
18:23–21:16	Off again: from Antioch to Jerusalem via Greece
21:17–26:32	Paul in prison and on trial
27:1–28:31	And so to Rome: the gospel at the heart of the Empire

essential to the story, because Jesus' crucifixion had been both God's plan and an act of dreadful wickedness (see 2:23; 3:13-15; 4:10).

So Luke shows God thoroughly involved in a messy story, preparing Saul even as Stephen is stoned, releasing Peter from prison after James's death, bringing good out of Paul and Barnabas's argument, and getting the gospel to Rome, but by a most tortuous and difficult route. Having been stoned at Lystra, Paul tells the Christians there that God's work of spreading the gospel would only be accomplished "through many tribulations" (14:22).

• *The relation between Jews and Gentiles before God.* The gospel begins within a Jewish context. But must Gentiles become Jews in order to benefit from it? Luke shows the Christians wrestling with this, and his own answer is clear: certainly not! He follows the first Jewish Pentecost (chapter 2) with another in Samaria (chapter 8) and another for Gentiles (chapter 10), thus showing that the Spirit treats all equally.

• *The fulfillment of prophecy.* Luke is describing something completely new in the history of Israel. Never since the election of Abraham has anything happened like this. So he is eager to show that these events are not novel, as well as new, but are the proper fulfillment of Israel's covenant with God. He makes this case chiefly in the speeches which are such an important feature of Acts: see 2:16-36; 3:21-23; 4:11; 7:2-53; 8:32-35; 13:16-47; 15:13-21; 28:25-28. This has to be a powerful and essential case, if Jews and Gentiles alike are to be convinced.

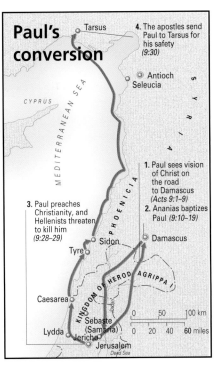

Paul's conversion

Tarsus

4. The apostles send Paul to Tarsus for his safety (9:30)

Antioch

Seleucia

CYPRUS

SYRIA

MEDITERRANEAN SEA

3. Paul preaches Christianity, and Hellenists threaten to kill him (9:28–29)

PHOENICIA

1. Paul sees vision of Christ on the road to Damascus (Acts 9:1–9)

2. Ananias baptizes Paul (9:10–19)

Sidon

Tyre

Damascus

Caesarea

KINGDOM OF HEROD AGRIPPA I

Sebaste (Samaria)

Lydda

Jericho

Jerusalem

Dead Sea

0   50   100 km
0   20   40   60 miles

"But you will receive power when the Holy Spirit has come upon you, and you will be my witnesses in Jerusalem and in all Judea and Samaria, and to the end of the earth."

Acts 1:8

Paul's early letters

The date of Galatians
The dating of Paul's letters is uncertain, and the date of Galatians particularly so. It is probably his earliest surviving letter, written to the churches he visited on his first missionary journey (Acts 13–14), during the period mentioned in Acts 15:35.

Faith or law?
We learn much about Paul, and what made him tick, from Galatians. He was deeply concerned that his converts were abandoning "the gospel of Christ" (1:7) by agreeing to be circumcised—under pressure from "the circumcision group" (2:12). These were Jewish Christians like those referred to in Acts 15:1, who taught (as summarized there): "Unless you are circumcised according to the custom of Moses, you cannot be saved." They seem to have followed Paul around his new Galatian churches, adding this requirement to the gospel that he had taught.

Paul was furious! "O foolish Galatians! Who has bewitched you?" (3:1). Passionately he argues that circumcision is a sign of a wholly different kind of relationship with God—a relationship based on law and requirement rather than on faith and grace (3:11-12; 5:3-6). His own experience on the Damascus Road is vital here (1:13-16): at that moment he "died to the law" (2:19), for he discovered, to his horror, that his zeal for the Law had led him to "persecute the church of God" (1:13). And since the Messiah had to die, the Law could not be God's answer to sin, as he had thought: "If justification were through the law, then Christ died for no purpose" (2:21, cf. 3:21f.).

So the thought that his Galatians might turn to the Law

for salvation felt to Paul like rejecting Christ and joining his enemies. He recounts how he spoke out in public against Peter himself, when the latter "wavered" under pressure from "the circumcision party" (2:11-16). How did you receive the Spirit? he pointedly asks the Galatians: by obeying the Law, or by believing in Jesus? (3:2).

1 and 2 Thessalonians
1 Thessalonians is probably Paul's second letter—written from Athens not long after the campaign in Thessalonica recorded in Acts 17:1-10. 2 Thessalonians followed, probably within months. Many scholars believe that 2 Thessalonians is not by Paul, because of its different teaching about the second coming of Christ (compare 1 Thessalonians 4:13–5:11 with 2 Thessalonians 2:1-12). But Paul is tackling different problems in the two letters, and drawing on different aspects of his teaching to do so. In the first letter he deals with the Thessalonians' concern about the premature death of some believers; in the second, with the strange view that the *parousia* (second coming) of Christ had already occurred.

Opposition in Thessalonica
The gospel met immediate opposition in Thessalonica. Some of the first Jewish converts were grabbed by a rioting crowd and dragged before the city authorities, charged with sedition against Rome. Paul and Silas had to escape from the city under cover of night.

What caused this opposition? It is clear that first Paul himself, and then his Thessalonian converts, felt the sting of the same passionate persecution that he himself had launched at the Church. The

reasons may have been different, but the fundamental motivation was the same: "zeal for the law."

Why Paul provoked such hatred we can see, for instance, in 1 Thessalonians 1:4–5. Paul calls the Thessalonians "brothers loved by God," and says that he recognizes their "election" (KJV) because the gospel had come to them in "power." The terms

Outlines of early letters

Galatians

1:1-10	The single gospel of Christ
1:11–2:21	The single gospel: received, agreed, and defended
3:1–4:31	The single gospel: promised beforehand to Abraham
5:1–6:10	The single gospel: practical consequences
6:11-18	The heart of the single gospel: the cross of Christ

1 Thessalonians

1:1–3:13	**Looking back—the gospel in Thessalonica**
1:2-10	The people who received it
2:1-12	The apostle who preached it
2:13-16	The enemies who opposed it
2:17–3:10	The messenger who encouraged it
3:11-13	Paul's prayer for them now
4:1-12	In the present —living a holy life
4:13–5:11	Looking ahead —to the coming of the Lord
5:12-28	Living now in the light of the End

2 Thessalonians

1:1-12	The shape of the Christian life
2:1-12	The "rebellion" and the coming of Jesus
2:13–3:5	Belonging to Jesus in the meantime
3:6-18	Business as usual?

Fact file: Paul

34 A.D.	Converted on the Damascus Road
37	First visit to Jerusalem (*Galatians 1:18; Acts 9:26-30*). Returns to Tarsus
47-48	Ministers in Antioch (*Acts 11:25-26*)
48	Second visit to Jerusalem (*Galatians 2:1-10; Acts 11:30*)
49	First missionary journey – to the Galatian churches (*Acts 13–14*)
49	Apostolic Council in Jerusalem (*Acts 15*)
50	Writes Galatians Second missionary journey begins (*Acts 15:36*) Ministers in Thessalonica, arrives in Corinth (*Acts 18:1*)
50-51	Writes 1 and 2 Thessalonians

Paul's second missionary journey

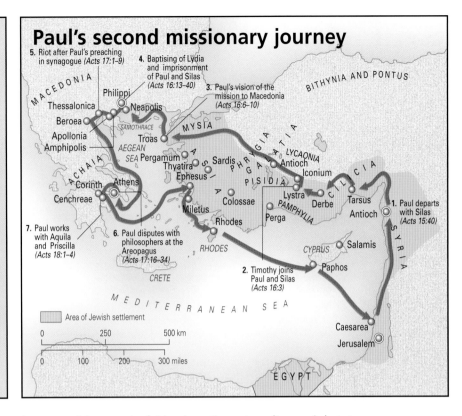

"loved" and "election" are both technical terms, special to Israel's relationship with God. Paul applies them without hesitation to these Gentile Thessalonians because he really believed, as he says in Galatians 3:28-29, that the old covenant distinction between Israel and the Gentiles had been abolished, and Gentiles had become "the seed of Abraham" through faith in Christ. Similarly in 1 Thessalonians 2:13 Paul insists that his message is "the word of God"—a description which ought to be reserved for the sacred Scriptures of Israel! No wonder those "zealous for the law" tried to stop him. They could not accept such a denial of Israel's special status.

Paul—missionary pastor
These three letters give us unique insight into Paul the missionary, pastor, and theologian. He was commissioned by God himself to preach a unique gospel, which he had received directly from Christ on the Damascus Road (Galatians 1:12). But if Galatians makes him seem rather fierce, 1 Thessalonians is full of moving expressions of love and concern for his converts. And in both of the Thessalonian letters we see the motivating conviction behind his missionary zeal—the belief that Christ would return soon as Savior and Judge of all.

Remains of the Roman aqueduct at Antioch, Asia Minor

> We know that a person is not justified by works of the law but through faith in Jesus Christ.
>
> Galatians 2:16

Paul and Corinth

Paul's two letters to the church at Corinth provide powerful insight into Paul the person, and into his teaching on a wide range of topics: not just the big "theological" topics like Christ, the Law, the cross and atonement, the Holy Spirit, resurrection, and final judgment, but also many practical issues such as church discipline, sex and marriage, relation to pagan society, the Eucharist, the use of "spiritual gifts," love and unity, giving, and attitudes toward suffering. Woven into this great mix is the constant thread of Paul's own relationship with the church in Corinth.

Conflict in Corinth

The opposition seems to have started soon after Paul left Corinth. He had ministered there for 18 months or more (Acts 18:11,18), before returning to his home church in Antioch. But soon he was off again—his third missionary journey—and before long he settled in Ephesus for a ministry of over two years (Acts 19:8,10). 1 Corinthians was probably written in his second year there (1 Corinthians 16:8-9). But by then he had already written to the church at least once, for in 1 Corinthians 5:9-11 he refers to an earlier letter which they had misunderstood.

2 Corinthians was written with much emotion from Macedonia (Acts 20:1; 2 Corinthians 7:5). Paul had left Ephesus and traveled north, deciding not to visit Corinth because an earlier visit (not recorded in Acts) had been so "painful," both to him and to the Corinthians (2:1; 13:2). Instead, he had written "out of much affliction and anguish of heart" (2:4), and then waited anxiously for Titus to return with their reply. Eventually Titus met Paul in Macedonia with good news (7:7-16). In response, Paul dashed off 2 Corinthians, vivid, passionate, disorganized, and sparkling in style and in theology—his most personal and revealing letter.

Remains of the ancient temple of Apollo, in Corinth

Troubles in the church

What was the problem? In 1 Corinthians Paul compiles a sad catalog, although he pointedly starts with warm encouragement (1:4-9). There was grave immorality, which for some reason they were happy to accept (5:1-2). Some of the wealthier Christians had been taking each other to court over grievances (6:1-8). Some church members had been using prostitutes, while others had been renouncing sex altogether, even within marriage (6:12-20; 7:1ff.). There was also disagreement—and hurt consciences—over whether it was right to eat meat which had been offered in temples and then sold in the market (chapters 8–10), and Paul was deeply concerned about their worship services, especially the conduct of some women (11:2-16), the divisions between rich and poor apparent at the Eucharist (11:17-34), and their overuse of the gift of tongues (chapter 14). If this were not bad enough, the church had divided into factions claiming favorite teachers (1:12), and some were denying the bodily resurrection of Christ (15:12).

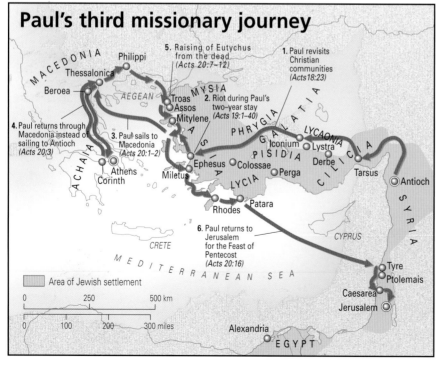

Paul's third missionary journey

5. Raising of Eutychus from the dead (Acts 20:7–12)

1. Paul revisits Christian communities (Acts 18:23)

2. Riot during Paul's two-year stay (Acts 19:1–40)

4. Paul returns through Macedonia instead of sailing to Antioch (Acts 20:3)

3. Paul sails to Macedonia (Acts 20:1–2)

6. Paul returns to Jerusalem for the Feast of Pentecost (Acts 20:16)

MACEDONIA — Philippi, Thessalonica, Beroea
AEGEAN, MYSIA, Troas, Assos, Mitylene
PHRYGIA, GALATIA, LYCAONIA
Iconium, Lystra, Derbe
PISIDIA, Ephesus, Colossae, Perga, Tarsus
ACHAIA, Athens, Corinth, Miletus
LYCIA, Rhodes, Patara
CRETE
CYPRUS
SYRIA, Antioch
Tyre, Ptolemais
Caesarea, Jerusalem
MEDITERRANEAN SEA
Alexandria, EGYPT

Area of Jewish settlement

0   250   500 km
0   100   200   300 miles

Attacks on Paul

By the time we get to 2 Corinthians, Paul is aware of accusations made against him personally: that he lacks the decisiveness expected of a Spirit-filled person (1:15-22), that he does not have "letters of recommendation" from other churches (3:1-3), that he is a poor and unimpressive speaker (10:1,10), that he cannot produce a proper list of miracles and visions to qualify as a true apostle (12:10-12, cf. 1 Corinthians 4:8-13), and that he pretended not to receive money from them but was actually feathering his own nest (12:14-18).

Paul's patience and love in the face of all this is truly moving, and deeply instructive for our understanding of him as a person and the conduct of his apostleship. He does not mince his words, yet leaves the Corinthians in no doubt about his concern and care for them.

The source of the problems

Paul tackles the problems theologically—that is, by taking his readers back to the fundamental principles of Christology, ecclesiology, anthropology, and eschatology offended by their behavior. This reveals that the rag-bag of problems in Corinth may have had a common basis. Some were claiming to be "wise" (1 Corinthians 3:18), to have "knowledge" (1 Corinthians 8:1), to be "rich" (1 Corinthians 4:8; cf. 2 Corinthians 8:9), and "spiritual" (1 Corinthians 3:1). They spoke the language of angels (1 Corinthians 13:1), performed miracles, and believed that they had already experienced the resurrection. ("There is no resurrection" in 1 Corinthians 15:12 means "there is no future bodily resurrection.") As "spiritual," they discounted the significance of the body—and so either indulged it with prostitutes or renounced sex completely, and had no objections to eating meat sacrificed to idols. "Everything's allowed!" was their slogan (1 Corinthians 6:12). Thinking

Outlines of Corinthians

1 Corinthians

1:1-9	Greetings and thanksgiving
1:10–3:23	The unity of the Church around the message of the cross
4:1-21	Paul's self-defense
5:1–6:20	The Church and the world: the necessary distance
7:1-40	Christians, sex, and marriage
8:1–11:1	Food sacrificed to idols: willingness to give up one's rights for others
11:2-34	Worshiping rightly in Christ
12:1–14:40	The Body of Christ—one in love and in mutual ministry
15:1-58	The resurrection—Christ's and ours
16:1-24	Wider fellowship: giving to others, greetings from others

2 Corinthians

1:1-11	Paul's sufferings for Christ and for the Corinthians
1:12–2:13	Paul and the Corinthians: pain, forgiveness, and longing
2:14–7:4	Life in Christ: freedom in suffering, the gospel in weakness, hope in the face of death, genuine love
7:5-16	Titus's news and Paul's response
8:1–9:15	Wider fellowship: giving to Paul's collection project
10:1–12:21	Paul, the "super-apostles," and the issue of boasting
13:1-14	Final warnings and greetings

Fact file: Paul

50–52	Ministers in Corinth. Returns to Antioch (Acts 18:22)
53	Starts third missionary journey. Begins ministry in Ephesus (Acts 18:23–19:1)
54	Writes 1 Corinthians
54/55	"Painful" visit to Corinth (2 Corinthians 2:1)
55	Leaves Ephesus. "Severe" letter to Corinth (2 Corinthians 2:4). Ministers in Troas and Macedonia. Writes 2 Corinthians. Arrives in Corinth for the winter (Acts 20:3)

about themselves in this way, it was easy to make distinctions between themselves and the less "wise," and thus to create factions in the church.

Correcting the errors

Paul affirms their spiritual enthusiasm and experience, but not their arrogance or bad theology. He insists that Christ rose from the dead physically; that our resurrection is also physical, and future; that our bodies are spiritually significant as "limbs of Christ"; that the "wise" and the "spiritual" do not divide into factions; that the Church is a unity as the Body of Christ, indwelt as a whole by the liberating Spirit of God; that he himself was appointed by God to bring the gospel to Corinth; that weakness and suffering (rather than supercharged victory) are the norms for the Christian life; . . . etc., etc.! The richness of these two letters cannot adequately be summarized.

> Who is weak, and I am not weak? Who is made to fall, and I am not indignant?
> 2 Corinthians 11:29

Paul and Rome

Paul's letter to the Romans is his longest and most influential. Martin Luther regarded Romans and the Gospel of John as "the chief pillars of the New Testament," containing "the purest gospel." He gave Romans this accolade because it contains the clearest exposition of Paul's doctrine of justification by faith, which Luther regarded as the heart of the Christian message. Romans contains the most complete explanation of the gospel to be found anywhere in Scripture. Paul may have provided this gospel summary to Rome because he wanted to introduce himself to them, so that they would willingly support him in his ministry (1:13; 15:22-24).

Paul's manifesto
However, Romans is not "the gospel in abstract." It is rooted in Paul's missionary work. After finishing his ministry in the east

(15:19, 23), he is now undertaking a dangerous journey to Jerusalem. He does not know whether he will survive it (15:30-31). So he sends to the Roman church, which he hopes to visit, a summary of the gospel for which he has fought, "the power of God for salvation" for Jews and Gentiles alike (1:16).

There is much drama, therefore, just under the surface. We catch echoes of the arguments, sometimes intense, through which Paul has come. And "justification by faith" is at the heart of it. In Galatians Paul argues his case directly and passionately. In Romans he reflects on the argument, draws wider implications, and spells out the consequences—but still passionately.

Justification by faith
The essence of the argument concerns the relation between Christ and God's covenant with

Israel. For many Jewish Christians, the covenant was the foundation of all relationship with God. It was forever—enshrined in the promises given to Abraham and sealed by the giving of the Law through Moses. It followed, therefore, that the blessings brought by the Messiah were available only within the covenant—to Jews, first and foremost, but also to Gentiles who committed themselves to the God of Israel through circumcision.

Paul's answer
Paul refused to accept this impressive argument. In a

Fact file: Paul

56	Writes to Rome from Corinth Travels to Jerusalem Riot, arrest, and hearing before Felix (*Acts 20–24*)
56–58	In prison without trial in Caesarea (*Acts 24:27*)
58	Hearings before Festus and Agrippa (*Acts 25–26*) Sea journey and shipwreck on Malta (*Acts 27:1–28:10*)
59	Arrives in Rome

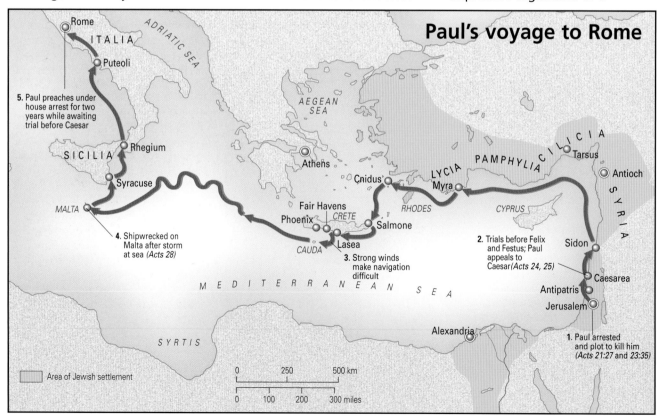

Paul's voyage to Rome

5. Paul preaches under house arrest for two years while awaiting trial before Caesar

4. Shipwrecked on Malta after storm at sea (*Acts 28*)

3. Strong winds make navigation difficult

2. Trials before Felix and Festus; Paul appeals to Caesar (*Acts 24, 25*)

1. Paul arrested and plot to kill him (*Acts 21:27 and 23:35*)

Area of Jewish settlement

0   250   500 km

0   100   200   300 miles

The Forum in Rome

Outline of Romans

1:1-17	Paul, set apart to preach the gospel of God
1:18–3:20	The need for the gospel: universal sin
3:21–4:25	The essence of the gospel, illustrated in Abraham
5:1-21	The Man of the gospel: the Christ who dies for us
6:1–8:39	The life of the gospel: death to sin, life in the Spirit
9:1–11:36	The people of the gospel: Jews and Gentiles in God's plan
12:1–15:13	The obedience of the gospel: community in Christ
15:14-33	Paul's ambitions, plans, and fears
16:1-27	Greetings to unite the church

nutshell, he says:

1. The covenant with Israel was never designed to bring blessing exclusively to those within it, but was meant to bring blessing to the Gentile world. Paul uses Old Testament quotations to make this point (2:22-24; 4:16-17; 9:25-26; 10:12-13, 20; 15:8-12).

2. Neither was the covenant ever a guarantee of salvation. In fact, it promised judgment on the disobedient as much as blessing on the circumcised (2:25-29; 9:27-29; 11:7-10, 20). Only Christ brings a guarantee of salvation (8:31-39), and he came not just to fulfill the promises to Abraham but to meet the need of the world caused by

Bust of the Emperor Nero

the sin of Adam (5:12-21).

3. Jesus brings salvation, through his atoning death, to all who believe, Jew or Gentile (3:21-31), because all have exactly the same need of deliverance from the penalty and power of sin (1:18-32; 3:9-20).

4. Abraham was not a Jew! In fact, he was "justified" before he was circumcised, and thus gives a pattern for today: uncircumcised Gentiles may be justified like him, and so claim him as their "father" (4:1-25).

5. And this has been Paul's experience: it is simply a fact that Gentile believers have received righteousness by faith in Christ— and this fact must revolutionize our understanding of the ways of God (2:14-16, 26-29; 3:22-24, 29-30; 9:30; 11:17). By the Holy Spirit, we have been transformed (6:17-18; 7:6; 8:9-10).

6. So trust in the righteousness of Christ and life in the Spirit, rather than obedience to the Mosaic Law, is what God now asks of his people. In any case, because of the power of sin, the Law could not deliver what it promised (7:4–8:8).

7. But God has not abandoned Israel! He is still faithful to his covenant promises. But these promises will be fulfilled in the

context of the worldwide salvation that he plans (11:1-36).

8. So the Church, made up of Jews and Gentiles together and defined not by loyalty to Moses but by the love of Christ, is the body that can now rightly claim to be the people of God, and it must live as such (12:1–15:13)!

An example to be heeded

It appears from chapter 14 that Paul probably also had a particular issue in mind—a conflict in the Roman church between Jewish and Gentile believers over practical issues arising from their life together— the observation of Jewish food laws and festivals. Amazingly, though he has argued strongly that "Christ is the end of the law" (10:4), Paul gently encourages the Gentile Christians simply to accept their Jewish brothers and sisters, and not to require them to go against their consciences (14:13-23).

Paul's later letters

Stone relief of a Roman soldier

The New Testament contains a string of seven shorter letters from Paul: Philippians, Ephesians, Colossians, Philemon, and the "Pastoral" letters (1 and 2 Timothy, and Titus). All of these (except possibly Philippians) date from the last few years of Paul's life.

Authorship
Modern scholars who read these letters notice that their language and style seem different from other Pauline letters. They also note that some of the theological concepts in these letters are not found elsewhere, or that theological themes found in other Pauline letters are not found here. For this reason, some scholars argue that Paul did not write these letters, suggesting that the letters are pseudonymous—that is, written by someone else and yet using Paul's name.

But evangelical scholars have offered convincing rebuttals to these claims. They point out that Paul's writings need not be monolithic, either in terms of style and language or in terms of theological themes. Our writing tends to develop over time—how and what we write often changes based upon differing situations. Furthermore, the differences in theology appear to be exaggerated. There is far more continuity than the critics have suggested. Finally, the prevalence of pseudonymous letters among the Jews was rare. The early Church regarded such a practice as dishonorable, and it explicitly rejected such spurious epistles (such as the apocryphal *Acts of Paul*, the *Epistles to the Laodiceans*, and *Gospel of Peter*). Further, there is no evidence for the idea that someone other than Paul wrote these letters.

At the end of the day, both the internal and external evidence rests with the judgment of the early church that these are indeed authentic letters penned by the apostle Paul.

Prison letters
Paul was in prison when writing all of the later letters except 1 Timothy and Titus. Which imprisonment is this? Acts mentions two (in Caesarea and in Rome), and Paul refers to frequent imprisonments (2 Corinthians 11:23). The best suggestion is that all except 2 Timothy were written from the Acts 28 Roman imprisonment, and 2 Timothy from a later imprisonment in Rome, immediately prior to Paul's execution.

The view that Paul was released at the end of Acts 28 rests (a) on the tradition that he was martyred in the persecution by Nero in A.D. 65, and (b) on the references in the Pastorals to various movements by him around the Mediterranean, which cannot be fitted into the Acts narrative.

These marvelous letters are gold mines of teaching and encouragement.

Philippians
This is a thank-you letter, written to acknowledge the church's gift to him (2:25; 4:18). But Paul fills it out into a powerful discourse on facing suffering and death, turning the example of Christ into a pattern for the Christian life (1:18-30; 2:5-11). He writes movingly of the way that pattern has been written into his own experience (3:4-14) and warns against people who dress up worldly ambition as religion (3:17-21).

Remains, dating from ancient times, of the prison at Philippi

Remains of the massive theater at Ephesus, site of the riot caused by Paul's visit

Fact file: Paul

59–61	Under house arrest in Rome (*Acts 28:30*) Writes Philippians, Ephesians, Colossians, and Philemon
61	Charges dropped and released?
61–64	Ministers again, possibly in Spain (*Romans 15:24*), Asia Minor (*Philemon 22; 2 Timothy 4:13*), Crete (*Titus 1:5*), Corinth (*2 Timothy 4:20*), Ephesus, and Macedonia (*1 Timothy 1:3; 2 Timothy 1:18*) Writes 1 Timothy and Titus
64–65	Writes 2 Timothy Rearrested, tried, and executed in Rome (*2 Timothy 4:6,16*)

Ephesians and Colossians

These letters have much in common and were clearly written at the same time. Ephesians may have been a circular letter, sent to several congregations in the Ephesus area, for Paul is aware that many of the recipients will not know him now (Ephesians 3:2-4). Ephesians compares with Romans for its power and intensity: Paul focuses on the person of Christ and displays his cosmic rule as the center of God's world plan. In Colossians he applies this cosmic picture of Christ to some of the religious conflicts his readers were facing.

Philemon

This letter is a little gem: by divine providence, Paul came into contact, in Rome, with a slave who had run away from his master in the Lycus Valley, 1,000 miles away—and the master turned out to be an old convert of Paul's. Through Paul, Onesimus (the slave) became a Christian, too—and now goes back to his master, Philemon, with this beautiful note entreating forgiveness and acceptance "no longer as a slave, but more than a slave, as a beloved brother" (verse 16). This letter speaks volumes about Paul's attitude toward slavery. Clearly he felt that it was incompatible with Christian fellowship that brothers in Christ should also be masters and slaves. But he never attacked slavery as such, preferring to let the gospel make its own appeal.

The Pastoral letters

These letters probably date from a few years later. Timothy and Titus have been coworkers with Paul for about 15 years and have become leaders of stature in their own right. Paul has left them in charge in Ephesus and Crete respectively, to appoint elders and deacons, to teach and to encourage and lead the churches. In addition, Timothy faced some difficult situations in Ephesus. The Pastorals are thus full of practical advice about church leadership. 2 Timothy contains Paul's moving testimony in the face of imminent death.

An artist's impression of the apostle Paul writing from his prison cell.

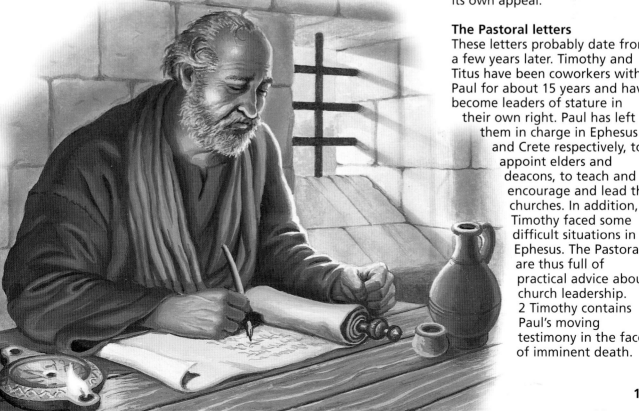

115

Hebrews

The letter to the Hebrews is an enigma. An enormously powerful piece of early Christian theology, clearly the product of a great and original mind—yet we do not know who wrote it, or to whom, or when, or where, or indeed why.

Is it a letter?
The first puzzle concerns its genre. Is it a letter, or a treatise? It has no opening greetings, but it ends like a letter (13:18-25). The style and contents have much in common with the treatises of Philo, the first-century Jewish philosopher, and yet we gather that the author is addressing a particular group of people (e.g.,

5:11-12; 10:32-34). The best solution is that the original letter-opening has been lost—which would have given us the author's and recipients' identities.

Who wrote Hebrews?
For many years Hebrews was ascribed to Paul, but this is no longer the majority view. Of the many suggestions, the most compelling is Luther's, that it was written by Apollos, Paul's coworker in Corinth (1 Corinthians 3:4-7), who came from Alexandria and is described in Acts 18:24 as "eloquent" and "competent in the Scriptures." His origin in Alexandria could explain the parallels with Philo,

who also came from there, and the author of Hebrews was certainly "mighty in the Scriptures"—see Acts 18:28.

The readers
Hebrews 13:24 possibly provides a clue about the recipients. "Those who come from Italy send you greetings" suggests that they are in Italy, being greeted by their fellow countrymen who are with the author outside Italy. If so, Rome would be the best bet. More broadly, they are clearly Jewish Christians who seem to form a distinct community, with their own history (6:10; 10:32-34; 12:4) and leaders (13:17). This would have been possible in Rome, where the church was divided into several house-churches (Romans 16:5, 14, 15).

Identity problems
For such Jewish-Christian groups, identity was a great problem. Where did they belong? Many still felt a strong loyalty to the synagogue, and yet the more they had fellowship with Gentiles, the more difficult their relationship with the synagogue became. If they ate with Gentiles, they would be branded law-breakers—and eventually apostates, if they persisted or deliberately broke off from the synagogue. Either way, they would lose their Jewishness. There seemed to be no cultural and religious middle ground.

The recipients of Hebrews are such a group! The author is clearly very concerned about them. The letter is peppered with warnings—against "neglecting" their salvation (2:3), "falling away" (3:12), "failing" (4:1), "shrinking back" (10:39); and with corresponding exhortations to "pay close attention" (2:1), "hold fast" (3:6), "strive" (4:11), "show the same earnestness until the end" (6:11), "draw near . . . in full assurance" (10:22; 4:16). These verbs illustrate the pastoral tone of the whole letter.

What was going on? Two theories have been proposed. Perhaps the recipients were so

Artist's impression of the Jewish high priest in his full regalia

linen turban with gold plate inscribed "Holy to Yahweh"

breastplate with twelve precious stones inscribed with the names of the twelve tribes of Israel

ephod of fine linen with colorful embroidery

pockets for sacred lots Urim and Thummim

blue robe with ornate hem decorated with gold bells and embroidered pomegranates

The Tabernacle

The author of the book of Hebrews assumes that his readers are well acquainted with the design of the Tabernacle. It was divided into two compartments. The first and larger was the "Holy Place." The further and smaller was the "Most Holy Place," the inner sanctuary. Here stood the Ark, surmounted by its golden lid, the mercy seat, where the Shekinah glory, the visible symbol of God's presence, appeared.

The two "Places" were separated by a thick curtain called the veil. By this arrangement the Holy One of Israel was teaching his people both his presence among them, and his inaccessibility to them. He was near and yet far; sinners could draw near, but were not permitted to penetrate into his holy presence beyond the veil. Access to God was limited by four conditions, listed in Hebrews 9:7: *only the high priest* might enter the inner sanctuary; but *only once a year* (on the Day of Atonement), and *only taking sacrificial blood* with him, to sprinkle on the mercy seat; and then he would secure remission *only for unintentional sins*.

For our author, these limitations showed "that the way into the Most Holy Place had not yet been disclosed" (9:8); once again, the Old Testament reveals its own inadequacy and its need of Jesus. In contrast to the old high priest, Jesus has "entered the Most Holy Place once for all by his blood, having obtained eternal redemption" (9:12).

Outline of Hebrews

1:1-4	Preface: the Son who is the final Word from God
1:5–2:18	The Son, superior to angels (through whom the Law was mediated)
3:1–4:13	The Son, superior to Moses and Joshua (the great old covenant deliverers)
4:14–5:10	Jesus, the Great High Priest (kernel statement, anticipating 5:11–10:39)
5:11–6:20	First exhortation to perseverance
7:1-28	The person of Jesus the High Priest (like Melchizedek)
8:1–10:18	The work of Jesus the High Priest (like Aaron)
10:19-39	Second exhortation to perseverance
11:1-40	Old Testament faith—confidently looking forward, in patient trust
12:1-29	New Testament faith—confidently looking to Jesus, in patient trust
13:1-25	Concluding exhortations and greetings

confused about their identity—Jewish or Christian?—that they were simply not making the progress in their faith that the author desired. He calls them "dull of hearing" (5:11) and "sluggish" (6:12). Alternatively, he may have heard that they were actually abandoning their Christian commitment in order to stay in fellowship with the synagogue. Hebrews 10:25 (NIV) reads like a mild encouragement to church attendance: "Let us not give up meeting together, as some are in the habit of doing"—but we need to read this against the background sketched above, where meeting with Gentiles seriously compromises Jewish identity.

Jesus or Judaism?

Either way, the author's strategy is clear: he presents Jesus as the fulfillment of the Scriptures to the extent that without Jesus the Scriptures are left without coherent meaning. So the readers are faced with a clear choice between the Old Testament, made complete and comprehensible only in Jesus, and Judaism, which has an incomplete Scripture, ineffectual rituals, and no answer to the deepest human needs.

The argument is deep and complex, and highly polemical. In current New Testament scholarship it is popular to suggest that the New Testament does not deny the validity of Judaism—it merely adds Christianity alongside it as another "pathway" to God. But the presence of Hebrews in the New Testament makes this suggestion impossible (though it is hard to square with other New Testament texts, also). The author seeks to claim the Old Testament for Christ, and Christ alone, arguing that, on its own, Israel's covenant with God is "growing old [and] is ready to vanish away" (8:13). Only in Christ do the Scriptures make sense, because Christ brings the promised "new covenant" under which sins are truly forgiven (10:11-18). Here Christianity's exclusive claim is expressed at its clearest.

Peter and John

The apostles Peter and John are often linked in the early stories in Acts (3:1; 4:13; 8:14), building on their association in Jesus' inner circle (Mark 5:37; 9:2; 13:3). So it is fitting that the New Testament should include letters from them both, written (probably) when both were in old age, Peter in Rome and John in Ephesus.

1 Peter

The ascription of these letters—two to Peter and three to John—is sometimes disputed. (We will look at 2 Peter on page 122.)

1 Peter is written in good, lively, idiomatic Greek: is it possible that a Galilean fisherman, whose first language was Aramaic, could have produced it? Though many reply "No," the better answer is "Why not?" Recent studies reveal that Galilee was bilingual. Almost certainly Peter would have spoken Greek as the language of trade. And we must not discount the effect of 25 years of mission in a Greek-speaking environment—nor the influence of Silas, who helped Peter to write the letter (5:12).

If by Peter, then this first letter was written from Rome (5:13— "Babylon" is a code for Rome) at a time when there were Jewish Christians throughout the Roman provinces listed in 1:1. These two factors give the letter a date perhaps in the late 60s. Early church tradition puts Peter in Rome for the last part of his ministry. The letter is addressed, like James, to "the diaspora," the technical expression for Jews scattered around the world, who are Peter's particular mission responsibility (Galatians 2:7).

Peter's readers

Persecution is clearly looming (1:6-7; 3:13-17; 4:12-19; 5:9-10). Peter knows that his readers feel isolated and vulnerable. They are "sojourners and exiles" (2:11; compare 1:1). Peter skillfully

The theater, Hierapolis, seat of Papias

modulates this sense of social alienation into the idea of election: they feel different because they *are* different (2:9).

Jews in Asia Minor were well integrated into local culture, and many of them participated happily in local festivals, as Peter reminds them (4:3). But now they have stepped back, and incurred suspicion and hostility as a result—especially by refusing to participate in the imperial cult by which people expressed their gratitude and loyalty to the emperor. Slaves and women were particularly vulnerable, for it was culturally unacceptable for them to adopt a religion different from the male head of the household. So Peter gives them special encouragement in the so-called "Household Code" (2:13–3:7).

Overall, Peter seeks to inspire his readers with a vision of what God has done for them in Christ, and to encourage them to "do good" in every situation, however difficult (2:12-14, 20; 3:6, 11; 4:19).

John

The letters of John do not identify their author by name, but the ancient manuscripts all include a heading which names "John." As in Hebrews, the opening greeting is missing from the first letter, but letters 2 and 3

Theater in Ephesus

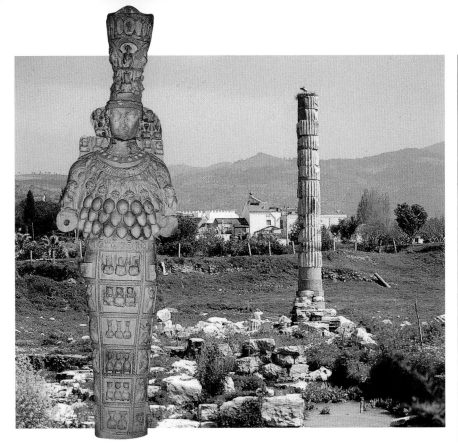
The remains of the temple of Artemis (Diana) in Ephesus, with (*inset*) statue of Artemis

Outlines:

1 Peter

1:1–2:10	**Suffering as a Christian**
1:1-9	The hidden inheritance, the hidden Lord
1:10–2:3	Focus on Jesus
2:4-10	Becoming a temple, enjoying fellowship with him
2:11–3:12	**Living as aliens in this world**
2:11-12	Keeping your inner self
2:13–3:7	Integrity in difficult relationships
3:8-12	Structuring your corporate self
3:13–4:19	**Suffering— the road to glory**
3:13-22	Suffering for doing good
4:1-11	Living for God
4:12-19	Sharing the sufferings of Christ
5:1-14	**Final exhortations and greetings**

1 John

1:1–2:2	The fundamentals of Christian life and truth
2:3-27	Knowing Jesus in practice
2:28–3:24	Abiding in Jesus in practice
4:1–5:5	Loving God in practice
5:6-21	The secure possession of eternal life through Jesus

are written by someone calling himself "the elder" (2 John 1; 3 John 1).

Uncertainty arises at this point, for Papias (bishop of Hierapolis *c.* A.D. 135) distinguished two "Johns" among the first-generation Christians known to him: the apostle and "the elder." So, even if the author was indeed "John," we do not know which! But the parallels in theme and style with the fourth Gospel support the traditional view that John the apostle wrote these letters in Ephesus toward the end of his long life. Letters 2 and 3 are addressed to particular churches over which "the elder" has authority (3 John 9), but letter 1 may be generally addressed to all the churches in the greater Ephesus area, or more widely still.

The two great themes of John's letters are love and truth (see 2 John 1-3). Both are firmly fixed to Jesus Christ, which gives them a particular spin. The great issue in the first letter, for instance, is the departure from the church of a group whom the author calls "antichrist." They have denied love because they have broken off from their fellow believers, and thus must be "walking in darkness," separated from God, who is the light. Fellowship with God is only possible for those who "walk in the light," which means living in fellowship with one another while "the blood of Jesus his Son cleanses us from all sin" (1:3, 7; 2:9-10, 18-19).

But this means that a denial of love is also a denial of the truth (that Jesus Christ, by his death for us, binds us into fellowship with himself and with each other). And in the case of this group, their denial of the truth is signaled by their explicit denial "that Jesus is the Christ" (2:22; 4:2-3). This probably refers to the idea, associated with Cerinthus in the late first century, that "Jesus" and "the Christ" were separate beings: the former an ordinary man, the latter a spiritual being who descended upon "Jesus" at his baptism, but departed again before the crucifixion.

> It is better to suffer for doing good, if that should be God's will, than for doing evil. For Christ also suffered once for sins, the righteous for the unrighteous.
>
> 1 Peter 3:17-18

Extent of the Church in A.D. 100

By the end of the first century, Christianity was more or less confined to the eastern Roman Empire, except for communities in Rome, Puteoli, and around the Bay of Naples. The only church that we know of outside the empire was a possible church at Edessa. Names of cities with Christians are known both from the New Testament—for example, the seven churches of Revelation—and from contemporary correspondence. The early Christian writer Ignatius tells of churches in Magnesia and Tralles, and later writers tell of a church in Alexandria, the home of Paul's helper Apollos.

Library of Celsus, in Ephesus

Rome ✠

Puteoli ✠

Pompeii ✠

Nicopolis

⁓ MALTA

MEDITERRANEAN SEA

✠ City/town with church

▨ Area with Christian communities

▬ Border of Roman Empire

0	250	500 km

0	100	200	300 miles

BLACK SEA

Thessalonica

Philippi

Troas

Pergamum

Thyatira

Smyrna

Philadelphia

Antioch

Iconium

Tarsus

Edessa

Berea

Ephesus

Sardis

Hierapolis

Lystra

Derbe

Magnesia

Colossae

Antioch

Corinth

Laodicea

Perga

Athens

CYPRUS

Salamis

PATMOS

Miletus

Paphos

Sidon

Damascus

CRETE

Capernaum

Tyre

Pella

Ptolemais

Caesarea

Sebaste (Samaria)

Joppa

Jerusalem

Lydda

Alexandria

Memphis

RED SEA

James, Jude, and 2 Peter

James and Jude belong together in that these two letters are both ascribed to brothers of Jesus (see Mark 6:3). Jude and 2 Peter belong together in that there is considerable overlap of material between them.

Who are the authors?
The traditional authorship of all three letters has been disputed, although the arguments for pseudonymity are strongly promoted only in the case of 2 Peter. This little letter is quite unlike 1 Peter and had some difficulty being accepted as genuine in the early Church. It may reflect a later period in its attack on the false teachers (chapter 2). In addition, it seems at pains to prove its genuineness, including references to the life of Peter (1:16-18) and to "our beloved brother Paul" (3:15).

The stylistic differences from 1 Peter are not, however, incompatible with common authorship, especially if Peter and Jude were using a common source or working together in composing the attack on the false teachers. The questions intertwine, for if Jude is genuine, then 2 Peter is likely to be genuine, for it is highly unlikely that a later writer would use it so fully in producing a pseudonymous letter ascribed to Peter. And Jude *is* likely to be genuine, for a pseudonymous writer would be unlikely to choose so obscure a figure as Jude, or to write something so short, or to make so little of Jude being the brother of Jesus (see Jude 1). So the early Church was right to set doubts aside and accept both as genuine.

Jude
We have no idea where Jude ministered, though we know from 1 Corinthians 9:5 that "the brothers of the Lord" had itinerant ministries. Possibly, while James led the church in Jerusalem, and Peter traveled west, Jude went east to the Jewish communities in Parthia, Media, Elam, or Mesopotamia (cf. Acts 2:9). Peter and Jude were becoming deeply concerned—possibly at the same time—about the influence of a "libertine" movement.

The false and the true
Paul tackles this libertine teaching in 1 Corinthians 6:12-20. It rested on a distorted dualistic conception of human persons and taught that, because the soul (the real, inner self) has been saved completely by Christ and can no longer be sullied by the "flesh," we can do what we like with our bodies. Gluttony and debauchery are back on the menu! Jude and

Outlines

2 Peter
1:1-11	God's call and plan for us: to reproduce his character in us
1:12–2:3	True and false prophecy: holding on to apostolic teaching
2:4-22	Rejecting false teaching and an immoral lifestyle
3:1-18	Living by grace in the light of the end of all things

James
1:1-27	The wise, tested, and reborn life—focused in the three virtues (verse 27)
2:1-26	*Virtue 1:* caring for the poor
3:1–4:12	*Virtue 2:* controlling the tongue
4:13–5:6	*Virtue 3:* keeping unspotted from the world
5:7-20	The foundations of the Christian life: patience and prayer

Jude
1-4	The need to contend for the faith
5-7	God's hatred of heresy
8-16	What the heretics are really like
17-25	How to respond: remember the faith, live a holy life of love

Ruins of the ancient black basalt synagogue at Chorazin near the Sea of Galilee

The death of James

Ananus, who . . . had been appointed to the high priesthood, was rash in his temper and unusually daring. He followed the school of the Sadducees, who are indeed more heartless than any of the other Jews . . . when they sit in judgment. Possessed of such a character, Ananus thought that he had a favorable opportunity because Festus was dead and Albinus was still on the way [that is, there was a vacuum of power between two Roman governors]. And so he convened the judges of the Sanhedrin and brought before them a man named James, the brother of Jesus who was called the Christ, and certain others. He accused them of having transgressed the law and delivered them up to be stoned. Those of the inhabitants of the city who were considered the most fair-minded and who were in strict observance of the law were offended at this. . . .
Josephus, *Antiquities* 20:199–201

A coin dating from the Jewish revolt, with the only known depiction of Herod's Temple, in Jerusalem. James continued to lead the Jerusalem church in worship there until his death.

2 Peter express sustained horror at this teaching: for Jude, it amounts to a denial of "our only Master and Lord, Jesus Christ" (verse 4; compare 2 Peter 2:1). They both insist that this is not the authentic Christian way (Jude 17-18; 2 Peter 3:2-3). Peter gives a moving defense of true Christian morality, which he builds upon intimate relationship with God (2 Peter 1:3-9), and upon the transformation of the world by Christ at his second coming (2 Peter 3:10-18). He argues that both of these provide a moral imperative for transformation now.

James

James is likewise passionately concerned with practical issues of Christian life. His letter is vivid, direct, and uncompromising, presenting essentials of Christian discipleship with an emphasis on prayer, how to cope with suffering and the testing of faith, care for the poor and the dangers of wealth, and the control of the tongue.

A strong argument in favor of the traditional ascription to James, the brother of Jesus, is the way in which the letter coheres with what Josephus, the Jewish historian, writes about James. He describes James's martyrdom in A.D. 62 at the hands of the high priest Ananus, who hated him and seized an opportunity to have him executed in the "gap" between two Roman governors. Just before this time, in A.D. 59, there was rioting in Jerusalem caused by the oppressive behavior of some Sadducean families, like that of Ananus, toward the poorer priests. Tithes were seized and some priests actually starved to death. In the light of James 4:1–5:6 and 2:14-17 it is not hard to imagine what James said about this, and how he thus made enemies in high places.

An attack on Paul?

James 2:14-26 has caused much discussion, with its apparent attack on Paul's doctrine of justification by faith. Whereas Paul taught that Abraham was "justified" by faith and not by "works," James says the opposite: "Was not our father Abraham justified by works when he offered his son Isaac on the altar?" (2:21). Partly because of this passage, Martin Luther called James "an epistle of straw."

Some maintain that James is issuing a warning against Paul's teaching, just as it was "men . . . from James" who argued that the Gentile Christians in Antioch should obey the Old Testament Law (Galatians 2:12). But we must take seriously Galatians 2:6-9, where Paul reports unanimity between himself and the Jerusalem leadership, including James (cf. Acts 21:17-26).

That James was not challenging Paul's message becomes more likely when we consider that James probably wrote his letter in or before A.D. 49–50, when Paul wrote his first surviving letter.

Furthermore, Paul himself stressed that faith should result in good works (e.g., Ephesians 4). The writings of Paul and James should be seen as complementary, not contradictory.

Revelation

Remains of the temple of Artemis, Sardis

The New Testament ends with one of its most remarkable books: "The Revelation (Greek "Apocalypse") of Jesus Christ" (1:1). The book is a colorful, evocative, awe-inspiring "removal of the veil" between heaven and earth (this is what "apocalypse" means), making events on earth transparent so that their real, hidden dynamic becomes clear. And, as the title suggests, the book is truly the revelation of Jesus Christ. Behind everything that happens lies the story of Jesus: his incarnation, suffering, death, rising, and exaltation to heaven, gift of the Spirit, and ultimate coming as Judge and Savior.

Type of writing
In form, Revelation is a letter from "John" (1:1, 4, 9; 22:8) to the seven churches of Asia, who each receive a brief letter from Christ himself (chapters 2–3), but to whom, in fact, the whole apocalypse is addressed (1:11; cf. 22:16). In genre, it is a prophecy (1:3; 22:7, 10, 18), because it bears "witness to the word of God" (1:2) by John: it is revelation from

God. We must imagine it being read aloud, at one hearing, in each of the churches (1:3), and this must affect the way we interpret it.

The writer
Christians traditionally have accepted John the apostle (author of the Gospel of John and 1, 2, and 3 John) as the author of Revelation. Some scholars, however, doubt his authorship because of the variance in writing style between the Revelation and those earlier books.

The province of Asia
The Roman province of Asia enjoyed a period of great prosperity in the first century (see 3:17). Revelation 18 pictures the vast network of Mediterranean trade, depending on huge numbers of merchant ships, by which imperial Rome sustained her power and wealth. But this prosperity came with a price tag: it involved trade in "human souls" as well as the luxuries of the East (18:13).

The ancient agora, Smyrna (Izmir)

Temple of Trajan, the acropolis, Pergamum

The two beasts
John does not just mean the slave trade. No one can buy or sell, he tells us, without the mark of the beast stamped upon them (13:16-17). Careful reading of chapter 13 suggests that the two beasts are respectively Rome, which enslaves the earth and makes blasphemous claims, persecuting the Church, and the imperial cult, by which the ideology of Roman power was promulgated and enforced. The cult of the goddess "Roma," or of the current emperor, was particularly strong in Asia (centered on Pergamum, "where Satan's throne is," 2:13). It was impossible to engage in the export or import trade without involvement in the imperial cult.

Some of the remaining stone arches of the stadium, ancient Laodicea, Asia Minor

Millennial interpretations of Revelation

Point of Interpretation	Amillennial	Historical Premillennial	Dispensational Premillennial	Postmillennial
Description of view	Viewpoint that the present age of Christ's rule in the Church is the millennium; holds to one resurrection and judgment marking the end of history as we know it and the beginning of life eternal.	Viewpoint that Christ will reign on earth for a thousand years following his second coming; saints will be resurrected at the beginning of the millennium, nonbelievers at the end, followed by judgment.	Viewpoint that after the Battle of Armageddon Christ will rule through the Jews for a literal 1,000 years accompanied by two resurrections and at least three judgments.	Viewpoint that Christ will return after a long period of expansion and spiritual prosperity for the Church, brought about by the preaching of the gospel; the Spirit's blessing; and the Church's work toward righteousness, justice, and peace. The period is not a literal thousand years but an extended time of spiritual prosperity.
Book of Revelation	Current history written in code to confound enemies and encourage Asian Christians; message applies to all Christians.	Immediate application to Asian Christians; applies to all Christians throughout the ages, but the visions also apply to a great future event.	Unveiling of theme of Christ among churches in present dispensation, also as Judge and King in dispensations to come.	Written to encourage Christians of all ages, but the visions also apply to a great future event.

The message to first-century Christians

The prosperity of the seven cities is built on the selling of their souls to Rome through their commitment to the imperial cult, and in the name of Christ John wants to call the churches to "come out of her, my people, lest you take part in her sins" (18:4). The message of the book thus has a strong relevance for the first readers. As with all letters, the first challenge in interpretation is "What did it mean to its first readers?" before further questions about later or contemporary significance are asked.

The message to all Christians

At the same time, however, the very fact that the Roman Empire is portrayed as a symbol—the beast from the sea—encourages us to ask where else this symbol might fit. Where else do we see totalitarian power, which opposes the Church of Christ and seeks to control people's minds by an all-embracing ideology? John would encourage us to see the power of the Dragon (representing Satan) behind all such worldly power (12:9–13:2).

The prophecy is presented as the narrative of a single visionary experience, not a series of separate visions like Daniel. The book thus has a powerful structural coherence and dramatic movement. The seven letters in chapters 2–3 are the first of several series of "sevens," which are carefully structured and follow on from each other. The message of the seven letters—that Christ knows his Church, holds her in his hand, and directs her destiny—turns out to be true for the whole world. So in the face of apparent chaos, persecution, and weakness, the Church can look behind the veil, hear and join the worship of heaven, and see the glorious destiny toward which the world is being steered (11:15; 21:1–22:5).

The New Testament could hardly end in a more fitting way. It begins with a baby called Jesus born in an obscure corner of the Roman Empire. It ends with the nations walking by his light, and all the kings of the earth surrendering their glory to his (Revelation 21:23-24). The movement from one to the other is the story—and vision—of the New Testament.

Outline of Revelation:

1:1-20	John's commission, and vision of Christ
2:1–3:22	The letters to the seven churches
4:1–5:14	Christ at the center: the vision of heaven, and of a unified universe
6:1–8:5	The seven seals including 7:1-17, the first interlude: the protection of the Church
8:6–11:19	The seven trumpets including 10:1–11:14, the second interlude: the preaching of the gospel
12:1–15:4	The seven great portents, explaining God's world
15:5–16:21	The seven bowls of God's wrath
17:1–19:5	The first woman: the fall of Babylon the Great
19:6–22:7	The second woman: the heavenly Jerusalem, the marriage feast of the Lamb
22:8-21	John's commission, and hearing of Christ

> Holy, holy, holy, is
> the Lord God Almighty,
> who was and is and is to come!
> Revelation 4:8b

Which are the seven churches of Revelation?

Ephesus *Revelation 2:1-7*
Ephesus, an ancient city with a population of up to 500,000 situated on a major trade route, was the leading port of Asia Minor in New Testament times. It was created a free city in 98 B.C., and its people—the Ephesians—were Roman citizens. The city was famed for the worship of Diana (Artemis), whose priestesses acted as cult prostitutes. Ephesus was also a center of the emperor cult, and a temple was built for the Emperor Domitian. The great theater of Ephesus, the remains of which still stand, held as many as 25,000 people.

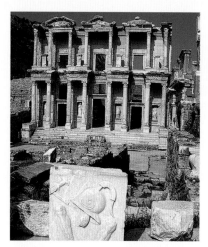

The reconstructed Library of Celsus, Ephesus

The Roman forum, Smyrna (modern Izmir)

Smyrna *Revelation 2:8-11*
Smyrna—modern Izmir—was a harbor with a population of around 200,000 in New Testament times. The city was famed for its "street of gold" with a temple at each end, and also boasted a wealthy academic community.

Remains of the Asclepium, Pergamum

Pergamum *Revelation 2:12-17*
Pergamum, the capital of the Attalid kingdom during the third and second century B.C., housed the second largest library in the Roman Empire—and was also renowned for its parchment. The city was home to the Asclepion where a healing cult was practiced, and also housed a great altar of Zeus and three temples to the Roman emperor cult.

Thyatira *Revelation 2:18-29*
Thyatira—modern Akhisar—was located on an imperial post road and had a great variety of trade guilds.

Sardis *Revelation 3:1-6*
Sardis was destroyed by a great earthquake in A.D. 17, and was subsequently rebuilt by the Emperor Tiberius. It was a wealthy fortress city set on a hill, and was easily accessible from Asia Minor's most fertile river basin.

Remains of the temple of Artemis, Sardis

Philadelphia *Revelation 3:7-13*
Like Sardis, Philadelphia—modern Alasehir—was destroyed by the major earthquake of A.D. 17 and was rebuilt by Tiberius. A fortress city on an imperial post road, Philadelphia was a significant Hellenistic educational center.

Ruins of ancient Laodicea

Laodicea *Revelation 3:14-22*
Laodicea—modern Eski Hisar—suffered two earthquakes during the New Testament period, and was rebuilt once without imperial aid. World-famous as the producer of black wool, the city was also a center for banking and boasted an important medical school.

Living in Bible Times

Clothing	128
Tent life	130
The house	132
Home life	134
Jerusalem: King David's city	136
Jerusalem: besieged, destroyed, rebuilt	138
Jerusalem: Herod the Great	140
Jerusalem in A.D. 30	142
Marriage	144
Children	146
Health and medicine	147
Eating and drinking	148
Olives and grapes	149
Craft workers	150
Travel	152
Weapons and war	154
Fishing	156
The shepherd	158
Growing grain	160
The farmer's year	162

Clothing

Men's clothes

Most Jewish men in Bible times wore an inner garment, an outer garment, and sandals. Unlike people today, they were not greatly influenced by fashion, and their dress did not change for centuries. Arabs today often wear similar clothes, because they are best suited to the hot climate of their lands in the Middle East.

The tunic

The inner garment, often called a tunic, was like a close-fitting shirt. It was made of wool, linen, or cotton. Some tunics just had slits for the arms; others had long sleeves. Sometimes men wore an undergarment called a loincloth beneath the tunic.

The tunic was often held in at the waist by a belt made of leather or cloth. Sometimes the belt had a pouch to keep money in (Mark 6:8). When a man needed to free himself for hard work, he tucked up his tunic into his belt.

In Bible times people had no special nightclothes. At night they simply loosened their belts and lay down in their tunics.

The cloak

Jewish men wore an outer garment called a cloak or robe. This cloak was made of woolen cloth and was wrapped around the body to help keep warm. It had slits for the arms. At night people used their cloaks as bedcovers.

Rich men often had cloaks made of expensive silk or linen, and with wide sleeves and blue fringes (Matthew 23:5).

Jewelry

Jewish men wore various sorts of jewels and decorations. They often wore a ring on the finger, or on a cord around the neck. These rings were sometimes used to press into wax on important letters. Each ring made a special mark, called a seal, to show who the letter came from.

Some people also wore magic charms, believing that they would keep away evil spirits.

Hairstyles

Jewish men cut their hair with scissors and long-bladed razors. Sometimes they made special religious vows and did not cut their hair for a long time. Men often wore skull-caps, with bands of cloth around the edge.

Below center: Costume of a Jewish man.

Below left: Men often hitched their tunic up when they were working in the fields.

Below right: Costume of a wealthy Eastern man. Notice his richly colored clothing.

Women's clothes

In Bible times, women wore clothes similar to what men wore.

The tunic
Like the men, women wore a tunic of wool, cotton, or linen. But women's tunics were usually worn right down to the ankles and were often blue in color. Women's tunics also had V-necks, with embroidery along the edges. Like the men, women lifted the hem of their tunics when they were doing heavy work, such as carrying water.

The woman's outer garment was also longer than the man's; it covered the feet and was fastened with a belt at the waist.

Headgear
Women wore squares of material on their heads, fastened with plaited cords. This helped protect them from the heat of the sun. Especially if they were unmarried, women often wore a veil over their faces out of modesty (Genesis 24:65).

Like the men, women often wore leather sandals. The strap went between the big toe and the second toe, and then around the heel (Luke 3:16).

Jewelry
Jewish women wore many pieces of jewelry, including bracelets on their wrists or above their elbows. They also wore bangles on their ankles, so that they jangled when they walked. The women often also wore earrings (Isaiah 3:18-21).

Jewish women used makeup, painting their eyelashes and sometimes staining their fingers and toes red with a dye called henna.

Perfume
Women perfumed themselves with scents. They used scents such as frankincense and myrrh from Africa, aloes and nard from India, saffron from Palestine, and many others.

Jewish women wore their hair long and often arranged it in plaits.

Sandals
The poorest people often went barefoot. Others wore simple leather sandals, sometimes with wooden soles. Jesus' disciples wore sandals of this kind (see Mark 6:9). Jewish people took off their shoes when they entered a house. They had their feet washed before going inside.

Left: Costume of a Jewish woman.

Above: Costume of a rich woman. Notice her elaborate headgear and the bright colors of her clothes.

Tent life

When Abraham and his family first came to the Promised Land they lived in tents (Genesis 18:1–15). The tents of that time were quite simple. The Bedouin people live in similar tents in the desert today.

Building the tent
To build a tent, they first stuck wooden poles into the sand. Then they stretched a covering of cloth or animal skin, such as goat's hair, over the poles. They secured this covering by tying cords to it and fastening the cords to tent pegs hammered into the ground.

The tent covering became waterproof after rain had fallen on it and made it shrink. If the covering got torn, it could be mended.

Inside the tent
The ground inside the tent was covered with mats and carpets. Curtains divided off different parts of the tent. Cooking pots, food, and family belongings were kept inside the tent, beside the tent poles. The family would dig a little hole in the middle of the tent and light a fire there to cook food on.

The tent door
The door was simply a flap of cloth that could be raised and lowered. No man was allowed inside the tent except for the father of the family. Other men had to stay outside at the porch, which had a cloth covering. If a stranger went inside the tent, he could be punished by being put to death (Judges 4:18, 21).

Furniture
Families living in tents had very little furniture. They were continually taking down the tent and moving on. They had to carry the tent poles and coverings with them on the backs of donkeys.

Tent people had straw mats to sit on, and they used animal skins as tables. They kept water, milk, and butter in bottles made from goatskins.

Right: The women of Bible times lived in a separate area of the tent, as Bedouin women do today.

Bedouin families still live in traditional style tents in the Judean wilderness.

The house

The poorest people lived in very simple houses with only one room. This room could be as small as 10 feet square.

The house was usually built of mud bricks or of rough stones and rubble. The walls were built very thick to keep the house cool in the hot summer days and warm during the cold winter nights.

Windows and door

There would be one small window, high up in the wall. It had no glass to keep out the wind and rain, but sometimes in winter the window was covered with an animal skin.

The house had a single small door, which was locked at night with a bar that was placed across it.

The lower area

There were usually two levels inside the house. The lower area, near the door, had a floor made of stamped-down earth. Often the family kept their animals, such as the donkey, sheep, and guard dog, in this section at night.

The family sometimes lit a fire in this part of the room, to warm the room and to cook their meals. Most houses had no chimney, so the walls and ceiling became black with soot, and the clouds of smoke made everyone cough.

The upper area

The second level inside the house was a raised stone platform. On this platform the family would eat their meals, sit talking together, and lie down to sleep at night. The family kept their food and pots on shelves or alcoves in the walls.

The roof

The house would have a flat roof made of branches laid across thick beams. After it rained, the roof had

Interior of the house

The house was lit by an oil lamp. The flat roof was made of branches laid across thick wooden beams. Notice the oil lamp on the upturned pot.

to be flattened down again with a roller; it was not very watertight. In spring, seeds that had blown onto the roof would start to sprout and make it look green.

The family made great use of the roof, which they reached by stairs up the outside wall of the house (2 Kings 19:26; Matthew 10:27; Acts 10:9). Often they dried grain and fruit on the roof, and stored part of the harvest there.

On hot summer nights, the family would take to the roof to sleep. Often the men would climb up on to the roof to pray, and they also stored their tools there. A law said there had to be a low wall round the edge of the roof to prevent people from falling off (Deuteronomy 22:8).

During the day the family did not spend much time inside the house. They were busy working in the fields, or doing jobs in the courtyard or in the garden.

Furniture

Families usually had very little furniture. Most important was the chest in which they stored food or clothes. Often poor families turned the chest upside down and used it as a dining table too. Some families had simple wooden stools or chairs to sit on, although many sat on the floor.

Poor people had only animal skins to sleep on. Richer people had rough mattresses, and sometimes even wooden beds. For pillows, people used goatskins stuffed with wool or feathers.

Every family had an oil lamp in the house. The cheaper lamps were made of clay; expensive ones were of bronze or other metals. These lamps burned olive oil, pitch, or wax and had wicks made of flax. They were left to burn all through the night. The light showed anyone outside that there were people indoors sleeping. It was unheard of not to have a light.

Artist's impression of a peasant's house. Notice the low wall around the roof's edge, built for safety's sake.

Home life

Because they lived in a very hot country, most people got up before daybreak so that they could do plenty of work before the sun got too hot. The mother would often get up before anyone else and light the fire, if it had gone out during the night.

After everyone had eaten breakfast, the men and the older boys would go off to the fields to work. The mother and the girls started their daily tasks. The young boys looked after the family's animals, such as the goat or the donkey, just as young Arab boys do today.

Milling
An important job was to grind the grain into flour to bake bread. Women ground the grain in a handmill made of two flat, round stones about 20 inches across. The bottom stone had a wooden peg in the center; the top stone, which had a hole in the middle, fit over this peg.

The woman would put handfuls of grain into the hole in the top stone. Then she slowly turned the handle on the top stone. As the two stones ground against each other, the grain was crushed between them. Fine flour poured on to the cloth that was laid beneath the two millstones. Often two women would do their milling together, to make the work less difficult (Matthew 24:41).

Fetching water
Another daily job was fetching water for the family (Genesis 24:11–13). Often the older girls would do this. They would take goatskin bottles to a nearby spring or well and fill them with water. Then they would carefully carry them back, balanced either on their hips or on their shoulders. At the well they might meet other women on the same errand and stop to chat.

Baking bread
Each day there was also bread to be baked. This, too, was usually done by the women. They mixed the flour that they had milled with a little water. If the bread was to rise, they added a little dough from the previous day's bread, to act as yeast or "leaven" (Matthew 13:33).

Then the dough was left to warm by the fire, so that the leaven could work its way through the dough. Finally the bread was ready to bake on the hot stones of a hearth.

Bread ovens
Sometimes bread was baked on a big, shallow bowl that was turned upside down over the fire. The dough was rolled out very thin and laid over the top of the dish to bake. Another type of oven looked like an upside-down earthenware cone. A fire was lit at the bottom, and the dough was put inside to bake.

Shopping
Although most families grew a lot of their own food, one or two extra things were usually needed for the evening meal. Some of the girls went to market most days to buy vegetables or meat.

Washing clothes
Sometimes clothes were washed in a fast stream; sometimes dirt was removed by beating dirt out of the wet clothes spread out on flat stones. The women used soap made of olive oil or from a special vegetable.

Rest time
At midday, when the sun was at its hottest, it was sometimes too uncomfortable to work. The family would find a shady place and take a couple hours of rest. People in hot countries today still rest in the middle of the day.

Artist's impression of a market in Bible times

Women ground the grain in a handmill made of two flat, round stones. Often two women would do their milling together, to make the work less difficult.

Jerusalem: King David's city

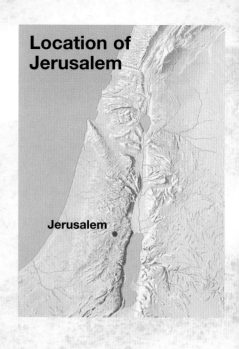

Location of Jerusalem

Jerusalem

Jerusalem was the city of David, Solomon's showcase, and the most important city in Israel's history.

The first time Jerusalem is named in the Bible is when Abraham met Melchizedek, a mysterious king from Salem (Jerusalem), who blessed the patriarch (Genesis 14:18–20). Egyptian records—the "Execration Texts," from as far back as the nineteenth century B.C.—probably refer to Jerusalem, as do fourteenth-century B.C. clay tablets found in Tell el-Amarna, central Egypt, known as the Amarna Letters. When the Israelites entered the Promised Land, they failed to drive the Jebusites from their fortified town of Jebus (Jerusalem). After David became ruler of the united kingdom of Judah and Israel, he needed a new capital city. Jerusalem was ideally positioned, belonging to neither of the two jealous kingdoms. David's commander, Joab, led a successful assault on Jerusalem, which now became known as "the city of David" (2 Samuel 5:6–10).

An artist's impression of Jerusalem in the time of King David

Tunneling into Jerusalem

The Jebusites boasted that Jerusalem—perched on the top of a hill with three steep sides—could never be captured. But David took Jerusalem by surprise when his men climbed a water shaft that tunneled beneath the city walls.

A rock-cut sloping shaft was discovered by the English nineteenth-century explorer Col. Robert Warren, and it leads to a vertical shaft through which a bucket could be lowered to a pool fed by the Gihon spring. The Jebusites enlarged the tunnels to ensure a good water supply during time of siege, and David gained entrance by this means (2 Samuel 5:8; 1 Chronicles 11:6).

King David strengthened Jerusalem's fortifications and brought the Ark of the Covenant to the city, making it the political and religious center for God's people. David bought a threshing floor from the Jebusite Araunah and on its site built an altar of sacrifice (2 Samuel 24:13–25). By tradition this is also Mount Moriah, where Abraham nearly sacrificed his son Isaac (Genesis 22:2). Jerusalem's most important building, the Temple, was to be built on exactly the same site (2 Chronicles 3:1–2).

Jerusalem: besieged, destroyed, rebuilt

Jerusalem reached its greatest glory under Solomon. There followed a pattern of decline, siege, surrender, deportation, repatriation, and rebuilding.

In 925 B.C. King Shishak of Egypt came to Jerusalem, plundering "everything" from the treasures of the Temple (2 Chronicles 12:9). Later, Jerusalem suffered famine when the Assyrian King Sennacherib laid siege to Jerusalem and shut up King Hezekiah "like a bird in a cage." The Bible records an amazing escape: "That night the angel of the LORD went out and struck down 185,000 in the camp of the Assyrians. And when people arose early in the morning, behold, these were all dead bodies. Then Sennacherib king of Assyria departed and went home and lived at Nineveh" (2 Kings 19:20–37).

Between the reign of Solomon and Jerusalem's destruction by King Nebuchadnezzar in 587 B.C., Jerusalem was plundered eight times. The last king of Judah in Jerusalem, Zedekiah, was placed in chains and taken to Babylon (2 Kings 25:1–21), along with the Temple treasures.

Exile and return

For 70 years the Israelites languished in Babylon, with their own beloved city and Temple in ruins. Then King Cyrus of Persia issued an edict allowing the Temple to be rebuilt. Gradually, Jerusalem was repopulated. Sheshbazzar was made governor of Judah in 538 B.C.; then Zerubbabel and Joshua led more exiles back to Jerusalem in 525 B.C.; as did Ezra in 458. Nehemiah came to Jerusalem in 445, with an armed escort. Nehemiah inspected the broken-down walls of Jerusalem and rebuilt them. After fifty-two days of work the entire wall was finished (Nehemiah 2:1–20; 6:15).

Jerusalem's fall

THE FALL OF JERUSALEM WAS THE SADDEST MOMENT IN THE HISTORY OF THE JEWS.

● "Shishak King of Egypt . . . took away the treasures" in the Temple.
(1 Kings 14:25–26)

● As the Assyrian army surrounded Jerusalem, King Hezekiah prayed, "O LORD our God, save us" from the Assyrians.
(2 Kings 19:1–19)

● King Nebuchadnezzar of Babylon destroyed Jerusalem and the people of Judah were "taken into exile."
(2 Kings 25:21)

Exile and return

Exile

Return

Babylon

Jerusalem

King Jehoiachin and the leading citizens of Jerusalem were exiled by Nebuchadnezzer in 597 B.C., followed by the rest of the able-bodied people, with King Zedekiah, in 587 B.C. The exiles returned to Jerusalem in waves, under Sheshbazzar, Zerubbabel, Joshua, and Ezra, from 538 B.C. to 458 B.C.

Nehemiah supervises the rebuilding of the walls of Jerusalem.

Jerusalem: Herod the Great

Herod the Great, renowned for his cruelty and ambition

The fortress of Herodium, built by Herod the Great near Bethlehem

Herod the Great was infamous for his cruel heartedness. He murdered his son and expected heir, Antipater, five days before he died himself. History also remembers him for his lavish building programs.

Herod rebuilt the temple at Samaria, "out of a desire to make the city more eminent than it had been before, but principally because he contrived that it might at once be for his own security and a monument of his magnificence" (Josephus). He renamed Samaria Sebaste (meaning Augustus) and built a theater and forum as a temple dedicated to Augustus.

Herod made Caesarea his capital, and built impressive breakwaters and a vast artificial harbor measuring 550 yards by 300 yards, making it into an impressive new port.

Impregnable

King Herod also built an impregnable fortress and summer retreat at Masada, which included two lavish palaces and his own private bath—with its changing room, cold plunge bath, warm room, and hot room—as well as a public bathhouse. At Herodium, near Bethlehem, he built a walled fortress on a hilltop, with four towers to protect it, from which heavy catapults could fire on any besieging force.

But Herod carried out his most ambitious building program in Jerusalem. He remodeled the *Baris* (fortress) north of the Temple, renaming it the "Antonia Fortress" in honor of Mark Antony. He built a second

Cleansing the Temple

A great struggle arose during the reign of Antiochus IV Epiphanes (175–163 B.C.), the Seleucid ruler of the Jews. His Jewish subjects were determined to retain their distinctive life and religion; the Seleucid king was equally determined to make Jerusalem a city in the Greek style. The Jews resisted fanatically when pigs (unclean animals for Jews) were offered in sacrifice on Jerusalem's new Greek altar and the Temple was rededicated to the Greek god Zeus. Judas, nicknamed "the Hammer," led a Jewish guerrilla war, known as the Maccabean Revolt, from the hills surrounding Jerusalem.

Surprisingly, the Seleucids were eventually forced to accept the terms demanded by the Jews. The Temple was reinstated as the focus of Jewish worship, and on December 14, 164 B.C., after ritual cleansing, it was rededicated (1 Maccabees 4:36–59). This is celebrated annually by the Jews at the festival of Hanukkah.

Judas's successors now ruled as the Hasmoneans, and they successfully governed Jerusalem until the Romans (under Pompey) captured the city in 63 B.C. King Herod the Great was a Hasmonean, but was primarily interested in retaining his throne, as he showed when he ordered the slaughter of all the male children in Bethlehem.

A special Hanukkah candlestick

The tomb of the family of Herod

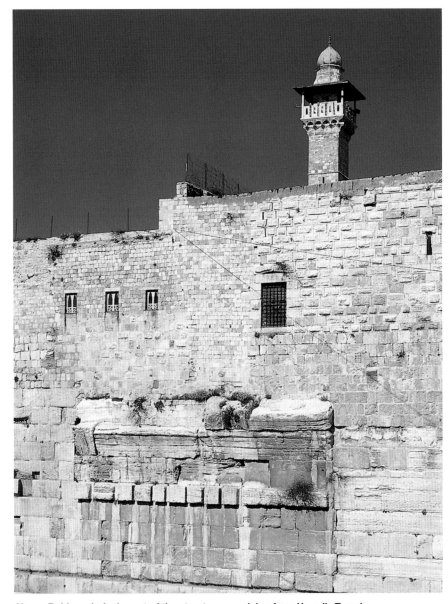

Above: Robinson's Arch, part of the structure remaining from Herod's Temple
Below: A model of Herodian Jerusalem, showing the hippodrome

fortress, with three massive towers, on the western side of Jerusalem, his Upper Palace linking the two fortresses with a great wall. Herod also built himself a more modest Lower Palace in the center of Jerusalem.

Far-reaching

Herod also constructed in Jerusalem baths, a theater, and a hippodrome, or stadium, where he promoted both Greek and Roman games. Two existing pools, just beyond the northeast corner of the Temple area, Herod replaced with the larger Pool of Israel.

Herod's far-reaching building program for Jerusalem meant that the street plan for the city had to be changed. Jerusalem changed little after his death in 4 B.C., before it was leveled by the Romans in A.D. 70.

Jerusalem in A.D. 30

In Jesus' day, Jerusalem was the center for Jewish faith and worship. It was also the setting for the last week of Jesus' life and for the most momentous events in God's plan of salvation.

This artist's impression of the city of Jerusalem in Jesus' day shows Herod's Temple, the greatest of Herod's building enterprises, which he started in 19 B.C. and which covered over 15 percent of the total area of Jerusalem.

Here, as a baby, Jesus was presented (Luke 2:22), and from its courts Jesus later witnessed the poor widow casting her two coins into the treasury (Luke 21:1–4).

Jesus spoke to his disciples about Jerusalem: "See, we are going up to Jerusalem, and everything that is written about the Son of Man by the prophets will be accomplished. For he will be delivered over to the Gentiles and will be mocked and shamefully treated and spit upon. And after flogging him, they will kill him, and on the third day he will rise" (Luke 18:31–33).

Jesus revealed his great love for Jerusalem when he said,

"O Jerusalem, Jerusalem, the city that kills the prophets and stones those who are sent to it! How often would I have gathered your children together as a hen gathers her brood under her wings, and you would not! See, your house is left to you desolate" (Matthew 23:37–38).

143

Marriage

In Bible times, young people did not normally decide for themselves whom to marry. Their parents usually chose for them.

The bride's price
Once a wife had been chosen for a son, there were financial arrangements to be made. The bride's mother and father had to be paid for losing their daughter. Also, the bride's father gave his daughter a gift of money, called a dowry.

Betrothal
Once all the arrangements had been made, the man and woman were bound by vows, or "betrothed," to be married (Matthew 1:18–20). The time of betrothal lasted a year, while everyone prepared for the wedding itself. The bride's family made her wedding clothes and arranged the wedding feast.

The wedding
At the wedding, the bride and groom made a legal agreement, and a blessing was said over them. Then came the wedding feast, when everyone dressed in their wedding clothes. The feast was usually given by the bride's family.

A bride wearing her traditional headdress

The procession
On the marriage day, there was a procession. The bridegroom, dressed in his best clothes and decorated with jewels, walked with his friends from his home to his bride's home. She would be waiting, having dressed after being bathed by her bridesmaids (Psalm 45:14–15). She wore a veil to cover her face.

The feast
Once the groom arrived, everyone walked back to his house, the guests holding oil lamps to light the way. When they entered the bridegroom's house, the bride and groom sat down under a decorated canopy, and the feast began.

Feasting could last as long as seven days (Judges 14:12), with much drinking, eating, dancing, and singing. Jesus once went to a wedding at the village of Cana, near his hometown of Nazareth (see John 2).

Artist's impression of a marriage ceremony in Bible times

Children

Jewish parents believed it was a sign of God's blessing if they had many children (Deuteronomy 28:4). The more children the better, especially if they were boys. If a woman was childless, people made fun of her or pitied her.

Birth

When a pregnant woman was ready to give birth, the midwife would be called to her house (Exodus 1:15–19). Birth took place at home; there were no hospitals as we know them.

The newborn baby was first washed, and then rubbed down with salt, water, and oil. People thought this was good for the baby's skin. After this, the baby was wrapped up very tightly with strips of bandage. People believed this would help the baby's legs and arms grow straight.

When a male child was eight days old, there was a special ceremony, called circumcision. The foreskin was cut off, as a sign that the boy was being given back to God (Genesis 17:10).

Names

At about the same time, the baby was named (Luke 2:21). Names were very important, and each name had its own meaning. For example, David means "beloved," and Sarah means "princess."

Childhood

Up to the age of three, children were taught by their mothers. From three to six, boys were taught by their fathers, and their fathers later trained them in their own trade. The mothers taught their daughters how to cook, spin, weave, and care for the home. Boys and girls might look after the family's sheep, goats, and donkey.

Growing up

When a boy reached the age of thirteen he was regarded as a

Children were taught to ask questions about their nation's past. As Moses described it, a child might ask, "What is the meaning of the testimonies and the statutes and the rules that the LORD our God has commanded you?" (Deuteronomy 6:20).

School

Until the time of Jesus, there were no schools. A child's parents taught him or her everything they knew. The children were told about the religious festivals, such as Passover, and what they meant.

By the time of Jesus, boys of six and over went to school at the "house of the book." The teacher was paid by the synagogue, the Jewish meeting place. The boys would learn by heart passages from Scripture and would be taught to read and write.

Classes

School lasted only about four hours each day. After morning class there was a long break until afternoon class started, at about three o'clock. But classes went on all the year round—there were no school holidays.

The teacher sat cross-legged on a little platform in front of the class. Before him was a little rack where he kept scrolls containing parts of the Scripture. The boys sat on the floor in front of their teacher. All the boys were in one class, whatever age they were.

The boys wrote on wooden tablets covered with a thin layer of wax, using pointed sticks to make marks in the wax (Luke 1:63).

man. There was a special ceremony to mark this stage in his life. When he was twelve, Jesus went to the Temple in Jerusalem with his parents for his last Passover as a child (see Luke 2:41–49). Jewish boys today have a ceremony called the bar mitzvah when they are about thirteen. Afterwards they can go as adults to the synagogue.

Toys and games

Children didn't have many toys to play with. They usually made do with sticks or bits of string and broken pottery. Balls have also been found. Some children had toys made out of clay, but Jewish children were not allowed to play with dolls or toy animals because of what the Law said about the making of "images."

Jesus talks about children playing games in the streets—they sound like dance games (see Matthew 11:16–17).

Health and medicine

The Jews had many rules promoting good health. They were to keep one day in seven as a day of rest. They were not to eat certain unhealthy foods. They were to make sure that their food and their homes were clean.

The Jews believed they should pray to God when they were ill. But sometimes they copied surrounding nations by wearing lucky charms to keep away evil spirits.

Medicines
The Jews gradually began to use simple natural drugs. They knew how to clean wounds and bandage them, using natural ointments for cuts. They used a herb called myrrh mixed with wine as a painkiller.

Diseases
We know from stories in the Bible that people suffered from many different illnesses and diseases, such as leprosy, blindness, deafness, epilepsy, and crippling disabilities (Mark 1:32–34). Many Jews believed that illness came as a result of their sins. If someone was ill, they might ask: "Who sinned, this man or his parents, that he was born blind?" (John 9:2–4).

Doctors
In Jesus' time some doctors were trained by the Greeks to do surgical operations. They took vows promising to put the life of their patient first, and not to give away personal details about their patients.

Artist's impression of a Roman surgeon treating his patient. Notice the various surgical tools, including a saw and tweezers.

Eating and drinking

Breakfast
Breakfast, the first meal of the day, was not a big meal. The family would usually eat bread and cheese and some dried fruit or olives. The men might take their breakfast with them to the fields.

Evening meal
The main meal of the day was in the evening, when work was finished and the sun was less hot. The women prepared a pot of vegetable stew or lentils (Genesis 25:29, 34), which was simmering over the fire when the men returned from the fields.

Everyone would scoop food out of the pot, using a piece of bread. There were no knives and forks to eat with. They might drink wine with the meal, and on special occasions they might have some meat too. They often finished the meal with fruit.

Feasts
The Jewish people enjoyed having special feasts. They held feasts when people got married, when a baby was born and when the child was weaned, at burials, and at sheep-shearing time. They also ate well if there were guests to entertain. There were religious festivals too—such as Passover, Purim, and Harvest (see pages 170–171).

At the festivals they often added meat to the usual stew. Also, they might have sweet pastries with the fruit. The feasts were very happy times, with plenty of singing and dancing. Wedding feasts lasted for days (see page 144), as they still do in many Arab villages.

Food

Bread
Bread, the basic food, was eaten at every meal. Jesus taught his followers to pray: "Give us each day our daily bread" (Luke 11:3).

Barley stew with lentils

Milk
The Jews drank the milk of sheep, and of goats and camels too. They used milk to make cheese and butter (2 Samuel 17:29). They also made a kind of yogurt by shaking milk in a skin bag (Genesis 18:8). The Bedouin people today make yogurt in a similar way.

Vegetables
The Jewish people grew and ate several different vegetables. They had beans, lentils, gherkins, and cucumbers for their stews (Ezekiel 4:9). They also had root vegetables, and herbs to flavor their stews.

Fruit and nuts
The Jews ate plenty of fruit. Many different fruits grow well in the warm climate of Israel. When Moses sent spies to explore the Promised Land, they brought back huge bunches of grapes to show how rich the land was.

The country was also rich in pomegranates, figs, dates, olives, almonds, and pistachio nuts (Jeremiah 24:2; Genesis 43:11; Deuteronomy 8:8).

Honey
The Jews obtained honey from wild bees (Judges 14:8–9). Honey was important as a sweetener because they had no sugar. Another sort of honey was made by boiling grape juice down until it was syrupy and sweet. They often spread this syrup on bread to eat.

Meat
Most families did not normally eat meat. They usually only tasted meat at special feasts. The Jews sometimes ate birds such as pigeons, geese, quails, and partridge. The most common meat was the kid, or young goat, but they also ate lamb.

Fish
Fish from the Sea of Galilee and from the River Jordan was a favorite food (Luke 11:11). In the time of Jesus many fishermen sailed on Galilee to bring in fish.

Wine
For most people the main drink was wine. Much of the grape juice was used to make wine. Water was often dirty and full of germs, so it was safer to drink wine.

Olives and grapes

Almost every family had olive trees, often growing in small groves. Olive trees grow well in dry lands like Palestine. They have very deep roots and can find water deep in the earth. It is about 15 years before an olive tree starts to bear fruit; but it can live many years longer than this.

Olive harvest
The olives were ready to pick in September and October. They were gathered in a cloth laid out under the tree. Boys would beat and shake the tree, and the ripe olives would drop into the cloth below. Some of the olives were eaten raw, and others were preserved in salted water. But most of the olives were crushed to make olive oil.

The olive press
The olives were crushed in an olive press. This was made up of a big stone with a hollow on top where the olives were placed for crushing. A stone wheel placed over the olives was turned, pressing the oil out of them. The oil was stored in jars.

Olive oil
Olive oil had many uses. It was used instead of butter on bread, and as cooking fat. It was also used to burn in lamps (Matthew 25:3-4), and to make soap. Olive oil was also rubbed into the skin to make it shine, and as an ointment for wounds.

Planting grapes
The grape harvest was nearly as important as the grain harvest. Grapevines were best planted on a hillside (Isaiah 5:1). The grapes would catch the sun well there, and the rain would run off the slope. Often the hillside would be stepped into a series of terraces running along the slope. The edge of each terrace was marked with a low wall of stones and rocks.

Before planting new vines, the farmer broke up the soil with his hoe or mattock. Then he planted the vines, leaving plenty of room between them. While some vines grew along the ground, others needed sticks to climb on.

Pruning
During the winter the farmer cut out dead or broken branches. This left the healthy branches to grow and bear grapes. Jesus talked about pruning grapes (see John 15:1–6).

Grape harvest
When the grapes were ready to pick, in July, August, or September, the farmer's family often went to live in a watch-tower among the vines (Isaiah 5:2). At night they could guard the grapes from thieves, and during the day they picked the grapes, collecting them in big baskets.

The grape harvest was a festival time (see page 170). There was much singing and dancing as well as plenty of hard work.

Using the grapes
Some of the grapes were eaten fresh. Some grapes were crushed to make fresh grape juice. Yet other grapes were spread out to dry in the sun to make raisins.

But most of the grapes were pressed to make wine. These grapes were put into a square tank cut into the rock. People would tread the grapes to press out the juice. As it ran out, the juice was collected in a pot or jar.

Storage
The juice was left for about six months to ferment into wine. Then it was poured into storage jars, carefully leaving behind the waste that had sunk to the bottom (Jeremiah 48:11). Sometimes wine was stored in goatskin bottles instead of jars.

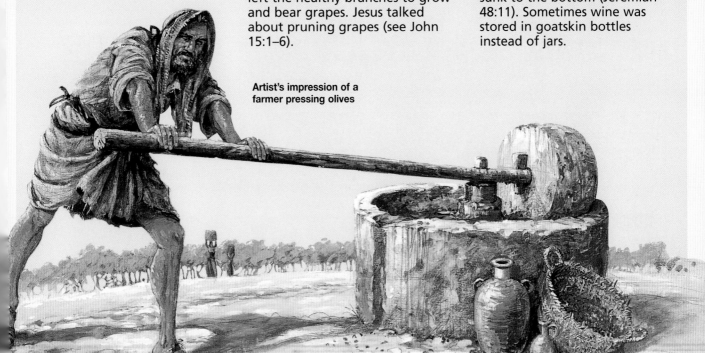

Artist's impression of a farmer pressing olives

Craft workers

The potter

In Bible times, clay was used to make pots for eating and drinking from, and for storing things. This clay was dug from the ground, and it had to be mixed with water to make it soft enough to shape.

Coil pots

The first potters made bowls and jugs by rolling out long snakes of clay and then coiling them up. Then they smoothed out the bumpy surface and left the pot to dry hard.

Later, potters found they could make smooth round pots by placing the clay on a flat turning wheel. This wheel was often turned by another worker. Then potters learned to turn it by pushing their feet on a second wheel attached below (Ecclesiasticus 38:29).

Decorating the pots

Once the pots had dried, they were often decorated. Sometimes

A potter of Bible times

red or black was added to make a pattern, or the clay was smoothed to give it a shiny surface.

The potter's mold

If he wanted to make complicated shapes, the potter could not use his wheel. Oil lamps, which had a lip on one side, were made by pressing clay into a wooden mold to shape it. The potter also made some things by hand, such as toys, ornaments, and seals.

Firing the clay

Once the clay had dried, the potter put it in a special oven to "fire" it. The clay pots would come out hard enough to use, but they broke very easily.

The leatherworker

Leather was used to make many different things, such as bottles, belts, soldiers' helmets, shields, and slings.

Skinning the animal

First the leatherworker had to prepare his leather. He would skin a goat or ox to get its hide (skin). Then he scraped the skin to remove all the animal's hair. Finally, he soaked the skin and put lime on it, to remove any remaining hair.

Softening the skin

Next the leatherworker softened the leather by soaking it in water with special leaves in it, by rubbing it with dog droppings, and by hammering it. His workshop could smell very bad!

Leather goods

Sometimes the tanner, or leatherworker, dyed the leather before starting to make sandals, belts, or other articles to sell.

The carpenter

The carpenter had two jobs – building houses and making furniture. Carpenters had to be tough, strong men.

Building a house

To build a house, the carpenter had to cut down trees. Then he shaped the logs he had cut to use as beams for the roof. He used tools such as a handsaw and an axe to do this work. The axe head was made of stone or bronze and was lashed to a wooden handle.

Making furniture

But the carpenter did many smaller jobs too. He made doors and doorframes, wooden locks, tables, stools, and chests for the home. He also made plows, yokes, and shovels for the farmer.

Working with cloth

The Jewish people made many of their clothes from sheep's wool.

Spinning

Before the wool could be spun, the women had to wash and comb it. Then they spun the wool into lengths on a wooden stick or spindle.

Dyeing

After this the women washed the wool again before dyeing it (Jeremiah 2:22). The dyes they used (Acts 16:14) were made of crushed shells, fruit, or even lice eggs and were mixed with water. The wool was dyed in big pots or basins, then rinsed in water and dried.

An Eastern woman weaves at an outdoor loom.

Weaving

Once the wool had been spun and dyed, it was ready to be woven into cloth. Often the loom was set up outdoors, on a simple wooden frame (Judges 16:13).

First the weaver would fix the long warp threads from end to end. Then she would push the yarn between the warp threads, using a wooden stick to guide it through. Gradually a piece of cloth would be formed, as the weft, or cross-threads, grew.

Important Roman Roads of Asia Minor

(map)

AEGEAN SEA

Troas
Pergamum
Sardis
Smyrna
Ephesus
Laodicea
Miletus
Colossae
Antioch
Perga
Lystra
Iconium
Derbe
Attalia
Tarsus
Germanicus
Antioch

MEDITERRANEAN SEA

CRETE
CYPRUS

| | 0 | 50 | 100 | 150 | 200 mi |
| 0 | 50 | 100 | 150 | 200 | 250 | 300 km |

Some rich Romans were carried in chairs by their slaves.

Travel

Because travel was so difficult and dangerous (2 Corinthians 11:26–27), people only left home if they had to, and traveled around in groups. Most people traveled on foot or on a donkey, while those who could afford it went on horseback or by horse-drawn carriage.

Difficult country
Much of Palestine was hilly, and there were few good roads. The best roads were built by the Romans. Their roads were straight and level. They enabled the Roman army to march rapidly if trouble arose.

Most people could walk 16 to 20 Roman miles in a day. We know from the Gospels that Jesus and his followers traveled on foot around Galilee. The book of Acts tells how the apostle Paul walked long distances through what we know as Turkey and Greece.

Danger, thief!
The roads were often dangerous, with thieves lying in wait for travelers. Jesus told a story about a traveler who was set upon by thieves (Luke 10:30–35). In his story, the Samaritan who found the wounded traveler took him to a roadside inn. There were many inns like this, where a traveler could find food and a bed for the night.

Chariots and carts
Sometimes farmers or merchants used carts drawn by oxen or by horses to carry grain and other goods. Some rich people could afford to travel in horsedrawn carriages (Acts 8:29).

Pack animals
Poorer people used a donkey or mule to carry their heavy loads, tying sacks onto the animal's back (Genesis 42:25–28). They also used donkeys to turn mill wheels and waterwheels.

The camel
The camel can store enough water to last several days, making it an ideal creature for traveling in hot deserts. In Bible times the camel was often used by merchants crossing the desert with their goods (Judges 6:5).

Military horseman

Mule
Horsedrawn carriage
Military chariot

Sea travel

The Jews didn't often travel by sea, because they thought it was very dangerous. Palestine is on the Mediterranean Sea, where it was unsafe to sail in winter because wild storms can arise.

In Jesus' time, the Romans sailed big ships to the ports of Palestine. They used them to carry soldiers, grain, and other goods. We know that the apostle Paul sailed to Rome in a grain ship that held 276 people, similar to the ship illustrated below (Acts 27:6, 37). These ships sometimes had only one sail on a single mast and were difficult to handle in stormy weather.

Horse-drawn carriage

Replica of a Roman siege engine and catapult (*background*) near Masada, Israel

Chariots

Some armies had horsedrawn chariots. The chariots were mainly used to carry archers, so that they could fire their arrows freely at the enemy. Sometimes their arrows had spikes, or barbs, to prevent their being easily pulled out of a wound.

Siege

Often enemy armies surrounded a town and set up a siege. Cities were built with high walls around them to protect them from enemies. An attacking army would try to tunnel beneath the walls, or knock a hole by using a battering ram. The Romans also used giant catapults that threw great rocks into a city.

The people inside a besieged city would throw stones or boiling oil at the soldiers outside.

The Roman army

The Roman army controlled Palestine in Jesus' time. They were very well organized and equipped; each soldier had armor consisting of a breastplate, helmet, and shield (Ephesians 6:13–17). He also had a full set of weapons: a dagger, long sword, and javelin. The Romans also trained specialist soldiers such as bowmen, horsemen, surgeons, and engineers.

Weapons and war

The Jews were surrounded by enemy nations, but it was not until the time of King Solomon that they could afford to have a regular army. Solomon raised taxes to pay for his army, and he built new strongholds to guard the roads.

Weapons

However the Jewish soldiers were often poorly armed. Enemy armies such as the Assyrians had fine coats of mail, and metal shields and helmets, whereas the Jewish soldiers often had only a simple weapon such as a sling. Shields usually consisted of a wooden frame covered with leather. Foot soldiers had a dagger and a throwing spear (1 Samuel 18:10–11), while some soldiers were trained to use slings or bows and arrows.

| Egyptian warrior | Philistine warrior | Assyrian spearman | Babylonian spearman | Greek soldier | Israelite archer |

A Roman centurion (*foreground*) and Roman legionary soldier (*background*). The legionnaire is armed with a long sword, a short sword, and a javelin, and he has a large shield for protection. The centurion commanded a force of 100 soldiers.

Fishing

In Jesus' time, many fishermen worked on the big lake called the Sea of Galilee, and many fishing villages surrounded the lake. Some of these fishermen used a rod and line, like anglers today.

Cast net

Some fishermen used a cast net (Mark 1:16–17). This was a circular net, about 17 feet across. It had weights tied around the edge and a rope tied to the middle. When a fisherman could see fish in shallow water by the water's edge, he would wade into the water and drop the net over them. The weights pulled the net down, trapping the fish.

Seine net
If they were fishing from a boat, fishermen would often use a seine net (Luke 5:4). This was a long net, about 10 feet wide, that was let out behind the boat. It had corks fixed to the top to make it float, and stones tied to the bottom to weigh it down.

Fish were caught in the net as the boat sailed along. Sometimes the boat turned in a circle so that the fish were caught in the middle of the net.

Fishing boats
The fishermen used small sailing boats that normally held only about four men. These boats had one big sail, and a long oar to steer with.

When they had finished a day's fishing, the men would lay out their nets to dry and mend any tears in them.

The shepherd

Sheep were highly valued in Bible times. They provided wool, meat, and milk. Even the sheep's horns were used—to make trumpets (Leviticus 25:9) or as containers for oil.

Sheep and goats
In Bible times, the shepherd looked after the goats and sheep together in the same flock. Goats gave a lot of milk, and some of it was used to make a kind of yogurt. Goat's hair was used to make a coarse cloth for covering tents and for rough clothes, while goatskin leather was used to make water bottles.

The shepherd often looked after the sheep and goats belonging to everyone in his village. After the rain had fallen in winter, there was plenty of grass near the village for the flocks to graze on, and when the grain had been cut at harvest, the sheep and goats grazed on the stubble left behind.

New pasture
But when the hot summer sun had dried the grass, the shepherd had to lead the flocks farther away to find pasture (1 Chronicles 4:39–40). He also had to find a brook or well where he could draw water for the sheep and goats to drink.

The shepherd also had to guard his flock from the wild animals that roamed the country (1 Samuel 17:34–36). Lions, bears, jackals, and hyenas were all looking for animals such as sheep to eat.

Shepherds' tools
The shepherd carried a heavy club spiked with sharp stones to beat off animals (Psalm 23:4). He also had a leather sling.

The shepherd had a staff about 6 feet long. He used this as a walking stick to navigate the rough terrain and to control his sheep (Ezekiel 20:37–38). Sometimes his rod had a hook, or crook, at one end.

The shepherd also had a leather bag, called a scrip, to carry his food. Some shepherds had a little reed pipe to play while they were watching the sheep and goats.

Shelter
At night the shepherd had to find a safe place to shelter his sheep (Luke 2:8). Often he would take his sheep to a cave and sleep in the doorway to prevent wild animals from entering (John 10:7). Sometimes, if there was no cave, he had to make a rough stockade out of stones or brushwood.

An Eastern shepherd tends his flock. For such men, little has changed since biblical times.

In the village, there would sometimes be a stone sheepfold, with a little shelter for the guarding shepherd.

The shepherd spent a lot of time alone with his sheep, and he learned to know them all by name (John 10:14). He knew which sheep belonged to which family and could return them to their owners.

An artist's impression of an eastern shepherd leading his flock. Note his stout staff and heavy club.

Sheep-shearing

At the end of summer the sheep would be sheared. When sheep-shearing was finished, the people celebrated with a feast, which included plenty of eating and drinking (1 Samuel 25).

Jesus described a shepherd looking for his lost sheep in Luke 15:3–7. There is also a fine description of the shepherd's job in Psalm 23.

Growing grain

Farmers in Bible times grew mainly wheat and barley, and sometimes a grain called millet. Barley could be grown on poorer land, but it was not as popular as wheat.

Sowing seed

The farmer scattered seed from a basket. As he sowed, he plowed the seed into the soil to stop the birds from flying off with it. Jesus describes a sower at work in Luke 8:5-8.

While the grain was growing, from December to February, the farmer had to weed the land so that the grain was not choked by weeds.

Harvest

Barley was ready to harvest in April or May. The farmer cut it

A farmer harvests the grain with his sickle.

down, using a sharp curved tool called a sickle (Jeremiah 50:16). He cut the barley stalks near the top and left the rest of the plant in the ground, so that his sheep could graze there afterwards.

The farmer left some grain standing in the corners of his fields. Poor people were allowed to come and take this grain, or any other grain that the farmer and his workers had missed (Ruth 2).

Threshing

Now the grain had to be separated from the straw stems. The grain was taken to a patch of hard ground (1 Chronicles 21:18-26) where it was beaten with sticks or trampled by oxen to separate it.

Sometimes the farmer used a threshing board. This was a wooden board with stones or iron spikes fixed underneath. Oxen pulled it over the grain to thresh it.

Plowing

The farmer started off by plowing up his land in October or November, when the rain came. The rain helped soften the parched earth and made it easier to plow.

Often the farmer plowed and sowed his seed at the same time. The plow was a T-shaped wooden tool with a sharp spike that cut through the soil. It was drawn by two donkeys or two oxen. If the field was on a hill or near trees, the farmer had to break up the soil by hand. To do this he used a tool like a hoe, called a mattock (Isaiah 7:25).

Artist's impression of a farmer plowing with two yoked oxen. Notice the farmer's goad.

Winnowing

After the threshing, the farmer had to separate the grain from the chaff—the bits of straw and the outer husk. He did this by tossing the grain in the air, using a wooden winnowing fork. The chaff was light and was blown away on the wind; but the grain was heavier and fell to the ground.

Finally the farmer shook his grain in a big sieve to get rid of any bits of waste or weeds (Luke 22:31).

Storage

Now the farmer could store his precious grain. He usually put his grain in great earthenware pots or jars.

Harvest was a very important time. It provided the grain for another year's bread. So the people celebrated the barley harvest and the wheat harvest each year with special feasts (see page 170).

An artist's impression of laborer winnowing grain

The farmer's year

In Bible times, most people had some involvement with farming, every family having at least a small plot of land.

Grain

The main crops were wheat and barley. Following the autumn rains, the farmer plowed the soil and sowed the grain by hand. If there were winter rains he could harvest the crop in April or May.

Harvest

The farmer would cut the grain with a sickle, leaving the sheaves in the field to dry. Next he threshed the grain on a threshing-floor, where oxen trod the grain. After this, the farmer winnowed the grain, throwing it in the air to separate the grain from the lighter chaff, which blew away. Finally, the grain was sieved and stored away in sacks or large jars.

Fruit

The Israelites also grew fruit such as grapes, figs, and olives, as well as melons, dates, pomegranates, and nuts. They also often cultivated vegetables such as beans, lentils, onions, and cucumbers, and some herbs.

Animals

Sheep and goats were herded both for their meat and their milk, and for their wool and hair, which could be utilized for making garments. Farmers would often use donkeys for load-bearing, and oxen for pulling the plow.

HEAVY WINTER RAIN

SPRING RAIN

DRY SEASON STARTS

VERY HOT

AUTUMN/EARLY RAIN

February

January

SHEBAT

March

April

December

ADAR

NISAN

Citrus harvest

Almonds blossom

Flax harvest

Barley harvest

TEBETH

ZIV (IYYAR)

WINTER STARTS

Almonds ripen

KISLEV

Vine tending

Wheat harvest

BUL (MARCHESVAN)

Wheat sown

SIVAN

Early Figs ripen

ETHANIM (TISHRI)

Plowing

Summer figs

AB

Walnuts ripen

ELUL

Winemaking starts

Dates, pomegranates ripen

Olive harvest

TAMMUZ

June

July

August

September

October

November

May

12 1 2 3 4 5 6 7 8 9 10 11

Religion in Bible Times

Religious life	164
People of the Law	166
Israel's God	168
The Jewish festivals	170
The Tabernacle—God's tent	172
The outer courtyard	174
The history of the Tabernacle	176
Solomon's Temple	180
The synagogue	184
Jewish sects and parties	185
Herod's Temple	186
The Temple destroyed	190
Varieties of religion in Bible times	192

Religious life

For the Israelites, worshiping God was not merely a matter of going to services three times a year, once a week, or even more often. Although services and other religious practices were important, they symbolized that for Israel, being God's people involved the whole of life. For the Jews, there was no difference between "religious" and "non-religious" activities. If they treated people unfairly or disobeyed the commandments, then religious observance counted for nothing.

Ways of worship

Worshiping God involved living one's life in the way that God had laid down. Family life, working life, social life, and political life all had to be carried out in a way that honored God and reflected his Law. Regulations about

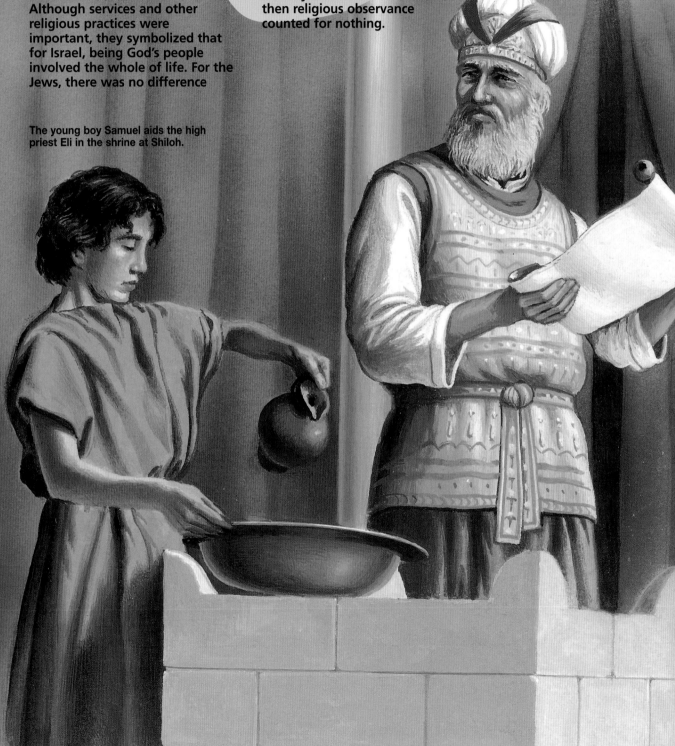

The young boy Samuel aids the high priest Eli in the shrine at Shiloh.

worship practice mingled with laws about farming, fighting, clothing, commerce, loving, and learning. All these areas were equally important in the people's relationship with God; all could be seen as part of worship.

But the occasions when people took part in specifically religious activities remained important. We look next at patterns of religious life in Israel.

The Levites
Israel was divided into twelve tribes, of which the tribe of Levi acted as assistants to the priests, looking after the religious aspects of national life. The Levites formed a kind of religious civil service, managing and administering religious activities.

In the early days, when Israel was still traveling in the desert, the Levites were responsible for the care of the Meeting Tent (Tabernacle) and for carrying the tent and Ark of the Covenant from place to place. Later, they were entrusted with cleaning the Temple and looking after the Temple furniture and implements. They also supervised the collection and distribution of gifts for the Temple and the poor.

The Levites did not have an area of the country assigned to them, as did the other tribes. Instead, they were allocated small sections of land throughout the country so that they could help with local religious activities. The land that the Levites owned was not enough to support the whole tribe, so they also received payment from national funds raised by gifts and taxes upon the whole people.

The priests
The main spiritual leaders of Israel were the priests, who came from one clan of the Levi tribe. The priests were all descendants of Aaron, Moses' brother. Every boy born into a priestly family was prepared from childhood for a priest's work, but worked as a priest only between the age of thirty and fifty.

The priests had to lead worship within the Temple and administer sacrifices. When the people brought sacrifices to offer to God, the priests had to ensure that they were properly prepared before they could offer them. However, only a few priests worked in the Temple at any one time; the rest taught and gave advice. People who had recovered from infectious illnesses or skin diseases such as leprosy had to have their recovery confirmed by priests.

The high priest
One priest was appointed high priest. Once a year, on the Day of Atonement, he alone entered the Most Holy Place in the innermost part of the Temple, where the Ark of the Covenant was kept. The high priest also worked alongside the king and the prophets in leading the nation.

The high priest wore special clothes, including a gold breastplate inlaid with twelve precious stones, to symbolize the unity of the nation gathered to worship God.

> And behold, I have taken your brothers the Levites from among the people of Israel. They are a gift to you, given to the LORD, to do the service of the tent of meeting.
> Numbers 18:6

Singers and servers
From the time of Solomon, some Levites were trained as singers and as musicians for Temple worship. Artists, woodworkers, and needle-workers, who helped design and decorate the Meeting Tent and the Temple, came from other tribes, as did those who served and helped when there were not enough Levites available.

The people
The servers, Levites, and priests did not, however, worship on behalf of the people or excuse the people from their religious responsibilities. All the people—men, women, and children—had an important part to play in Israel's religious life and should be counted among Israel's "religious personnel."

Death and burial

In Bible times, many people died before old age. They died through illness, poverty, or famine.

When someone died
As soon as someone died, friends and relatives began to wail and lament. This let neighbors know somebody had died. The family would come together to wail.

Sometimes rich families would pay for other people to come and wail for them (Jeremiah 9:17-18). While they were in mourning, people often wore rough goat's-hair clothes, sometimes called sackcloth. Or they tore their clothes, to show how sad they were.

Burial
Because the weather was often very hot, it was important to bury the dead before the body started to decompose.

Usually the body was washed and wrapped up in linen before being carried on a stretcher to the burying place.

People were often buried in caves, or in specially dug-out tombs in the rock (Judges 8:32). But there were not enough caves for all the bodies. So, when bodies had rotted away, the bones were collected and saved in special bone-boxes (called ossuaries) to make room in the caves for new bodies.

Burial caves
These burial caves were closed up with huge rocks. Sometimes the door was a circular stone that was rolled across the opening in a slot (see Luke 24:1-2).

Poorer people were sometimes buried more simply (Luke 7:14). The stretcher with the body was laid on the ground, covered with earth, and surrounded by rocks.

People of the Law

The people of the Law

To Israel, the Law was not merely a list of rules that had to be kept; it was a gift from God to them, an agreed basis for national life and the means by which they could remain in relationship with God. The Law confirmed that God loved them and that they were his own special people. In this sense, it brought them freedom—not a list of impossible requirements. We can begin to see why godly Israelites were so enthusiastic about the Law, and such statements as, "Oh how I love your law! It is my meditation all the day" (Psalm 119:97) make sense.

A law for all seasons

Because God cared about the whole life of his people, the Law deals with every aspect of living. Rules about family and social life, treatment of neighbors, work, the army, food, justice, health, and hygiene are combined with rules about national government and religious belief. Everything mattered to God: how you harvested your crops, whom you married, how you treated your animals, which feasts you attended, how you looked after your servants and where you worshiped. All these issues—and countless others—are related to the central question: What does it mean to be God's people?

The Law was not merely for lawyers. Of course there were special rules for judges, as there were for kings, employers, husbands, mothers, and almost every other group. But the Law was a gift from God to the whole community, providing a means by which he could bless his people.

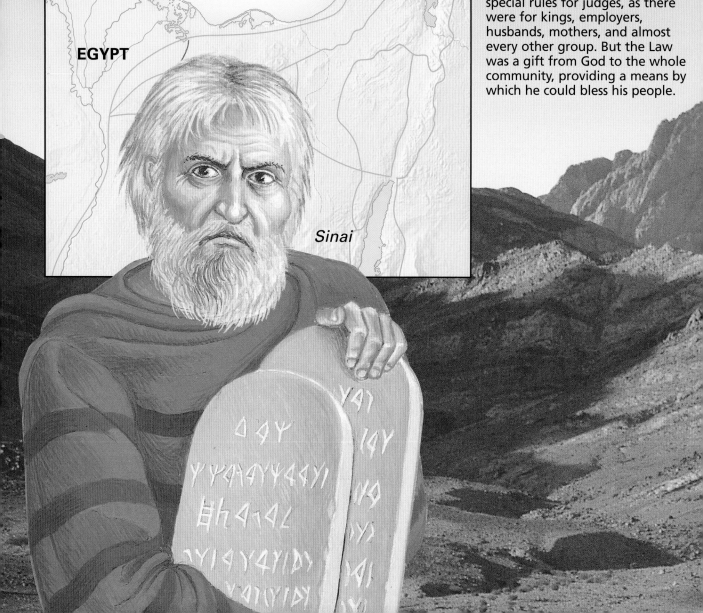

EGYPT

Sinai

The Ten Commandments

The Ten Commandments provide a summary of the Law. The rest of the Law expands on these rules, exploring what they mean in different situations. The covenant (see page 47) meant that the Israelites could relate to God, but it also affected their relationships with each other. Similarly, the Ten Commandments deal with relationships with both God and each other.

The commandments covered many areas, and the Jews applied them to almost every imaginable situation. While individual rules were important, it was still more important to have a "feel" for the Law, a sense of what it meant to belong to God, in applying the general principles in a particular situation.

Jesus and the Law

In New Testament times the requirements of the Law were often summarized even more concisely as: love God and love your neighbor:

And behold, a lawyer stood up to put him to the test, saying, "Teacher, what shall I do to inherit eternal life?" He said to him, "What is written in the Law? How do you read it?" And he answered, "You shall love the Lord your God with all your heart and with all your soul and with all your strength and with all your mind, and your neighbor as yourself." And he said to him, "You have answered correctly; do this, and you will live." (Luke 10:25-28).

St. Catherine's Monastery, near Mount Sinai, in Egypt

The Ten Commandments

And God spoke all these words, saying,

"I am the LORD your God, who brought you out of the land of Egypt, out of the house of slavery.

■ "You shall have no other gods before me.

■ "You shall not make for yourself a carved image, or any likeness of anything that is in heaven above, or that is in the earth beneath, or that is in the water under the earth. You shall not bow down to them or serve them, for I the LORD your God am a jealous God, visiting the iniquity of the fathers on the children to the third and the fourth generation of those who hate me, but showing steadfast love to thousands of those who love me and keep my commandments.

■ "You shall not take the name of the LORD your God in vain, for the LORD will not hold him guiltless who takes his name in vain.

■ "Remember the Sabbath day, to keep it holy. Six days you shall labor, and do all your work, but the seventh day is a Sabbath to the LORD your God. On it you shall not do any work, you, or your son, or your daughter, your male servant, or your female servant, or your livestock, or the sojourner who is within your gates. For in six days the LORD made heaven and earth, the sea, and all that is in them, and rested the seventh day. Therefore the LORD blessed the Sabbath day and made it holy.

■ "Honor your father and your mother, that your days may be long in the land that the LORD your God is giving you.

■ "You shall not murder.

■ "You shall not commit adultery.

■ "You shall not steal.

■ "You shall not bear false witness against your neighbor.

■ "You shall not covet your neighbor's house; you shall not covet your neighbor's wife, or his male servant, or his female servant, or his ox, or his donkey, or anything that is your neighbor's."

Exodus 20:1-17

But this is the covenant that I will make with the house of Israel after those days, declares the LORD: I will put my law within them, and I will write it on their hearts. And I will be their God, and they shall be my people.
Jeremiah 31:33

Israel's God

If we see in the Old Testament nothing but Israel's sorry history, a collection of literature, or a description of a religion, we have missed the point. At the heart of it is a picture of Israel's glorious God.

We learn about God primarily from the way in which he involves himself in the lives of human beings in real-time situations, not just from theological sermons or doctrinal statements.

Nevertheless, gathering together some of what we learn about him helps us understand why belonging to him, being part of his people, was seen as so special and desirable.

Four starting points:
1. *God exists*. This is taken for granted; it is assumed that only a fool would question it (Psalm 14:1).
2. *God allows himself to be known*. He wants people to know him, and he reveals himself in many varied ways, through creation, through the Law and the prophets, through visions, and by acting in people's lives.
3. *God relates*. The purpose of God's self-revelation is not just to give people an intellectual appreciation of who he is, but to allow them to relate to him.
4. *God is majestic and transcendent*. God makes himself known and, despite his greatness, he enters into relationship with human beings. Yet he is also incomprehensible, greater than any human being can conceive. The prohibition against depicting God in human or any other form stems from this belief in God's transcendence (Deuteronomy 4:15-16).

The nature of God
• *He is living*. God is active, not static; he interacts with his people. He is Life, and no single picture of him could possibly be adequate. "Here is how you shall know that the living God is among you" (Joshua 3:10).
• *He is personal*. The Old Testament knows nothing of the impersonal "life-force" of ancient philosophy and modern science fiction. He is a living person; he has a will and reveals his personal name. It matters to God what happens (Exodus 3:13-15).
• *He is spirit*. God is personal but must not be limited by human ideas of personality. He is not a human being. "For I am God and not a man, the Holy One in your midst" (Hosea 11:9).
• *He is eternal*. "Before the mountains were brought forth, or ever you had formed the earth and the world, from everlasting to everlasting you are God" (Psalm 90:2).
• *He is one*. God is a unity and God is unique. God is One, and there is only one God "That there is none besides me; I am the LORD, and there is no other" (Isaiah 45:6).
• *He is three*. Although the term "Trinity" does not occur in Scripture, Christians believe that the one God exists in three Persons—Father, Son, and Holy Spirit—but all of one essence (see, e.g., Matthew 3:16-17, where all three appear together).
• *He is hidden*. Sometimes God is found at the point where he seems to be missing. "Truly, you are a God who hides yourself, O God of Israel, the Savior" (Isaiah 45:15).
• *He is always present, always available*. God is not limited to the Temple, or even to the land of Israel, but is equally accessible in Egypt, Babylon, or anywhere else.

The character of God
• *God is holy*. Holiness implies purity and apartness. It is a kind of awesome goodness that is simultaneously attractive and terrifying. "Who is able to stand before the LORD, this holy God?"

And the glory of the LORD shall be revealed, and all flesh shall see it together.

Isaiah 40:5

SOME OLD TESTAMENT NAMES AND DESCRIPTIONS OF GOD

Ancient of Days
(Aramaic *Attiq yomin*)
Daniel 7:9
The ultimate authority as judge of the world.

Creator *Isaiah 40:28*

Everlasting God
(Hebrew *El Olam*)
Genesis 21:33

Father (Greek *Theos ho Pater*) *Malachi 2:10*

God Almighty
(Hebrew *El Shaddai*)
Genesis 17:1; 49:25
God is all-powerful.

Most High (Hebrew *El Elyon*)
Genesis 14:18-20
God, the maker of heaven and earth.

God of All Flesh
Jeremiah 32:27

God of the Covenant
(Hebrew *El Berit*)
Judges 9:46
Maker and keeper of his covenants.

God of Heaven
Nehemiah 2:4

God of Israel
(Hebrew *El Elohe-Yisra'el*)
Genesis 33:20

Holy One *Job 6:10*

Holy One of Israel
(Hebrew *Qedosh Yisra'el*)
Isaiah 1:4

I AM *Exodus 3:14*

Judge (Hebrew *Shapat*)
Genesis 18:25

King *Jeremiah 10:7*

Living God
Deuteronomy 5:26

LORD (Hebrew *Yahweh*)
Exodus 3:13-16

LORD of hosts
(Hebrew *Yahweh-seba'ot, Sabaoth*)
1 Samuel 1:11; 17:45
God is all-powerful.

LORD Is My Banner
(Hebrew *Yahweh-nissi*)
Exodus 17:15
God gives us victories.

The LORD Is Peace
(Hebrew *Yahweh-shalom*)
Judges 6:24
God brings us inner harmony.

The LORD Is There
(Hebrew *Yahweh-shammah*)
Ezekiel 48:35
God will be with his people at the end of history.

Lord, Master (Hebrew *Adonai*) *Psalm 2:4*
God has authority.

The LORD Will Provide
(Hebrew *Yahweh-jireh*)
Genesis 22:14

The LORD Is Our Righteousness
(Hebrew *Yahweh-tsidkenu*) *Jeremiah 23:6*
By God's acts he declares and makes his people righteous.

Most High (Aramaic *Illaya*)
Daniel 7:18
God has final authority.

> The LORD is the everlasting God, the Creator of the ends of the earth… He gives power to the faint, and to him who has no might he increases strength.
> Isaiah 40:28-29

(1 Samuel 6:20). God's holiness brings demands for his people. Because he is holy, they also must be holy (Leviticus 19:2).

• *God is all-powerful.* His power is not arbitrary, but purposefully applied, working toward a goal. God is able to fulfill his eternal purpose.

• *God is righteous and just.* Righteousness, sometimes seen as an aspect of his holiness, includes—but is more than—doing what is ethically right. For humans, it involves conforming to a norm—to an accepted standard or ideal pattern. So it makes sense to talk about righteous weights and balances, or righteous behavior, which conforms to the Law. God's righteousness makes him concerned to see that justice is done.

• *God is faithful.* There is no adequate equivalent in English for the Hebrew word *chesed*, which is sometimes translated as loving-kindness or steadfast love, but also includes faithfulness, loyalty, and total dependability. It is one of the commonest words used to describe God's attitude toward Israel.

• *God is love.* God's love for Israel is what makes the covenant more than a formal agreement. Many words are used for God's love, meaning desiring, taking pleasure in, attaching oneself to, knowing, caring about—and there is a strong link with *chesed*. Love involves both the will and strong emotion. God's love for Israel is spontaneous; it is not a result of Israel's deserving it. God chose to love them.

• *God is jealous.* God's jealousy is linked to his holiness and power—but also to his love. He is sovereign and cannot share the love and worship of his people with other gods. The Hebrew word for this includes no sense of petulance or envy, so perhaps the term "jealous" is misleading; "zealous" might be a better translation.

• *God is angry.* God's jealousy may express itself in anger, which is linked with his holiness. It is different from human anger, and is never malicious or capricious. God is angry about evil. Unlike his love, his anger is momentary. "His anger is but for a moment, and his favor is for a lifetime" (Psalm 30:5).

• *God is merciful and gracious.* This too is linked with *chesed* and with love. God's sovereignty means that he is free to give human beings more than they deserve, and he delights to do this. Mercy and forgiveness are pictured as freely available to those who, in repentance and faith, turn back to God. God cares about human beings and longs for their restoration. His mercy is never grudging.

The Jewish festivals

Passover (Pesach) and Unleavened Bread
Commemorated Israel's deliverance from Egypt
Exodus 12:11-30; Leviticus 23:4-8; Numbers 28:16-25; Matthew 26:17
Each family celebrated the deliverance of the Hebrews from slavery in Egypt and symbolically reenacted the first Passover as they ate their own special meal. The celebration continued for seven days as they commemorated the Exodus and wilderness wanderings by eating unleavened bread, recalling the haste with which they left Egypt when they did not have time to let the bread rise.

Firstfruits
Leviticus 23:9-14; Numbers 28:26-31
A barley harvest feast at the end of the seven-day Passover festival

Second Passover
Numbers 9:9-13; 2 Chronicles 30:2-3
For those unable to keep the first Passover

Pentecost
(Shavuot, Weeks, Firstfruits, Harvest)
A celebration of harvest
Leviticus 23:9-22; Deuteronomy 16:9-12; Acts 2:1
At Pentecost, seven weeks after Passover, the Jews celebrated the gathering in of the wheat harvest. The priests symbolically offered two loaves made from new flour. This feast also celebrated the giving of the Law to Moses at Mount Sinai.

Trumpets
(Rosh Hashanah, New Year, Judgment, and Memorial)
A time of reckoning with God
Leviticus 23:23-25; Numbers 29:1-6
This two-day celebration, marked by the blowing of trumpets to greet the civil new year, was also the beginning of the most solemn month in the year. The Israelites prepared themselves for Yom Kippur, which comes ten days later, by praising God, whose standard they had failed to meet, and by recounting his greatness, love, and mercy.

Day of Atonement
(Yom Kippur)
The most holy day in the Jewish year
Leviticus 16; 23:26-32; Numbers 29:7-11
On Yom Kippur Israel confessed the nation's sins and asked for forgiveness and cleansing. A scapegoat was sent into the desert, symbolically carrying the people's sin. The high priest entered the Most Holy Place of the Temple on this day alone. Recognizing this day as the holiest of feast days, Jews neither ate nor drank for 24 hours.

Tabernacles
(Succoth, Booths, Ingathering)
Commemorated Israel's wanderings in the wilderness
Leviticus 23:33-44; Numbers 29:12-40; John 7:2
A joyful harvest festival celebrating the gathering of the grapes. During the seven-day celebration the people thanked God for protecting them in the wilderness and for the harvest. For seven days they lived in shelters made of branches, to remind them of their time living in tents in the wilderness.

The Hebrew calendar

Month	Name (name before Exile)	Modern equivalent
1	**Nisan** (Abib)	March/April
2	**Iyyar** (Ziv)	April/May
3	**Sivan**	May/June
4	**Tammuz**	June/July
5	**Abu** (Ab)	July/August
6	**Elul**	August/September
7	**Tishri** (Ethanim)	September/October
8	**Heshvan** (Bul) = Marcheshvan	October/November
9	**Chislev**	November/December
10	**Tebeth**	December/January
11	**Shebat**	January/February
12	**Adar**	February/March

The Jewish year is strictly lunar, with lunar months averaging 29.5 days, giving 354 days in a year. A thirteenth month, Veader, was added about every three years to align the calendar with the solar year.

A Jewish family celebrate Passover in modern Israel.

the expulsion of the Syrians by Judas Maccabeus in 164 B.C., and the cleansing and rededication of the Jerusalem Temple, which the Syrians had desecrated. Lighting a new candle each day for eight days, the Jews commemorated the miracle of the Temple's holy candelabrum: for the rededication they had only one day's worth of consecrated oil, but it burned for eight full days, the time required to consecrate more oil.

Purim (Lots)
Celebrated the failure of Haman's plot to destroy the Jews
Esther 9:21-28
A time of feasting and joy when the people celebrated the deliverance of the Jews from death through the bravery of Queen Esther of Persia.

Simhath Torah
(Rejoicing in the Law)
Marked the end of the annual reading of the entire cycle of the Law A joyful celebration giving thanks for the Pentateuch—the first five books of the Hebrew Bible.

Dedication
(Hanukkah, Lights, Maccabees)
Commemorated the rededication of the Temple in 164 B.C.
1 Maccabees 4:41-49;
John 10:22
On Hanukkah the Jews celebrated

Weather	Harvests/agriculture	Festivals/Holy days
Rain ("latter rain")	Flax harvest	•14th Passover •15th–21st Unleavened Bread •16th Firstfruits
Dry	Barley harvest	•14th Second Passover
Warm and dry	Wheat harvest	•6th Pentecost (= Harvest, Firstfruits, Shavuot, Weeks)
Hot and dry		
Very hot and dry		
Very hot and dry	Date harvest Grape harvest Summer fig harvest	
Rain begins	Olive harvest Grape harvest	• 1st Trumpets (= Rosh Hashanah) •10th Day of Atonement (= Yom Kippur) •15th–21st Tabernacles (= Ingathering, Succoth, Booths) •22nd Simhath Torah (= Solemn Assembly)
Rainy ("former rain") Plowing	Olive harvest	
Cool and rainy	Winter fig harvest Sowing	•25th–2nd Tebeth Dedication (= Hanukkah, Lights)
Cold, hail and snow	Sowing	
Warmer and rainy	Almond blossoms Sowing	
Thunder and hail	Citrus fruit harvest Sowing	•14th–15th Purim (= Lots)

The Tabernacle—God's tent

About 50 chapters of the Bible are concerned with the Tabernacle, indicating its importance in the development of the religious life of Israel.

Why the Tabernacle?
The Tabernacle was a portable sanctuary—a holy place for worshiping God—created in the desert in response to the demand for mobility. It symbolized God's presence with his people and was a place where his will was communicated.

When the people of Israel were journeying from Egypt through the wilderness toward the Promised Land they were living in tents, so the Tabernacle was also a tent. It was designed so that it could easily be dismantled when the Israelites moved their camp and reassembled at the next halting place.

The Tabernacle and the Temple

The Israelites anticipated that once peace and security had been secured, a permanent national shrine would be set up (Deuteronomy 12:10-11). However, this was not realized until the time of King Solomon, when the first Temple was erected (2 Samuel 7:10-13; 1 Kings 5:1-5). The Tabernacle was thus a forerunner of the Temple. The Tabernacle and Temple are closely linked both historically and by their similarity in construction and underlying theology.

How we know about the Tabernacle

The fullest and most reliable source of information about the Tabernacle is in the book of Exodus. Exodus 25–28 prescribes the construction and furniture of the Tabernacle, while Exodus 35–40 describes how it was made. We are also helped by the specifications for Solomon's Temple (1 Kings 6; 2 Chronicles 3–4), and the Temple seen in a vision by the prophet Ezekiel (Ezekiel 40–43), both of which followed the basic plan of the Tabernacle.

An artist's impression of the Tabernacle in the wilderness near Mount Sinai. Notice that the camp of Israel is set up around the central Tabernacle.

The outer courtyard

The courtyard
(Exodus 27:9-18; 38:9-20)
The courtyard was a rectangle,
100 cubits (about 150 feet) long
on its north and south sides and
50 cubits (about 75 feet) wide on
its east and west sides.

See page 117 for a
description of the
Tabernacle.

The framework of the fence

Enclosing this space was a fence, with a framework consisting of 60 acacia wood pillars, 5 cubits (about 7.5 feet) high (Exodus 27:18). The pillars were probably round, and about 5 inches in diameter, with 20 on each side and 10 at each end. The base of each pillar stood in a brass socket, and each pillar was held upright by cords (Exodus 35:18) fastened to brass tent pegs (Exodus 27:19) driven into the ground, both inside and outside the court.

Curtain rods rested on hooks near the top of the pillars, serving as the top rail of the fence, and keeping the pillars the right distance apart. These rods were made of acacia wood, covered with silver; the hooks and protecting caps on the pillars were also made of silver (38:17, 19). There were also hooks at the bottom of the pillars, to which the bottom edge of the curtains was fastened.

The curtains

Curtains of fine twined linen (probably like modern duck) and probably white or natural in color were sewn together end to end, to form a continuous screen all around the Tabernacle area. Each curtain was 22.5 feet long, and the curtains were 7.5 feet high so that no one could look over the fence.

The entrance

(Exodus 27:16-18; 38:18)
A central entrance about 30 feet wide and 5 cubits (about 7.5 feet) high was located in the eastern end of the Tabernacle court. The entrance was screened by an embroidered curtain woven from blue, purple, and scarlet material and "fine twined linen" (Exodus 38:18)—that is, the warp consisted of bleached linen threads and the woof of strips of wool dyed alternately blue, purple, and scarlet. The entrance curtain was probably set back from the fence, allowing entry at both ends. This was the only entrance into the Tabernacle courtyard.

The altar of burnt offering

(Exodus 27:1-8; 38:1-7)
Anyone entering the Tabernacle court immediately confronted the bronze altar of burnt offering, where sacrifices were offered to God. According to the Mosaic Law, this was the only place where sacrifices could be made. The altar stood at the east end of the court, probably about halfway between the entrance and the Tabernacle itself (Exodus 40:29), reminding the people that they could not approach God except by the place of sacrifice.

The altar was a hollow box of acacia wood, 5 cubits (about 7.5 feet) square by 3 cubits (about 4.5 feet) high—small compared with the gigantic altar in Solomon's Temple (2 Chronicles 4:1). It was lined with sheets of bronze inside and out to protect it from the heat, and it was light enough to be carried on bronze-covered poles that passed through bronze rings fixed at each corner.

An artist's impression of sacrifice at the altar of burnt offering

The history of the Tabernacle

The wilderness years

It was at Mount Sinai, today identified with Jebel Musa, at the base of which stands St. Catherine's Monastery, that Moses received the Law. When the Jews turned from God and started to worship the golden calf in the wilderness, Moses angrily shattered the tablets of stone inscribed with the Ten Commandments. After the people repented, Moses climbed Mount Sinai again to intercede with God.

Constructing the Tabernacle

God renewed his covenant with Israel, gave them a second copy of the Law, and invited them to offer materials with which to construct the Tabernacle. The people responded generously and gave much more than was needed (Exodus 36:5-6); the work went ahead under the direction of Bezalel and Oholiab (Exodus 35:30; 36:2).

The Tabernacle was completed on the first day of the first Jewish month (Abib, March-April) in the second year after the Exodus from Egypt. The cycle of sacrifices and worship that God had laid down for the new sanctuary now began (Exodus 40:2).

The Tabernacle in the camp

Unlike the provisional tabernacle (Exodus 33:7-14), this permanent Tabernacle stood in the very center of the Jewish encampment. It must have appeared very impressive, with Mount Sinai as its backdrop. Moses and Aaron set up their tents on the east side of the Tabernacle, and the other three families of priests on the other three sides—the family of Kohath to the south; the family of Gershon on the west; and the family of Merari on the north—acting as the "bodyguard" of Israel's ruler, God. This prevented any unauthorized intrusion into the sacred area. This pattern is still followed by tent-dwellers in the Middle East. In a Bedouin camp the chieftain's tent occupies a central position with the families grouped around it in their allotted positions.

Outside the inner square, in a wider square, the tribes of Judah, Zebulun, and Issachar camped on the eastern side, under the standard of Judah; Ephraim, Manasseh, and Benjamin to the west, under the standard of

An artist's impression of the Tabernacle, showing the series of coverings draped over the wooden structure. *Bottom*: The arrangement of the tribes around the Tabernacle.

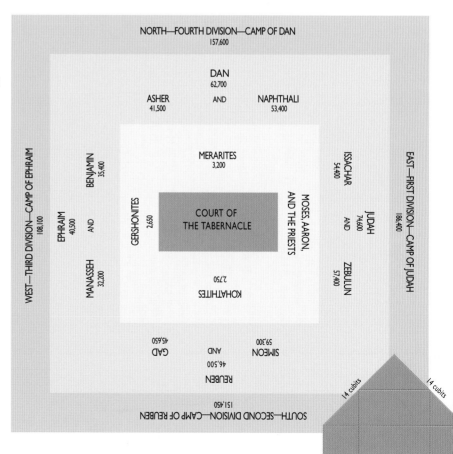

NORTH—FOURTH DIVISION—CAMP OF DAN
157,600

DAN
62,700

ASHER 41,500   AND   NAPHTHALI 53,400

WEST—THIRD DIVISION—CAMP OF EPHRAIM

BENJAMIN 35,400

MERARITES 3,200

ISSACHAR 54,400

EAST—FIRST DIVISION—CAMP OF JUDAH

EPHRAIM 40,500   AND   MANASSEH 32,200

GERSHONITES 2,650

COURT OF THE TABERNACLE

MOSES, AARON, AND THE PRIESTS

JUDAH 74,600   AND   ZEBULUN 57,400

KOHATHITES 2,750

GAD 45,650   AND   SIMEON 59,300

REUBEN 46,500

SOUTH—SECOND DIVISION—CAMP OF REUBEN
151,450

14 cubits   14 cubits

5 cubits   10 cubits   5 cub
20 cubits

A nineteenth-century engraving of Mount Sinai, or Mount Horeb.

named in the itinerary in Numbers 33 are today unknown. Two sites can be definitely identified: Hazeroth and Kadesh. Hazeroth has usually been identified with Ein Hudra, an oasis west of the Red Sea. Kadesh-barnea is today usually identified with the valley of Ein el-Qudeirat, a lush oasis based around the biggest spring in the area. It is situated in northern Sinai, at the crossroads of two major routes across the desert, a site surveyed by the British archaeologist Leonard Woolley and T. E. Lawrence—"Lawrence of Arabia"—just before World War I.

Rebellion in the camp

The Israelites arrived at Kadesh nearly a year after leaving Sinai, and it was from here that Moses sent out twelve spies to scout out the Promised Land (Numbers 13). When all the spies except Joshua and Caleb returned with discouraging reports, the Israelites panicked. Their fear turned to fury, and there was a mass uprising. Moses' and Aaron's lives were saved only by the direct intervention of God at the Tabernacle (Numbers 14:1-10). Because of their failure to trust God, the Israelites were condemned to remain in the wilderness until all the adults who had left Egypt had died (Numbers 14:20-25).

A fresh start

It was 38 years before the Israelites, with the Tabernacle in their midst, again set out for the Promised Land. After leaving Kadesh-barnea, circling around Edom, and defeating the Amorites and Og, king of Bashan, they encamped on the Plains of Moab (Numbers 33:48-49), at the oasis formed by springs in the foothills of Moab. From here, Moses climbed Mount Pisgah (also known as Nebo; Deuteronomy 34:1) to look at the Promised Land which he was not to be permitted to enter (Deuteronomy 3:27).

Ephraim; the less conspicuous tribes, Dan, Asher, and Naphtali to the north, under the standard of Dan; and Reuben, Simeon, and Gad on the south side, under the standard of Reuben.

Breaking camp

The Israelites remained at the foot of Mount Sinai for a year, until the Tabernacle and its furnishings were completed. Then they set out again, heading for the Promised Land (Numbers

10:11). When the Israelite army organized the people for the march, the Tabernacle, carried on the shoulders of Levites, remained at the center, with the tribes from the east and south sides of the camp marching in front of it, those from the north and west to the rear (Numbers 2).

En route

Although the Bible records the route taken by the Israelites in the wilderness, most of the places

Into the Promised Land

Crossing the River Jordan

When Moses died, Joshua took over the leadership of the people. After sending two spies across the Jordan and into the ancient city of Jericho, he prepared the Israelites to enter the promised land of Canaan. The Ark of the Covenant was taken to the head of the Israelite marching column, and the people were ordered to follow the Ark, carried as usual by the Levites, across the River Jordan (Joshua 3:3-4), which dried up for their crossing.

Gilgal, the site of the Israelites' first camp on the west side of the Jordan, became their first permanent settlement, and during the early stages of the Israelite conquest of Canaan, the Tabernacle was located here (Joshua 4:19; 5:10; 9:6; 10:6, 43).

Taking Jericho

The Ark figured prominently in the destruction of Jericho, being carried around the walls of the city every day for seven days, before the "great shout" on the seventh day, when the city walls fell.

After the Israelites failed to take the city of Ai, through the sin of one man, Achan, Joshua, and the elders of the nation fell in front of the Ark and asked God's help.

The central sanctuary

When the Israelites had captured the central highlands of Palestine, the Tabernacle was transferred there. Although the exact location is not clear, it was probably sited in turn at Shiloh, near Bethel, in the mountains of Ephraim (modern Seilun; Joshua 18:1, 10; 22:9, 12); Shechem, a city lying between Mount Gebel and Mount Gerizim, where the covenant was renewed (Joshua 8:30-35; 24); at Mizpah (Judges 20:1); and at Bethel (Judges 20:18, 26).

Finally the Ark was moved back to Shiloh, perhaps because of the town's central position.

The Tabernacle remained in Shiloh for the entire period of the judges; but the Ark of the Covenant was taken from it in the time of Eli (1 Samuel 4:4) and never returned.

By the time of the prophet Samuel, the sanctuary at Shiloh, now called the "house of the LORD," appears as a more permanent structure with doors (1 Samuel 1:7; 3:3, 15; see also the Mishnah). Probably this building replaced the earlier Tabernacle, which, with the passing of years and the wear and tear of moving, had deteriorated. It is certainly unlikely that the Moses Tabernacle survived beyond the period of the judges.

The capture of the Ark

During the time of Samuel, the warlike Philistines, who lived along the Mediterranean coast, threatened the existence of the Israelites. In about 1050 B.C., after a major defeat at Aphek, the leaders of Israel took the Ark into battle with them to try to compel God to fight for his people (1 Samuel 4:1-11). But the Philistines were again victorious. They captured the Ark and destroyed the sanctuary at Shiloh (as archaeologists have shown).

After the battle, the Philistines first took the Ark to Ashdod, where its presence caused the Philistine deity Dagon to fall over, and plague to break out. It was therefore moved on to Gath and then to Ekron, but the plague went with it. At last, seven months after its capture, the terrified people of plague-ridden Ekron returned the Ark to Beth-shemesh in Israel (1 Samuel 6:12).

From Beth-shemesh, the Ark was sent to Kiriath-jearim, above the modern village of Abu Ghosh, only 8 miles from Jerusalem, where it was kept for 20 years (1 Samuel 7:1-2). Here Eleazar looked after it in his own house.

King David's Tabernacle

When David became king over all Israel, he made Jerusalem his capital city. Here, on Mount Zion, next to his palace, he set up a new tabernacle for the Ark.

In his first attempt to bring the Ark to its new home, David did not observe the scriptural instruction for it to be carried on priests' shoulders, but transported it in a cart. When the oxen stumbled, Uzzah held the Ark to steady it and was killed for his lack of reverence (2 Samuel 6:1-7).

Frightened by this disaster, David now stored the Ark for a further 20 years in the house of the foreigner Obed-Edom (2 Samuel 6:10).

The Ark was finally carried into Jerusalem on the shoulders of Levites (1 Chronicles 15–16), with David dancing before it.

Other tabernacles

There are references to a tabernacle at Nob in the reign of King Saul (1 Samuel 21:1-6) and at Gibeon (1 Chronicles 16:39; 21:29). In David's day the bread of the Presence was kept

The Ark of the Covenant

The Ark was the portable holy chest built to hold the most sacred relics from Israel's history. It was made according to instructions given to Moses by God and is sometimes also known as "the ark of the Testimony" and "the ark of God." It measured 45 x 27 x 27 inches, and was made of acacia wood overlaid with gold. Two cherubim stood on top.

The Ark served as a container for the two tablets of the Law that Moses brought down Mount Sinai, a sample jar of manna, and Aaron's rod that budded. The Ark's cover, also known as the "mercy-seat," was the place where the high priest came once a year on the Day of Atonement to spill blood to atone for the people's sins. The Israelites believed that God's presence was manifest between the two cherubim on the lid of the Ark. This made the Ark the holiest item in the worship of ancient Israel.

The Philistine deity Dagon

The capture of the Ark

Yarkon

Aphek

Ebenezer

Capture of the ark

Shiloh

P H I L I S T I A

Mizpeh

Ekron

Ark recaptured

Kirjath-Jearim

Jebus

Ashdod

Beth-shemesh

Ark kept at the temple of Dagon

Gath

| 0 | 10 | 20 km |
| 0 | 4 | 8 | 12 miles |

➡ Ark in possession of Israelites

➡ Ark in possession of Philistines

Jordan R.

Artist's impression of the Ark of the Covenant

Upon its return to Israel, the Ark was kept at Kiriath-jearim for 20 years.

at Nob (1 Samuel 21:1-6), implying that at least some of the Tabernacle's sacred furniture was also situated there.

We know that at the close of David's reign the high place at Gibeon possessed relics from the original Tabernacle, including the altar of burnt offering, which was still in use (1 Chronicles 16:39; 21:29; see also 1 Kings 14; 2 Chronicles 1:3-6).

Solomon's Temple

An artist's impression of Solomon's Temple, with the great laver, or bronze ritual washing basin. The capitals of the pillars on either side of the Temple doorway were each decorated with 200 pomegranates.

King David was not permitted to build a Temple, though he collected money and materials for its construction. His son, Solomon, built the first Temple in Jerusalem. It was twice the size of the portable Tabernacle that it replaced and on which it was modeled.

Solomon used the forced labor of foreigners living in the country—80,000 quarrymen and 70,000 porters—to cut and transport the huge stones for building the Temple; 30,000 Israelites collected cedar and juniper wood from Lebanon; and there were 3,850 supervisors. The Temple was paneled with cedar, on which skilled Phoenician craftsmen carved cherubim, flowers, and palm trees, before the whole interior was overlaid in gold.

Outside the Temple stood a three-tiered bronze altar and a great bronze basin (the laver) for ritual washing. It was supported by twelve bronze oxen, three at each point of the compass.

The double doors of cypress wood, which opened into the Holy Place, were flanked by two pillars, which were named Jachin and Boaz.

Solomon's Temple, a fulfillment of King David's dream, was a monument to the glory of God (see 1 Kings 6–7; 2 Chronicles 3–4).

Plan of Solomon's Temple

1. Holy Place
2. Most Holy Place
3. Ark of the Covenant
4. Altar
5. Laver
6. Jachin
7. Boaz

A reconstruction of Solomon's Temple

David purchased the site for a temple for 50 silver shekels from Araunah the Jebusite. This site is identified with Mount Moriah—today the Temple Mount, Jerusalem—where Abraham had years before been told to sacrifice his son Isaac. The building of the Temple began in the fourth year of Solomon's reign, about 959 B.C., and took seven years to complete. It was a national project of immense size. To preserve the holiness of the Temple site, and to minimize noise, most of the masonry and carpentry was completed elsewhere, before the components were assembled on the actual site. Detailed accounts of the Temple's construction in the Bible enable us to make a quite accurate reconstruction of Solomon's Temple.

Bronze lamps on marble stands

One of the most impressive objects outside the Temple was the "sea of cast metal," a huge, round tank made of bronze which stood opposite the great altar. This tank was supported on the back of twelve bronze oxen, four at each point of the compass, and held about 10,000 gallons of water. It was used by the priests for ceremonial washing.

The high priest had a breastplate, inlaid with twelve precious stones, each symbolizing one of the tribes of Israel. His most solemn role was to enter the Most Holy Place on the Day of Atonement to present the blood of a sacrifice for the people's sins.

The Ark of the Covenant was placed in the Most Holy Place of the Temple. The Ark, the only major item surviving from Moses' Tabernacle, still contained the tablets of the Law, but the pot of manna and Aaron's rod had disappeared.

Inside the Holy Place were ten golden lampstands—five on each side—which had to be trimmed regularly by the priests to ensure that they were never extinguished.

The huge altar of sacrifice was probably cast in sections at a foundry in the Jordan Valley and then transported to the Temple site for assembly.

King Solomon, David's son and successor, built the first Temple in Jerusalem. Famed for his wisdom, later in his reign he turned away from God, married many wives, and built pagan temples for the use of his foreign wives.

The synagogue

In Jesus' time, there was at least one synagogue in nearly every town and village (Luke 4:14-30). The Jews started having services in synagogues during the Exile, when they had no access to the Temple. The synagogues developed their own form of service, parallel to that of the Temple.

There were synagogue services every Sabbath, and on the Jewish festival days. The synagogue was also open for prayer three times a day.

In the main room of the synagogue stood a seven-branched lampstand, or *Menorah*, and a lamp of eternity. During worship there would be prayers, Scripture readings, and praise.

The sacred rolls of the Law (the *Torah*) were kept in a special cupboard.

Sometimes in larger buildings there would be a courtyard with small rooms leading off it built on to the main structure.

Women and children
Women and children were allowed only into the gallery of the synagogue.

Above: The fourth-century Capernaum synagogue has been carefully excavated and partially reconstructed.

Below: Artist's cutaway illustration of the synagogue at Capernaum, probably built on the same site as the synagogue at which Jesus taught

gallery for women and children

reading desk

men's area

cloister

entrance

Jewish sects and parties

In New Testament times there were a number of political, religious, and social groups.

RELIGIOUS

Pharisees
First called the *Hasidim* ("pious ones"), this religious group supported the Maccabeans in the revolt against Antiochus. They studied both the Jewish Law (written Law) and the traditions that had been added to the Law (the spoken Law) They believed that their strict observance of these traditions made them the only righteous Jews. Later they became known as Pharisees ("separate ones,") and held religious power in Jerusalem during Jesus' ministry (Matthew 5:20; Luke 11:42), when some of them were Jesus' most bitter opponents.

Sadducees
A small but very powerful Jewish sect made up mainly of priests and members of the Sanhedrin council (Acts 4:1; 5:17). Their dislike of all change and a desire to keep everything as it was led to frequent quarrels with the Pharisees. Their name

means "righteous ones" in Hebrew. Their Bible was limited to the Pentateuch, and they rejected doctrines not found there. They held that no oral law or tradition was equal to Scripture. In contrast to the Pharisees, they did not believe in a resurrection, angels, or spirits (Mark 12:18; Acts 23:8). The Sadducees kept on good terms with the Romans when they came to power.

Essenes
A Jewish sect whose members lived a form of monastic life. Living in isolated communities such as Qumran, their name means "saintly" ones. They sought purity and communion with God through self-denial, temperance, and contemplation.

POLITICAL

Herodians
A sect of Jews who agreed to subject themselves to Roman rule. They believed that Herod

and his descendants were the last hope for Israel to maintain their own national government. They helped plot the death of Jesus (Mark 12:13; Matthew 22:16).

Zealots
A strongly nationalistic Jewish sect. They combined the religious practices of the Pharisees with hatred for any non-Jewish government. They believed it was God's will for Jews to take military action against Rome *(Matthew 10:4)*.

Galileans
A sect that believed that foreign control of Israel was against Scripture, and therefore refused to acknowledge foreign rulers. Similar politically to the Zealots, the Galileans were eventually absorbed into that sect (Acts 5:37).

SOCIAL

Scribes
Jewish men who copied, taught, and explained the Law. Many scribes were Pharisees and, like them,

believed in the authority of oral traditions (Luke 20:46). As teachers of the Law, they were important in Jewish society and also served as judges or lawyers.

Nazirites
Jews who took a vow of separation for a limited time or for life. Easily recognized because they vowed never to cut their hair, Nazirites separated themselves by their lifestyle to be close to God (Numbers 6:2, 4-6; Judges 13:5; 1 Samuel 1:11; Acts 18:18; 21:23-24).

Proselytes
Non-Jews who had been converted to Judaism. By being circumcised, a convert was thought to have joined the family of Abraham and was expected to follow the Law.

Publicans
Jews who collected taxes for the Roman government. Their willingness to work in the government was seen as disloyalty to Israel (Luke 19:1-9).

Some of the Levites (Temple assistants) served as Temple guards.

Pharisee

Sadducee

High priest

Herod's Temple

From Solomon to Herod

Solomon's splendid Temple had a history of neglect, plunder (by King Shishak of Egypt), misuse (by King Manasseh), and looting and destruction under the Assyrian King Nebuchadnezzar in 587 B.C. The Ark of the Covenant disappeared at the time of the Exile and was never recovered or replaced.

Under the leadership of King Zerubbabel and the high priest Joshua, the Israelites rebuilt Solomon's Temple, but on a far inferior scale. When the foundation stone of this Temple was laid, many of the older priests wept in disappointment (Ezra 3:7-13).

The prophets of the Old Testament encouraged the returned Jewish exiles to complete the restoration of the Temple and worship God faithfully there. The prophet Haggai asked pointedly, "Is it a time for you yourselves to dwell in your paneled houses, while this house [the Temple] lies in ruins?" (Haggai 1:4).

The Second Temple was probably improved and more elaborately adorned during the third and second centuries B.C., but we know little about this period in its history. On December 15, 167 B.C., Antiochus IV, the Seleucid king, set up a pagan altar in the Temple, thereby ritually polluting it for the Jews. When the Jewish heroes the Maccabees defeated the Seleucids, they had to cleanse the Temple and rededicate it (1 Maccabees 4:36-59). In 63 B.C. the Roman general Pompey captured Jerusalem.

A political move

King Herod now rebuilt the Temple. While his Temple was unquestionably the largest and most magnificent of the three Temples, it was not built by him for the glory of God, but to curry favor with the Jews, whom he had to keep in order if he wanted to remain a puppet king within the Roman Empire.

The Court of the Women was also known as the Court of Prayer; beyond it women were not allowed to penetrate the innermost courts of the Temple. Worshipers came to the Court of Prayer to meet the priests at the hour of prayer, bringing with them their various sacrifices. Within the Court of Prayer stood four enormous lampstands, lit on special occasions, such as the Festival of Lights.

The Court of Priests was the innermost court of the Temple, and also the holiest; as its name implies, only priests could enter it. At its center stood the Temple sanctuary itself, with other buildings and porticoes surrounding it.

Herod the Great

Herodium

Herod loved grandiose building projects. The Herodium ranks as one of the largest fortresses ever built for the protection of one man and as the greatest engineering feat yet discovered in the inter-Testamental period. Built on top of a huge cone-shaped mount 7 miles south of Jerusalem, with four towers (three semi-circular, and one rounded), it was protected by an outer double wall with a 10-foot passageway between the walls.

When Jerusalem was destroyed in A.D. 70, the Herodium was one of three major sites of Jewish resistance outside Jerusalem. The second-century Jewish Bar Kokhba Revolt also used the Herodium as its headquarters.

Masada

Masada, Herod's other palace fortress, was located overlooking the western shore of the Dead Sea, and it served as his summer resort. This virtually impenetrable refuge was lavishly furnished, as the excavated bathhouse and storerooms have revealed.

Fanatical Jewish zealots made their last stand against Rome in A.D. 73 at Masada. Rather than be captured by the Romans, they entered into a suicide pact, first killing their wives and children and then themselves.

The remains of Herod's northern palace in profile at Masada

The Temple
and its courts

This overall view of the Temple constructed by Alec Garrard gives a fine impression of the structure and extensive surrounding courts.

Herod's magnificent 150-foot-high structure greatly impressed the disciple who said to Jesus, "Look, Teacher, what wonderful stones and what wonderful buildings!" And Jesus said to him, "Do you see these great buildings? There will not be left here one stone upon another that will not be thrown down" (Mark 13:1-2).

Jesus also used the Temple to illustrate his resurrection, when he said, "Destroy this temple, and in three days I will raise it up." The Jews then said, "It has taken forty-six years to build this temple." John then explains, "But he was speaking about the temple of his body" (John 2:19-21).

The Temple destroyed

In A.D. 66 the Jews rebelled against their Roman masters. Herod's Temple became the focal point of resistance, from where the Jews held out against the might of Rome. By August of A.D. 70 all of Jerusalem except the Temple was in Roman hands.

As the Temple was one of the wonders of the ancient world, the Romans hesitated before destroying it. But the stubborn zealots refused to surrender, even though they stood no chance against the overwhelming numbers, war machines, armaments, and discipline of the world's best army.

The Romans, under Titus, responded by torching the Temple, setting fire to all its woodwork, and even throwing a lighted torch into the sanctuary itself. Before the building was reduced to a heap of rubble the Romans grabbed some of its priceless furnishings, thinking what excellent trophies they would make for their victory parade back in Rome.

In literal fulfillment of Jesus' prophecy that "there will not be left here one stone upon another that will not be thrown down" (Matthew 24:2), all that remained of Herod's Temple by the time the Roman army had finished was the platform on which it was built.

The massacre
The Romans were always ruthlessly efficient in warfare. In crushing the resistance of the Jewish zealots, the Romans massacred all the inhabitants who had failed to flee to the surrounding mountains. From the time that Titus had laid siege to

The emperor Vespasian, A.D. 69-79

the city, to the time the last stone of the Temple was pulled down, it is estimated that more than one million Jews were slaughtered.

The Titus Arch, Rome, built to commemorate Titus's victory over the Jews

The Temple plundered

Rome was no friend to the early Christians. Under Nero, the emperor who preceded Vespasian, the Christians had been persecuted and blamed for its great fire, and the apostle Paul had been martyred.

Rome was proud of her military victories. The Titus Arch (*opposite*) was built in Rome and showed soldiers carrying off the priceless treasures they had plundered from the Jerusalem Temple in A.D. 70.

The relief below shows the Romans triumphantly carrying the seven-branched golden lampstand and the table of the showbread. This is the only contemporary depiction of furniture from the Temple extant today.

Titus, the successful Roman commander who crushed the Jews and destroyed their Temple in A.D. 70

A hoard of silver shekels, dating from A.D. 66–70, with the oil lamp within which they were discovered by archaeologists. They were probably hidden by a frightened Jewish family during the Roman assault on Jerusalem in A.D. 70.

Varieties of religion in Bible times

False gods of Bible times

Name	Country	Description	Scripture
Artemis (Diana)	Asia	many-breasted fertility goddess	*Acts 19:28*
Asherah	Canaan	goddess of the sea wife of Baal symbol—a pole	*Judges 3:7* *1 Kings 18:19* *2 Kings 21:3* *2 Chronicles 15:16; 24:18*
Ashtoreth (Astarte, Queen of Heaven)	Canaan Sidon	mother-goddess fertility goddess	*Judges 2:13; 10:6* *1 Samuel 12:10* *1 Kings 11:5, 33* *Jeremiah 7:18; 44:17-25*
Baal	Canaan	young storm god chief god of Canaan until the Exile; the name Baal is often linked with place names, such as Gad, Peor, etc.	*Judges 2:13;* *1 Kings 16:31-32;18:18-29*
Baal-Zebub	Philistia	god of Ekron	*2 Kings 1:2*
Castor, Pollux	Greece	twin sons of Zeus	*Acts 28:11*
Chemosh	Moab ?Ammon	national god of war	*Numbers 21:29* *Judges 11:24* *1 Kings 11:7, 33* *Jeremiah 48:7*
Dagon	Philistia	national god of rain/agriculture	*Judges 16:23* *1 Samuel 5:2-7*
Hermes (Mercury)	Greece	messenger god, god of cunning, theft	*Acts 14:12*
Marduk (Bel)	Babylon	young storm/war god chief god	*Isaiah 46:1* *Jeremiah 50:2; 51:44*
Molech (Malcam) (Milcom) (Moloch) (?Rephan)	Ammon Israel	national god worshiped with child sacrifice	*Zephaniah 1:5* *Jeremiah 49:1, 3* *1 Kings 11:5, 7, 33* *Acts 7:43* *Acts 7:43*
Nebo (Nabu)	Babylon	son of Marduk god of wisdom, literature, arts	*Isaiah 46:1*
Nergal	Babylon	god of hunting/the underworld	*2 Kings 17:30*
Rimmon (Hadad)	Damascus	god of thunder, lightning, rain	*2 Kings 5:18*
Tammuz	Babylon	fertility god	*Ezekiel 8:14*
Zeus	Greece	chief of Greek gods	*Acts 14:12*

( ) = alternative name

Men and Women of the Bible

The first families	194
Into Egypt—and out	196
Judges	198
The first kings	200
Judah's prophets and kings	202
Israel's prophets and kings	204
Exile and return	206
Jesus of Nazareth	208
The Twelve	210
Jesus' friends and foes	212
The first Christians	214
Paul and his circle	216
Paul's converts and opponents	218

The first families

The families of Adam and Eve, Noah, and Abraham and Sarah

Adam and Eve

Adam *"mankind"*
Adam was the first person created by God. When he ate the forbidden fruit from the tree of the knowledge of good and evil, he brought sin into the world and, with Eve, his wife, had to leave the Garden of Eden.
Genesis 2–3; Luke 3:38; Romans 5:14–19; 1 Corinthians 15:22, 45

Eve *"life"*
Eve, created out of Adam's side, was the first woman and became the mother of all human beings. Tempted by the serpent, she disobeyed God and gave Adam the forbidden fruit to eat.
Genesis 2:18–3:20

Cain *"acquire"*
Cain, Adam and Eve's eldest son, was a farmer. God rejected Cain's offering of produce, but accepted his brother's animal sacrifice. This so infuriated Cain that he murdered his brother.
Genesis 4:1–25; Hebrews 11:4

Abel *"shepherd"*
Abel, Adam and Eve's second son, sacrificed the firstborn of his flock, which was accepted by God. Abel was murdered by his jealous brother, Cain.
Genesis 4:1–25; Hebrews 11:4

Noah *"rest"*
Noah, a "preacher of righteousness," was the only blameless man in a corrupt world. On God's instructions he built a three-tiered ark, 450 feet long, in which he and his family were kept safe during the great flood. After the flood, God made a covenant with Noah and gave the rainbow as a sign that he would never again destroy the world with a flood.
Genesis 5–9; Luke 3:36; 1 Peter 3:20; 2 Peter 2:5

Ham *"hot"*
Ham was Noah's youngest son. After the flood, Noah cursed Canaan, one of Ham's four sons, because of Ham's indecent behavior when Noah was drunk.
Genesis 5:32; 9:18–10:6

Shem *"name"* or *"renown"*
Shem, Noah's eldest son, was an ancestor of Jesus Christ.
Genesis 5:32; 9:18–23; 10:21–29; 11:10–26; Luke 3:36

Japheth *"may God enlarge"*
Japheth was Noah's second son.
Genesis 5:32; 9:18–23; 10:2–5

Methuselah *"man of the javelin"*
Methuselah is renowned for being the oldest man to have lived—he was 969 when he died.
Genesis 5:21–27; Luke 3:37

Enoch *"teacher"*
Enoch is one of only two people (the other is Elijah) whom the Bible records as being taken directly to heaven without dying.
Genesis 5:18–24

Job *"persecuted"*
Job, a godly man who lived in Uz, endured terrible and undeserved sufferings. He lost his family, fabulous wealth, status, and health. Job's three friends, Eliphaz, Bildad, and Zophar, tried unsuccessfully to counsel him, as did a younger man, Elihu. Nothing helped Job until he humbled himself in God's presence. After Job had prayed for his friends, God restored his health and his fortune.
Job 1–42

Noah and his family leave the ark after the great flood.

Abraham (Abram) *"father of multitudes"*

Abraham was the founder of the Jewish nation. His life was characterized by outstanding faith and by prayer. He lived about 2000 B.C., growing up in the prosperous town of Ur in Mesopotamia. At God's call he set off into the unknown with his wife, Sarah, his father, Terah, and his nephew, Lot. After spending some years in Haran, where his father died, he traveled to Canaan. There he lived in the highlands, probably as a wealthy nomad. He believed God's promise that a great nation would descend from him, and he believed that his wife, Sarah, would have a son, though she was past child-bearing years. Later he was willing to obey God's command to sacrifice his son Isaac, believing that God would raise Isaac from the dead. Abraham "believed God, and it was counted to him as righteousness."
Genesis 11:1–25:11; Matthew 1:1–2; Acts 7:2–3; Hebrews 11:8–19

Sarah *"princess"*

Sarah was Abraham's wife. In fulfillment of God's promise she became the mother of Isaac in her old age.
Genesis 17:1–18:15; 20:1–21:7; Hebrews 11:11; 1 Peter 3:6

Terah *"turning"*

Terah, born in Ur, traveled with his son Abraham to Haran, where he died.
Genesis 11:24–32; Luke 3:34

Lot *"covering"*

Lot, Terah's grandson and Abraham's nephew, chose to live in the evil town of Sodom. He escaped just before Sodom was destroyed, but his wife was turned into a "pillar of salt" because she looked back as she fled.
Genesis 11:31–14:16; 19

Isaac *"laughing"*

Isaac was the long-awaited son whom God had promised to Abraham and Sarah. Isaac and his wife, Rebekah, had twin sons, Esau and Jacob. In Isaac's old age, he was tricked into blessing Jacob with the blessing he had reserved for Esau.
Genesis 21:1–27:40; Matthew 1:2

Jacob *"supplanter"*

Jacob was the son of Isaac and Rebekah, and the younger twin brother of Esau. By devious means, he supplanted his brother and so inherited God's blessing to Abraham. Jacob escaped to Mesopotamia, where he married his uncle Laban's two daughters, Rachel and Leah. As he was returning to Canaan he had an all-night wrestling match with an angel of God and was told, "Israel shall be your name" *(Israel means "he struggles with God").* His twelve sons were the founders of the twelve tribes of Israel.
Genesis 25:21–35:29; 37:1; 42:1–50:14

Rachel *"ewe"*

Jacob worked for Laban for 14 years to win his daughter Rachel in marriage. Joseph and Benjamin were her sons.
Genesis 29–30; 35:18–20

Rebekah *"flattering"*

Rebekah was the granddaughter of Abraham's brother, Nahor, who had remained in Mesopotamia, and she was Laban's sister. She married Isaac. It was Rebekah's idea to trick Isaac into giving Jacob the blessing.
Genesis 24–28

Esau *"hairy"*

The son of Isaac and Rebekah, and elder twin of Jacob, Esau became a skillful hunter. He was the founder of the nation of Edom.
Genesis 25:1–28:9; 32–33; 36; Hebrews 12:16–17

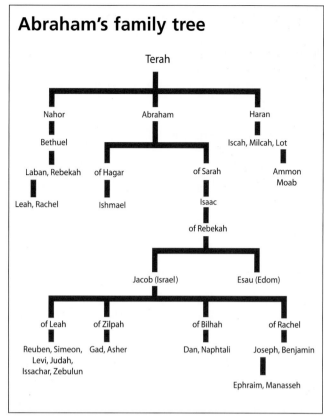

Abraham's family tree

Terah
— Nahor
  — Bethuel
    — Laban, Rebekah
      — Leah, Rachel
— Abraham
  — of Hagar
    — Ishmael
  — of Sarah
    — Isaac
      — of Rebekah
        — Jacob (Israel)
          — of Leah
            — Reuben, Simeon, Levi, Judah, Issachar, Zebulun
          — of Zilpah
            — Gad, Asher
          — of Bilhah
            — Dan, Naphtali
          — of Rachel
            — Joseph, Benjamin
              — Ephraim, Manasseh
        — Esau (Edom)
— Haran
  — Iscah, Milcah, Lot
    — Ammon, Moab

Hagar *"flight"*

Hagar was Sarah's Egyptian servant, who, at Sarah's suggestion, became Abraham's secondary wife. Sadly, when Ishmael was born to Hagar and Abraham, Hagar despised the childless Sarah, and Sarah was jealous of Hagar. After the birth of Isaac, Hagar and Ishmael were sent away.
Genesis 16; 21:8–21; Galatians 4:21–31

Ishmael *"God heard"*

Ishmael, son of Hagar, Sarah's servant, and Abraham, teased his young half-brother Isaac. Sarah forced Abraham to expel Ishmael and Hagar into the desert, where an angel led them to water. Ishmael had twelve sons, each of whom became a tribal chief.
Genesis 16–17; 25:12–18; 1 Chronicles 1:28-31

Melchizedek *"king of righteousness"*

Melchizedek is one of the Bible's most mysterious people, "without father or mother or genealogy, having neither beginning of days nor end of life . . ." He was king of Salem (Jerusalem), priest of God most high, and he blessed Abraham. Melchizedek was a "type," or prophetic symbol, of Jesus Christ, who was both king and priest.
Genesis 14:18–20; Psalm 110:4; Hebrews 5:6; 7

Into Egypt—and out

God cares for the Israelites, making Joseph prime minister and Moses their rescuer.

Joshua

Joseph with two of his brothers

Joseph *"increaser"*
Joseph, Rachel and Jacob's first son, was given an ornamented coat ("robe of many colors") by his doting father. Joseph's brothers sold him as a slave to passing traders, who in turn sold him to Potiphar in Egypt. Wrongfully thrown into prison, he was set free after he had correctly interpreted Pharaoh's mysterious dreams. Pharaoh appointed him prime minister of Egypt, responsible for collecting and storing food in preparation for the seven years of famine that he had predicted. Famine forced Joseph's family to come to Egypt, where Joseph cared for them all.
Genesis 30:22–24; 37–50

Pharaoh *"great house"*
Some eleven pharaohs are mentioned in the Bible. The pharaoh of Joseph's time was probably not Egyptian but a foreign "Hyksos" ruler, a Semite like the Hebrews. The "new" pharaoh in the time of Moses was Rameses II, who reestablished an Egyptian dynasty. He treated the Hebrews with great cruelty,

forcing them to be slaves.
Genesis 40–41; Exodus 1–15

Benjamin *"son of the right hand"*
Benjamin was Jacob's youngest son and Joseph's brother. His mother Rachel died as he was born. When Benjamin went to Egypt, Joseph kept him there, accusing him of stealing a silver cup. As a result of this trick, Jacob was persuaded to go to Egypt, where he was reunited with Joseph.
Genesis 35:18, 24; 42:4, 36; 43–45

Ephraim *"fruit"*
Ephraim was Joseph's second son and brother of Manasseh. Even though he was the younger of Joseph's sons, his grandfather Jacob gave him the blessing reserved for the firstborn son. Ephraim was an ancestor of one of the twelve tribes of Israel.
Genesis 41:52; 46:20; 48; 50:23

Zipporah *"bird"*
Zipporah was one of seven daughters of Jethro, a priest in Midian, who gave Moses a home when he fled from Egypt. Zipporah became Moses' wife, and they had two sons, Gershom and Eliezer.
Exodus 2:16–22; 4:24–26; 18:2–4

Miriam *"loved by God"*
Miriam was Moses' sister. As a child she helped her mother hide her baby brother and kept watch until he was rescued. As an adult, she was a prophetess. For a time she opposed Moses' leadership and was temporarily punished with leprosy.
Exodus 2:4, 7–8; 15:20–21; Numbers 12; 20:1

Aaron *"enlightened"*
Aaron was Moses' elder brother. Because Moses had protested to God that he was not a good speaker, Aaron became Moses' spokesman to Pharaoh. In the desert Aaron gave in to the Israelites' demand for gods and helped them

make a golden calf. He became Israel's first high priest and was in charge of God's tent of worship, the Tabernacle.
Exodus 4:14, 30; 5–12; 28–29; 32

Joshua *"God is salvation"*
Joshua had courage and faith. He was both a spiritual and military leader. As Moses' right-hand man in the wilderness, he went to spy out the land of Canaan and, with Caleb, encouraged the people to attack. Though this advice was ignored, he eventually led the people to victory in Canaan, having taken over the leadership upon Moses' death. At the end of his life, Joshua challenged the Israelites to follow God faithfully, and said, "As for me and my house, we will serve the LORD."
Exodus 17:9–13; 24:13; Numbers 13–14; Joshua 24:15

Shrine built over the traditional site in Hebron of the Cave of Machpelah, burial place of the patriarchs

Judah *"praise"*
Judah, the fourth son of Jacob and Leah, gained the birthright Reuben forfeited. After his brothers had planned to kill Joseph, Judah persuaded them to sell him to traders instead. Judah was the ancestor of the Davidic kings and of Jesus the Messiah.
Genesis 29:35; 37:26–28; 38; 43:3–10

Levi *"joined"*
Levi was the third son of Jacob and Leah. With his brother Simeon, he avenged his sister Dinah's rape in a dreadful slaughter of the people of Shechem. Levi was the ancestor of the Levites, the Israelite tribe who served God and his priests in the Tabernacle and later in the Temple.
Genesis 29:34; 34:25–31; 49:5–7

Manasseh *"one who causes forgetfulness"*
Joseph's elder son, Manasseh, was adopted, with his brother Ephraim, by his grandfather Jacob, and so became an ancestor of one of the twelve tribes of Israel. Jacob, however, gave the blessing for the firstborn son to Ephraim and not to Manasseh.
Genesis 41:51; 48

Potiphar *"belonging to the sun-god"*
Potiphar was a captain of the guard, a high-ranking Egyptian official. He bought Joseph from the Ishmaelite traders, and when he saw that "the LORD was with Joseph" he put him in charge of all his household. Potiphar later threw Joseph into prison, after his wife falsely accused Joseph of attempted rape.
Genesis 37:36; 39

Reuben *"see, a son"*
Reuben, the first of Jacob and Leah's six sons, tried to rescue Joseph after his brothers had planned to kill him.

Moses and Aaron plead with Pharaoh to let their people go.

Moses *"drawer out"*
When Moses was a baby he was saved from death by Pharaoh's daughter, who found him hidden in a reed basket among the bulrushes. She brought him up as her son, a prince of Egypt. But when he was a young man he "refused to be called the son of Pharoah's daughter, choosing rather to be mistreated with the people of God than to enjoy the fleeting pleasures of sin." After killing an Egyptian taskmaster, he fled to Midian, where he became a shepherd and married Zipporah.

The Exodus
When he went to look at a burning bush in the desert, Moses received God's call to return to Egypt and rescue the people, with his brother Aaron as his spokesman. Moses confronted Pharaoh, but only after the land had been devastated by plagues and all the firstborn Egyptian sons had died did Pharaoh give permission for them to leave—an event remembered every year in the Jewish Passover festival.

In the desert
After leading the people to safety on dry land through the sea, Moses brought them to Mount Sinai, where God gave him the Ten Commandments. He also gave detailed rules for daily living and instructions for the building of the Tabernacle. Moses led the often rebellious people through the desert for 40 years, supervising their conversion from a rabble of discontented slaves to a fighting force. His fiery temper cost him the privilege of entering the Promised Land.

Moses was the first and greatest of the prophets. He gave the Law and revealed God as *"Yahweh"* ("I AM"). He was a man to whom "God spoke face to face, as a man speaks to his friend."
Exodus 2—Deuteronomy; Luke 9:28–36; Hebrews 11:23–29

Genesis 29:32; 35:22–23; 37:21–29; 42:37–38

Simeon *"hearing"*
Simeon was Jacob and Leah's second son. With his brother Levi, he avenged his sister Dinah's rape by slaughtering the people of Shechem.
Genesis 29:33; 34:25–30; 49:5–7

Caleb *"dog"*

Caleb was one of the twelve men Moses sent to spy out the Promised Land. He and Joshua submitted a minority report that, with God's help, they could conquer the land, a courageous stand that almost cost Caleb his life. Out of all those who left Egypt, only Joshua and Caleb eventually entered Canaan.

Numbers 13–14; 26:65
Achan *"troubler"*
Achan stole some of the rich treasures of the conquered city of Jericho and hid them in his tent. This led to Israel's defeat in the battle against Ai. When Achan's crime was discovered, he was stoned to death, and Ai was then captured.
Joshua 7:1–8:29

197

Judges

Judges were rulers of Israelite tribes when the Israelites were settling down in the Promised Land. A judge was a military leader who rescued his tribe, or a group of neighboring tribes, from the enemy and became a peacetime governor.

Samson *"distinguished"*
Samson, famed for his superhuman strength, ruled Israel for 20 years. Often single-handedly, Samson tried to free the Israelites from the 40-year-long domination of the Philistines. As a Nazirite dedicated to God, Samson never cut his hair. His downfall, which proved to be fatal, was his attraction to women. He revealed to Delilah that the secret of his strength lay in his long hair. While he was asleep, she had his hair cut off.

Philistines, hiding in her room, seized him and blinded him, making him their prisoner. As his hair grew, Samson's strength returned. One day when he was in the Philistine temple, he pushed down its two central pillars. The building collapsed, killing Samson and all the leading Philistine rulers and warriors.
Judges 13–16; Hebrews 11:32

Jael *"mountain goat"*
Jael is remembered for the gruesome way in which she killed the commander of the Canaanite army, Sisera. As he slept in her tent, Jael drove a tent peg through his head.
Judges 4:17-21; 5:24-27

Sisera *"meditation"*
Sisera commanded Canaan's army for King Jabin. He deployed 900 iron chariots to oppress the Israelites. After one battle he took refuge in

Samson and Delilah

the tent of Jael, who, after welcoming him with traditional oriental hospitality, drove a tent peg through his head as he slept.
Judges 4–5

Barak *"lightning"*
After 20 years' oppression at the hands of the Canaanites, Barak, commander of the Israelite army, gained an important victory over Jabin, king of Canaan, thus freeing the Israelites.
Judges 4–5

Deborah *"honey bee"*
Deborah was one of the most successful judges of Israel (and the only woman judge). She made Barak her commander, and he defeated the Philistines, ushering in a period of 40 years of freedom from foreign domination.
Judges 4–5

Gideon overcomes the Midianites by his midnight surprise attack.

Gideon *"great warrior"*
Though Gideon's family, with at least ten servants, must have been a leading family, Gideon himself had little self-confidence. When called upon by an angel to rescue his tribe from Midianites—fierce nomads from the desert—he protested his insignificance and inability. Told to pull down his father's Baal idol, he did so at night. Instructed to summon an army, it took two "signs" of a wet, and then a dry,

fleece to encourage him, and a dream whose retelling he overheard, to strengthen his resolve. However, at God's command he reduced his army to a mere 300, and, with a brilliant midnight ploy, his small force terrified and overcame the vast numbers of the enemy. After this victory Gideon became a judge over his tribe. Sadly, he let go of his hard-won dependence on God, allowing his family and tribe to worship a golden ephod.
Judges 6–8

Delilah *"dainty"*
Using her beauty and charm, Delilah badgered Samson into revealing the secret of his strength—the fact that his hair had never been cut. Delilah, who was herself a Philistine, then betrayed Samson into the hands of her people. For this treachery she received a large reward.
Judges 16

Jephthah *"he opens"*
Before Jephthah, Israel's eighth judge, went into battle against the Ammonites he rashly vowed that, if he won, he would sacrifice the first thing that came out of his house upon his return. His only daughter met him, dancing and singing, and Jephthah did as he had vowed.
Judges 11–12

Naomi *"pleasantness"* or *"my joy"*
Naomi was Ruth's mother-in-law. With her husband, Elimelech, she moved from Bethlehem to Moab, where her husband and their two sons, Mahlon and Kilion, died. Naomi would have been destitute if Mahlon's wife, Ruth, had not returned with her to Bethlehem. As a result of Ruth's second marriage, Naomi became the great-great-grandmother of King David.
Ruth

Ruth *"companion"*
Ruth married one of Naomi's sons, Mahlon. Ruth's husband, father-in-law, and brother-in-law all died. But Ruth left her home country of Moab to return to Naomi's home in Bethlehem, saying, "Where you go I will go, and where you lodge I will lodge. Your people shall be my people, and your God my God. Where you die I will die, and there will I be buried." In Bethlehem Ruth married a relative of Naomi's, Boaz. Ruth's son, Obed, was the father of Jesse, whose son was King David.
Ruth; Matthew 1:5

Boaz *"quickness"* or *"strength"*
Boaz, a wealthy landowner, lived in the time of the judges. When the foreigner Ruth gleaned for grain in his fields, he protected her from the rough workmen and gave her extra grain. Boaz is

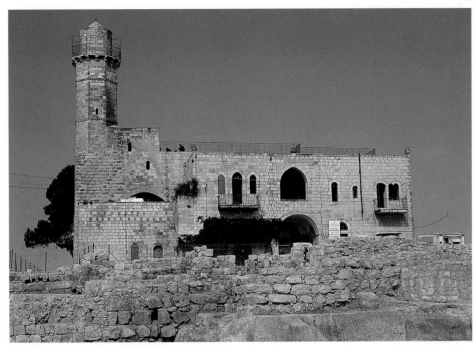

Nebi Samwil, by tradition the burial place of Samuel

Samuel *"asked of God"*
Samuel, the son of Elkanah and Hannah, was the last great warrior-judge of Israel, and one of the first prophets. His call to be a prophet came when he was still a child serving God in the tabernacle in Shiloh. He did not recognize the voice that spoke his name in the night, and the first three times he thought that the old priest Eli was calling him. Samuel's rule marked the transition between the period of judges and the kings. In his old age, much against his better judgment, Samuel yielded to the Israelites' desire to be like the other nations and have their own king. Samuel anointed Saul as Israel's first king. But, to Samuel's intense disappointment, Saul betrayed his early promise. Samuel broke off all contact with Saul and anointed David as Saul's successor.
1 Samuel 1–4; 7–16

called a "kinsman-redeemer" as he was a relative (kinsman) of Naomi (Ruth's mother-in-law). When Boaz married Ruth he bought back (redeemed) the property Naomi and her husband had lost when they left Bethlehem. Boaz became the great-grandfather of King David.
Ruth; Matthew 1:5; Luke 3:32

Abimelech *"my father is king"*
Abimelech, Gideon's son, ruled Israel as judge for three years, but killed 70 of his half-brothers to achieve this. He came to a violent end himself, being crushed to death by a millstone.
Judges 8–9

Hannah *"grace"*
Hannah, married to Elkanah, had no children, but Elkanah had children, and Hannah suffered the taunts and jeers of her husband's second wife. During her annual visit to the shrine of Shiloh, Hannah prayed for a son and vowed that she would dedicate any son of hers to God's service. When God gave her the gift of a son, Samuel, she waited until he was weaned and then gave him to Eli to serve in the sanctuary at Shiloh. Each year Hannah brought Samuel a coat. As a result of Eli's prayers, Hannah had five more children.
1 Samuel 1–2

Eli *"God is exalted"*
Eli was both a priest and a judge over Israel. As priest in the sanctuary at Shiloh, he trained the boy Samuel. But his failure to discipline his two sons, Hophni and Phinehas, brought God's judgment on Israel. The sons were killed by the Philistines, God's covenant box, the Ark, was captured, and Eli, on hearing the news, fell from his chair, broke his neck, and died.
1 Samuel 1–4

The first kings

Israel's most illustrious king was David, whom God called "a man after my own heart."

King Saul

Saul *"asked"*
Saul, a Benjamite, the son of Kish, was anointed by Samuel to be Israel's first king. As a young man Saul was outstandingly good-looking. A courageous and charismatic military leader, he was also a genuinely humble and trusting man of God. Sadly, he grew proud and disobedient, and God rejected him. In his times of madness, David calmed Saul by playing the harp, but Saul became jealous of David's popularity and drove him from the court and from the country. In a battle against the Philistines at Mount Gilboa, Saul was wounded and killed.
1 Samuel 8–31; 2 Samuel 1

Jesse *"God exists"*
Jesse, who lived in Bethlehem, was the grandson of Ruth and Boaz, and the father of King David.
Ruth 4:16–22;
1 Samuel 16–17

Jonathan *"God is given"*
Jonathan was King Saul's eldest son. Even though he knew that David, and not he, would be the next king, he was David's best and closest friend. A brave warrior, Jonathan was killed in battle by the Philistines.
1 Samuel 13–14, 18–20, 23, 31; 2 Samuel 1

Goliath *"an exile"* or *"soothsayer"*
Goliath was the Philistine champion and over 9 feet tall. He was heavily armored, the iron point of his spear alone weighing 15 pounds. A stone from David's sling silenced his jeers; he fell unconscious to the ground, and David cut off his head.
1 Samuel 17; 22:10

David *"beloved"*
Despite some spectacular failures, including adultery with Bathsheba and the murder of Bathsheba's husband, Uriah, David was Israel's greatest king. He was the youngest son of Jesse and had numerous talents. He played the harp, composed music, wrote poetry (including some of the most beautiful psalms), killed the giant Goliath, defeated Israel's enemies, established Jerusalem as the capital city, and ushered in a golden age for Israel. His passionate love for God made him "a man after [God's] own heart." Through his lineage would come the Messiah, Jesus.
1 & 2 Samuel;
1 Chronicles 11–29

David meets the Philistine champion, Goliath.

Absalom *"father of peace"*
Absalom was the deeply loved and ill-disciplined son of David. In his quest to take over the throne, Absalom stole the hearts of the Israelites from his father, King David. A fierce civil war followed. As Absalom was fleeing for his life, his mule went under an oak tree, and his long hair was caught in the branches. Against David's orders, Joab then killed him.
2 Samuel 3:3; 13–19

Michal *"who is like God?"*
Michal was Saul's younger daughter and David's first wife. She saved David's life when Saul tried to kill him.
1 Samuel 18–19; 25:44;
2 Samuel 3:13; 6

Bathsheba *"the seventh daughter"*
One evening as David was walking on the palace roof, he saw Bathsheba bathing. David committed adultery with her, had her husband Uriah killed, and then married Bathsheba. David was severely rebuked by the prophet Nathan for his sin. Bathsheba and David's first son died, but their next son, Solomon, succeeded David as king.
2 Samuel 11–12; 1 Kings 1–2

Nabal *"foolish"*
Nabal, a wealthy man from Carmel, refused hospitality to David and his men, whereupon his wife, Abigail, sent food. Ten days later, "the LORD struck Nabal, and he died."
1 Samuel 25

Joab *"God is father"*
Joab was King David's commander-in-chief and his nephew. He was notorious for his ruthlessness, and he killed David's son Absalom when he rebelled against David. Solomon had Joab killed for killing Abner and Amasa, two other army commanders.
2 Samuel 2–3; 14; 18–20; 1 Kings 2:28-35

Solomon *"peace"*
Solomon, son of Bathsheba and King David, whom he succeeded as king of Israel, built and dedicated to God the magnificent Temple in Jerusalem. Unlike his father, Solomon was not a man of war, but excelled at diplomacy. Inheriting a peaceful kingdom, he strengthened it by means of lucrative trading partnerships and marriage alliances. His kingdom became a byword for wealth and luxury. Solomon was internationally renowned for his wisdom. But his many foreign wives led him to lose his first love for God. High taxes, introduced to finance his building projects, left his country poorer and the people angry.
2 Samuel 12:24; 1 Kings 1–11; 1 Chronicles 22; 28; 29; 2 Chronicles 1–9

Uriah *"God is my light"*
Uriah the Hittite was a totally loyal officer in David's army. David, who had committed adultery with Uriah's wife, Bathsheba, arranged for Uriah to fight in the most dangerous position, where he was killed.
2 Samuel 11–12

Abigail *"source of joy"*
Abigail saved her husband, Nabal, from David's fury with gifts of food for him and his men, including 200 cakes of pressed figs. David, who greatly appreciated her good judgment, married Abigail when her husband died.
1 Samuel 25; 27:3; 30:5; 2 Samuel 2:2

Adonijah *"God is my lord"*
Adonijah, David's fourth son, tried unsuccessfully to gain the throne of Israel from his weak and very elderly father. Although David forgave Adonijah, Solomon had Adonijah executed for threatening the throne again.
2 Samuel 3:4; 1 Kings 1:1–2:25

Hiram *"my brother is exalted"*
As king of Tyre, Hiram was an ally of both David and Solomon. He supplied cedars from Lebanon and pine logs for the building of the Temple.
2 Samuel 5:11; 1 Kings 5; 9:11-14

Ish-bosheth *"man of shame"*
When King Saul was killed, the commander of Saul's army, Abner, crowned Saul's son Ish-bosheth king of the eleven northern tribes of Israel. After Ish-bosheth's death, David became king of both Judah and Israel.
2 Samuel 2–4

Amnon *"faithful"*
Amnon, King David's firstborn son, raped his half-sister Tamar. Though David was furious, he failed to punish Amnon. Absalom, who was Tamar's full brother, could never forgive Amnon and killed him two years later, against David's wishes.
2 Samuel 3:2; 13:1-39

Abner *"my father of light"*
Abner, the commander of Saul's army and King Saul's cousin, crowned Ish-bosheth as king on Saul's death.

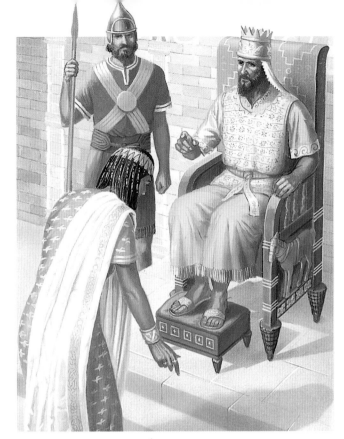

The Queen of Sheba visits King Solomon.

Abner became disenchanted with Ish-bosheth and joined David's army, only to be killed by David's commander, Joab, in revenge for Abner's slaughter of Joab's brother.
1 Samuel 14:50; 17:55-58; 26:7-16; 2 Samuel 2:12–3:39

Ahithophel *"brother of foolishness"*
When David's son Absalom revolted against his father, Ahithophel deserted David's service and joined Absalom. Ahithophel's advice was highly respected. When Absalom refused Ahithophel's advice, preferring the advice of Hushai, who was in fact a "mole" planted by David, Ahithophel committed suicide.
2 Samuel 15–17

Abiathar *"father of abundance"*
King Saul had Abiathar's father and the other 84 priests of Nob slaughtered because they had assisted David. Abiathar, the sole survivor, became joint high priest with Zadok under King David. When David was old and ineffective, Abiathar was one of those who supported David's son Adonijah in his usurpation of sovereignty, and for this he was banished by Solomon.
1 Samuel 22–23; 2 Samuel 8:17; 1 Kings 1:7, 19; 2:26-27; 1 Chronicles 15:11-15; 18:16

Zadok *"righteous"*
Zadok was joint high priest with Abiathar in King David's reign. While Abiathar supported Adonijah's claim to the throne, Zadok remained faithful to David and crowned Solomon as the next king of Israel. Solomon kept Zadok as high priest.
2 Samuel 8:17; 15:24-36; 17:15; 19:11; 1 Kings 1:8; 2:35

Judah's prophets and kings

After Solomon's death, the united kingdom of Israel split into two, with ten tribes forming the northern kingdom of Israel and two tribes forming the southern kingdom of Judah.

Rehoboam in a war chariot

Rehoboam *"freer of the people"*
Rehoboam, King Solomon's son and successor, inherited a kingdom that was seething with discontent. When he refused to lessen the burden of taxes, threatening instead to increase it, the Israelites rebelled. Only the tribes of Benjamin and Judah stayed loyal to Rehoboam and the house of David.
1 Kings 12; 14:21-31;
2 Chronicles 10–12

Abijah *"the Lord is my father"*
Abijah, Judah's second king, was the son of King Rehoboam. He ruled for three years. Though not a godly king, when an emergency came and his army was threatened, he cried to God for help. His troops rallied, and he won a great victory.
1 Kings 14:1–15:8;
1 Chronicles 12

Asa *"healer"*
Asa, Judah's third king, attempted to remove pagan worship from Judah.
1 Kings 15:9-24;
2 Chronicles 14–16

Jehoshaphat *"God is judge"*
Jehoshaphat, Asa's son, was Judah's fourth king. Though he allied himself with wicked King Ahab, he was himself a godly king, destroying idols and ¹ upholding God's laws.
1 Kings 22; 2 Kings 3;
2 Chronicles 17:1–21:3

Jehoram *"God is high"*
Jehoram, the son and successor of Jehoshaphat, married Athaliah, daughter of Israel's Queen Jezebel and King Ahab, who led him away from his father's right ways. He murdered his six brothers and allowed the people to worship idols. As Elijah predicted, he died of an incurable disease.
2 Kings 8:16-24;
2 Chronicles 21:4-20

Ahaziah *"God sustains"*
Son of Jehoram, Ahaziah was the sixth king of Judah. Influenced by his mother, Athaliah, he "did evil in the sight of the LORD." He ruled for less than a year, being murdered by a military commander, Jehu, while visiting his uncle Joram, king of Israel.
2 Kings 8:25–29; 9:14–29;
2 Chronicles 22:1–9

Athaliah *"God is strong"*
Judah's only queen. When Athaliah's son King Ahaziah died, she murdered her grandchildren in order to gain the throne, and she behaved like her evil mother, Jezebel. Unbeknown to her, one grandchild, Joash, survived and was kept hidden till he was seven years old. He was then proclaimed king, and soldiers murdered Athaliah.
2 Kings 11;
2 Chronicles 22:10–23:21

Joash *"God has given"*
Joash, son of King Ahaziah, became king of Judah when he was seven years old. Under the influence of Jehoiada, the priest, Joash restored the Temple and removed Baal worship. When Jehoiada died, Joash lost his commitment to God and allowed idol worship to creep back. He ruled for 40 years before his courtiers murdered him.
2 Kings 11–12;
2 Chronicles 24

Amaziah *"God has strength"*
Amaziah, the son of Joash, began well but gradually turned away from God's ways, reintroducing idols. He was assassinated at Lachish after ruling for 29 years.
2 Kings 14:1–22;
2 Chronicles 25

Azariah *"God has helped"*
Azariah, also called Uzziah, was Amaziah's son. He became king when he was 16. Though he served God, Azariah failed to remove the idolatrous "high places." For usurping the role of a priest and attempting to offer incense in the Temple, he was afflicted with leprosy and had to live in isolation.
2 Kings 15:1–6
2 Chronicles 26

Isaiah *"salvation of God"*
Isaiah prophesied in Jerusalem during the reigns of Uzziah, Jotham, Ahaz, and Hezekiah, a period of about 40 years. Isaiah was married to a prophetess, and his two sons were given symbolic names: Shear-Jashub, meaning *"a remnant will return,"* and Maher-Shalal-Hash-Baz, meaning *"quick to the plunder."* Isaiah's call to be a prophet came in an awe-inspiring vision of the holiness of God, recorded in Isaiah 6. His book speaks strongly of the power of God, combining outrage against sin and prophecies of catastrophic judgment with tender and beautiful visions of future peace and blessing. It is Isaiah who first portrays the Messiah as a suffering servant, killed for the sins of his people. He was a courtly adviser of kings, strongly warning against foreign political alliances and preaching the necessity of total trust in God.
Isaiah (especially 1:1; 6; 7:3; 8:1; 53; 61)

Jotham *"God is perfect"*
Jotham followed in the godly ways of his father, King Azariah. He was crowned king in Azariah's lifetime, when leprosy forced Azariah to live in isolation.
2 Kings 15; 32–38;
2 Chronicles 27

Ahaz *"he holds"*
Ahaz, the son of Jotham, encouraged Baal worship, and even made human sacrifices of his own sons. When the armies of Aram and Israel marched against him, he panicked. Ignoring Isaiah's advice, he went to Tiglath-Pileser III of Assyria for help, but ended up being subject to him.
2 Kings 16; 2 Chronicles 28;
Isaiah 7

Hezekiah *"God is strength"*
Unlike his father, Ahaz, Hezekiah held fast to God and introduced wide-ranging and thorough religious reforms. His dependence on God led him to rebel against Assyria. In preparation for an Assyrian attack, he built a famous aqueduct 1,745 feet long through solid limestone, so that the city of Jerusalem would always have a secret water supply when under siege. When the Assyrians called on him to surrender, he turned to God for help, and God routed the army.
2 Kings 18–20;
2 Chronicles 29–32;
Isaiah 36–39

Manasseh *"causing forgetfulness"*
Manasseh was as evil as his father, Hezekiah, had been good. He burned his own son as a child sacrifice, took advice from mediums and fortune-tellers, and practiced magic. He "filled Jerusalem from one end to another" with the blood of innocent people. He was captured by the Assyrians and exiled to Babylon, but he returned to Judah a reformed man, trusting God.
2 Kings 21:1–18;
2 Chronicles 33:1–20

King Hezekiah

Amon *"workman"*
Amon, the son of Manasseh, succeeded his father to the throne, and followed the same evil practices. After two years, he was murdered by his court officials.
2 Kings 21:18–23;
2 Chronicles 33:20-25

Josiah *"God supports"*
Josiah, the boy-king of Judah, was crowned when he was eight, when his father, Amon, was killed. Under Josiah, idolatry was purged, and the Temple in Jerusalem was repaired. In the Temple, a copy of the lost scroll of the Law was found, and Josiah obeyed the instructions found there.
2 Kings 21:26–23:30;
2 Chronicles 33:20–25:27

Jehoiakim *"God establishes"*
King Jehoiakim reversed the godly reforms introduced by his father, Josiah, and reinstated Baal worship. He opposed the prophet Habakkuk and had Jeremiah's scrolls burned.
2 Kings 23:36–24:7;
2 Chronicles 36; Jeremiah 36

Jehoiachin *"God will establish"*
The Babylonians appointed King Jehoiachin in the place of his father, Jehoiakim. Fourteen weeks later he was exiled to Babylon by King Nebuchadnezzar.
2 Kings 24:8–16;
2 Chronicles 36:9-10;
Jeremiah 52:31-34

Zedekiah *"Yahweh is my righteousness"*
Zedekiah was the last king of Judah, taking over from his nephew Jehoiachin. Although he was King Nebuchadnezzar's puppet king, Zedekiah rebelled. This brought about Jerusalem's destruction.
2 Kings 24:17–25; 2 Chronicles 36:10–23; Jeremiah 21; 32; 34; 37–39

Habakkuk *"God is strength"*
Habakkuk wrote his prophetic book during the reigns of Jehoiakim and Josiah. He warned that the Babylonians would capture Judah, and this would be God's punishment for their violence, idolatry, and corruption. Habakkuk emphasized the importance of personal faith, writing that the "righteous shall live by faith."
Habakkuk

Nahum *"comforter"*
Nahum's short prophecy encouraged the people of Judah as they faced defeat by the Babylonians. Nahum predicted the overthrow of Nineveh, the capital of the Assyrians, who had long oppressed the Israelites. This took place in 612 B.C.
Nahum

Jeremiah *"God is high"*
Jeremiah, whose prophecies are recorded in the books of Jeremiah and Lamentations, lived in the grim days of the last five kings of Judah: Josiah, Jehoahaz, Jehoiakim, Jehoiachin, and Zedekiah. Jeremiah was hated and called a traitor because he urged the people not to resist the Babylonian armies, declaring that the impending destruction of Jerusalem was God's judgment against idolatry. His book vividly communicates the horror and misery he felt as he contemplated the destruction of his beloved homeland. Jeremiah was probably taken off to Egypt after Jerusalem fell into the hands of King Nebuchadnezzar in 587 B.C. His prophecy that the Jews would return to Jerusalem 70 years after its fall also came true.
Jeremiah; Lamentations

Micah *"who is like God?"*
Micah prophesied against the southern kingdom of Judah (during the reigns of

Hezekiah's tunnel, Jerusalem

Jotham, Ahaz, and Hezekiah), and also against the northern kingdom of Israel (during the reigns of Pekah and Hoshea). While Micah spoke out against evil practices and God's impending judgment (saying that Samaria would become "a heap of rubble" [NIV]), he was also a prophet of hope, and he predicted that a great ruler over Israel would come from Bethlehem.
Micah

Zephaniah *"God has treasured"*
The prophet Zephaniah was the great-great-great-grandson of King Hezekiah. His message of judgment on Judah was delivered during Josiah's reign. He predicted that a small number (a "remnant") would return to Jerusalem.
Zephaniah

Obadiah *"servant of God"*
Obadiah prophesied against the people of Edom, Judah's persistent enemy.
Obadiah

Huldah *"weasel"*
Huldah, a prophetess, was consulted by Hilkiah the priest, on behalf of King Josiah, after the book of the Law had been discovered in the Temple.
2 Kings 22:14–20;
2 Chronicles 34:22–28

Israel's prophets and kings

In the 210 years from Jeroboam I to Hoshea, the northern kingdom of Israel had nine dynasties and nineteen kings. Kings' sons did not succeed their fathers, as in the southern kingdom (which had a single dynasty); in fact, some of the kings were merely ambitious officials or military leaders.

Jeroboam I *"the people multiplied"*
Jeroboam was a talented young officer in Solomon's court, in charge of the entire labor force of the country, when the prophet Ahijah met him and prophesied that he would be king over the ten northern tribes. When Solomon consequently tried to kill him, he fled to Egypt until Solomon's death. Jeroboam became Israel's first king, after Israel had split into the two kingdoms of Judah (in the south) and Israel (in the north). In order to stop the people in Israel from traveling to Jerusalem to worship God, he set up rival religious sanctuaries in Bethel and Dan, where the same religious festivals were held, but on different days, and sacrifices were offered by priests not descended from the family of Aaron. This counterfeit system of worship was supported by all the subsequent kings of Israel.
1 Kings 11:26–14:20

Omri *"God apportions"* or *"people"*
Omri, a commander-in-chief in King Elah's army, came to Israel's throne as its sixth king by defeating commander Zimri, who had killed King Elah. Omri "did more evil than all who were before him." He established the strategic hill town of Samaria as Israel's new capital.
1 Kings 16:15-28

Ahab *"father is brother"*
Ahab, son and successor of Omri, was one of Israel's most successful (yet evil) kings. He married evil

Jezebel, daughter of Ethbaal, king of the Sidonians, and so began to worship Baal. He set up an altar for Baal in a temple that he built. Ahab's death, during his third war against Syria, was seen as God's punishment on one of Israel's most wicked kings.
1 Kings 16:29–22:40

Ahaziah *"God sustains"*
Ahaziah followed in the evil footsteps of his father, Ahab, and consulted the god of Ekron, Baal-Zebub, rather than the Lord. When he fell from his balcony, he never recovered, as Elijah the prophet had pronounced.
1 Kings 22:51-53; 2 Kings 1

Jehoram (Joram) *"God is exalted"*
Jehoram did evil in the eyes of the Lord, but not to the extent that his father (Ahab) and mother (Jezebel) had done, because he did at least make an attempt to end Baal worship. He was murdered by Jehu.
2 Kings 3; 9:14-29

Jehu *"he is Yahweh"*
Jehu was an army commander when he was anointed by a prophet to be the next king of Israel. He killed Jehoram, Jezebel, all members of the royal family, and all the priests of Baal. Though he claimed that he would worship God, he maintained the false worship introduced by Jehoram.
2 Kings 9–10

Black obelisk, showing Jehu giving tribute to Shalmaneser

Jehoahaz *"God has grasped"*
Israel's eleventh king, Jehoahaz, was a failure. He led the Israelites away from worshiping God and was defeated by two kings of Syria, Hazael and Ben-Hadad.
2 Kings 13:1-9

Jehoash *"God has given"*
Jehoash (sometimes known as Joash) consulted the dying prophet Elisha and was told that he would defeat Syria three times. Although he did this, he still worshiped idols.
2 Kings 13:10–14:16

Jeroboam II *"the people multiplied"*
Jeroboam II's military achievements in recovering Damascus and Hamath for Israel were notable, but he continued Baal worship.
2 Kings 14:23-29

Elisha *"God is Savior"*
Elisha was Elijah's disciple, assistant, and successor as God's faithful prophet in Israel. He worked as a prophet for 55 years during the reigns of Joram, Jehu, Jehoahaz, and Joash. Fourteen miracles were performed through Elisha, most notably the healing of commander Naaman's leprosy.
1 Kings 19:16, 19–21; 2 Kings 2–9; 13:14–20

Naaman *"pleasantness"*
Naaman, the Syrian army commander, was a valiant warrior, but also suffered from leprosy. A captured Hebrew girl told him about the prophet Elisha. Naaman visited him and was told to dip himself seven times in the River Jordan. Naaman at first proudly refused, but when he complied, he was immediately cured.
2 Kings 5

Gehazi *"valley of vision"*
Gehazi, Elijah's dishonest servant, secretly accepted gifts of silver and clothes from Naaman, which Elijah had declined. Gehazi was punished and became "as white as snow" with Naaman's leprosy.
2 Kings 4:25–5:27; 8:1-6

Amos *"burden-bearer"*
Amos was a shepherd and cultivator of sycamore–fig trees in Judah when God sent him to Israel to prophesy against the moral corruption, dishonesty, mistreatment of the poor, and luxurious living that was rampant in the northern kingdom of Israel.
Amos

Naboth *"a sprout"*
Naboth refused to sell his vineyard to King Ahab, and for this Queen Jezebel had him killed.
1 Kings 21; 2 Kings 9:30-37

Hoshea *"deliverer"*
Hoshea, the last king of Israel, acquired the throne by killing his predecessor,

Elijah's sacrifice on Mount Carmel is consumed by fire from heaven.

Elijah *"the Lord is my God"*
Elijah, the most prominent prophet of his day in Israel, opposed King Ahab and his foreign queen, Jezebel, in their attempts to make Baal worship the official religion of Israel. God sent a severe drought, during which Elijah was fed with food brought by ravens. He also multiplied food for a widow and brought her son back to life. Elijah challenged Ahab and the 450 prophets of Baal to a contest on Mount Carmel. While Baal's prophets could do nothing, fire came on Elijah's sacrifice, in answer to his prayer. The prophets of Baal were then all killed, and God again sent rain. After this "mountaintop" experience Elijah suffered deep depression. He traveled to Mount Horeb in the wilderness and there God spoke to him in a "low whisper." Elijah did not die in the normal way, but was "translated" and caught up in a chariot of fire. With Moses, Elijah appeared at Jesus' transfiguration.
1 Kings 17–19; 21; 2 Kings 1:1–2:18; Luke 9:28-36

King Pekah. It was during his reign that final disaster struck the northern kingdom. After a three–year siege in the ninth year of Hoshea's reign the king of Assyria (Shalmaneser) captured Samaria (the capital of Israel) and deported the Israelites to Assyria. In this way the prophetic warnings came true, and Israel was punished for its sin of worshiping other gods and refusing to obey God's law of justice and love.
2 Kings 15:30; 17-18

Joel *"the Lord is God"*
Joel warned the southern kingdom of Judah that God's judgment ("the day of the LORD") would fall on Judah like a devastating plague of locusts, if they did not return to following God.

Joel
Hosea *"God has saved"*
Hosea denounced the people of Israel for their idolatry, likening them in their unfaithfulness to God to his adulterous wife, Gomer. In his deeply moving prophecies Hosea shows that, just as he loved his wife and brought her back, so God loves his wayward people and brings them back to himself.
Hosea

Jonah *"dove"*
Jonah was the first Hebrew prophet sent to a pagan country. God told him to warn the ungodly people of Nineveh to turn away from their sins. Jonah, trying to run away from this thankless task, found himself swallowed by a great fish. When he

eventually preached to the people of Nineveh, and they repented and turned to God, Jonah was furious. Jonah, and through Jonah the Jewish people, had to learn that God cares for people of all nations. The book of Jonah takes its name from the prophet.
Jonah

205

Exile and return

After a 70-year exile in Babylon, the Jews of Jerusalem returned to rebuild their ruined city.

Sennacherib *"Sin [the moon-god] has multiplied the brothers"*
Sennacherib, king of Assyria, defeated the Babylonians and then besieged King Hezekiah of Judah. In fulfillment of Isaiah's prediction that God would save Jerusalem, 185,000 Assyrian soldiers mysteriously died in the night, killed by "the angel of the LORD." Sennacherib returned to Nineveh, where two of his sons killed him.
2 Kings 18:17–19:37; 2 Chronicles 32; Isaiah 36–37

Nebuchadnezzar *"may the god Nebo defend the boundary"*
Nebuchadnezzar, the powerful king of Babylon, defeated the Israelites of Judah, captured Jerusalem, and exiled the majority of the people to Babylon. Nebuchadnezzar built many beautiful buildings and temples in Babylon, including the fabulous hanging gardens of Babylon, which were later counted among the seven wonders of the ancient world. For seven years Nebuchadnezzar was insane—God's punishment on him for his great pride. His sanity was restored when he gave glory to God.
2 Kings 24–25; 2 Chronicles 36:6-20; Daniel 1–4

Ezekiel *"God strengthens"*
The son of Buzi the priest, Ezekiel lived in Jerusalem until he was deported in 597 B.C. and taken to Babylon, along with the king and most of the ruling families of the city. Until 587 B.C., when Jerusalem was destroyed, Ezekiel lived by the River Kebar, from where he urged the

people left in Jerusalem to repent. Later, after the destruction of Jerusalem, Ezekiel preached a message of hope and prophesied a future return to Jerusalem. In this way he comforted the captured Jews, who had lost their homes, their land, and their Temple, and who felt as if they had been abandoned by God. He showed that faith in God could continue even in a foreign land, and without the Temple. He often acted out his prophecies in dramatic, and sometimes bizarre, ways.
Ezekiel

Abednego *"servant of Nego"*
Abednego was one of Daniel's three close friends among the Jewish exiles in Babylon. With Shadrach and Meshach, Abednego refused to bow down and worship the statue of Nebuchadnezzar. For this rebellion he was thrown into a blazing furnace, but miraculously survived unscathed.
Daniel 1–3

Belshazzar *"Bel protect the king"*
As coregent and successor to King Nebuchadnezzar, Belshazzar was Babylon's last king. During a banquet Belshazzar called Daniel to interpret strange writing that had appeared on the wall. Daniel's interpretation was that Belshazzar had been weighed in God's balances of judgment and had been found deficient. As a result he was about to lose his throne to the Medes and Persians. "That very night," we are told, "Belshazzar . . . was killed," bringing to an

end the vast power of Babylon.
Daniel 5

Cyrus *"sun, splendor"*
Cyrus, founder of the Persian Empire, captured Babylon in 539 B.C. He was noted for his enlightened and humane rule. In keeping with this, he allowed the exiled Jews to return to Jerusalem and rebuild the Temple, at the expense of his royal treasury.
Ezra 1–6

Daniel *"God is my judge"*
Daniel, who came from an aristocratic Jerusalem family, was exiled to Babylon when he was in his teens. Sent to court to train to be an administrator, he rose to high rank in the Babylonian, and then the Persian, kingdoms. Daniel was a man of outstanding faith and prayer. He was noted for his courage and his wisdom, including the ability to interpret dreams. Because of his refusal to deny his faith he was thrown into a lions' den, where he was miraculously preserved. He was a visionary, and the second half of the book named after him records the revelation God gave him of future world events.
Daniel

Darius *"he that informs himself"*
Darius the Mede, who succeeded Belshazzar as king of Babylon, was tricked by his officials into having Daniel thrown into the lions' den. When he saw Daniel's miraculous deliverance, he said, "In all my royal dominion people are to tremble and fear before the God of Daniel."
Daniel 5–6

Daniel in the lions' den

Nehemiah oversees the rebuilding of the walls of Jerusalem.

Nehemiah *"the Lord comforts"*

Nehemiah grew up in Babylon during the time of the Jewish Exile. He rose to the influential position of cupbearer to King Artaxerxes of Persia. When Jews were allowed back to Jerusalem, Nehemiah's family stayed behind. He was deeply upset when he heard that the returned exiles had not succeeded in rebuilding Jerusalem's walls. After praying and fasting for four months, Nehemiah asked if he could return to Jerusalem and organize the people to rebuild the ruined walls of the city. Nehemiah's building program was opposed by Sanballat, Tobiah, the Arabs, the Ammonites, and the men of Ashdod, but as a result of hard work and prayerful vigilance the wall was rebuilt.
Nehemiah

Ezra *"the Lord helps"*

Ezra, a priest and scribe, led the third group of Israelites from exile in Babylon back to Jerusalem. He had written permission to enforce God's Law as the law of the land. The Temple had been rebuilt, but he found the people had grown lax and were neglecting God's laws. Thirteen years after Ezra's arrival, Nehemiah came to Jerusalem as governor, and the people experienced a spiritual revival.
Ezra

Zerubbabel *"seed of Babylon"*

Zerubbabel was the leader, and later governor, of the first group of Israelites to return to Jerusalem from exile in Babylon. With the encouragement of the prophets Haggai and Zechariah, and against violent opposition, he rebuilt and dedicated the Temple.
Ezra 1–5; Haggai

Queen Esther

Esther *"myrtle"*

Esther, a beautiful young Jewess, grew up in Susa, the capital of Persia. She was an orphan, cared for by her cousin Mordecai. King Xerxes chose her to be his consort after Queen Vashti fell from favor. At first Esther did not reveal that she was a Jewess, but when Haman planned to massacre all Jews in his empire, Esther, after prayer and fasting, devised a courageous plan to save her nation.
Esther

Xerxes (or Ahasuerus)

Xerxes was the king of Persia who married the Jewess Esther after dismissing his wife, Vashti.
Esther

Haggai *"born on a feast day"*

Haggai rebuked the returned exiles for living in expensively paneled houses while the Temple was still in ruins. Zerubbabel, Judah's governor, and Jehozadak, the high priest, followed Haggai's instructions and rebuilt the Temple.
Haggai

Haman

Haman became prime minister to Xerxes, king of Persia, and in his hatred for Mordecai used his wealth and position to mastermind the massacre of all the Jewish people in Persia. His evil plan would have succeeded but for Esther. Haman was hanged on the 75-foot-high gallows he had built for the execution of Mordecai the Jew.
Esther 3–9

Malachi *"my messenger"*

Malachi rebuked the Jews for replacing enthusiasm for God with the ritual of services in the new Temple.
Malachi

Mordecai *"consecrated to Merodach"*

Mordecai was a Jewish exile who lived in the Persian capital of Susa. His cousin, Esther, became King Xerxes' wife. By exposing a plot to kill Xerxes, Mordecai saved the king's life. He later incurred Haman's fury for his fearless refusal to bow down to him. In his anger, Haman resolved to slaughter all Jews and have Mordecai hanged on a gallows. It was Mordecai who made sure that Esther received news of the plot and acted to save her people. Mordecai was then made prime minister.
Esther

Sanballat *"the god Sin has given life"*

Sanballat, governor of Samaria, with Tobiah and Geshem, opposed Nehemiah's governorship and did all he could to prevent the rebuilding of Jerusalem's walls.
Nehemiah 2:19-20; 6:1-14; 13:28-29

Tobiah *"the Lord is good"*

Tobiah the Ammonite, with Sanballat and Geshem the Arab, fought against Nehemiah's rebuilding of Jerusalem. Tobiah taunted the Jews, saying that if a fox were to tread on their walls they would collapse.
Nehemiah 2:19-20; 4:3-9; 6:28-29; 13:1-9

Zechariah *"the Lord remembers"*

Zechariah's prophecies roused the Jews who had returned to Jerusalem out of their apathy, spiritual sloth, and evil ways. He was a priest as well as a prophet, a descendant of one of Judah's ancient high-priestly families. He had been born in exile in Babylonia, but returned with the first group of Jews and prophesied alongside Haggai.
Zechariah

207

Jesus of Nazareth

All the prophecies about God's promised Messiah were fulfilled in the birth, life, death, resurrection, and ascension of Jesus.

John the Baptist

Mary *"loved by God"*
Mary, a young Jewish virgin who was engaged to a carpenter named Joseph, was chosen by God to conceive and bear his Son, Jesus Christ, by the power of the Holy Spirit. The angel Gabriel announced this to Mary in Nazareth, and she responded with humility and trust. Her *Magnificat,* or song of praise to God, which she sang when she went to visit her cousin, Elizabeth, shows her love and devotion for God. Mary's deeply thoughtful nature is shown after Jesus' birth in Bethlehem and the visit of the shepherds with their astounding story of angels in the sky. Mary, we are told, married Joseph and had several other children. Jesus' first sign, when he changed water into wine,

Mary

was performed at the instigation of Mary, who was with him during at least this part of his three-year public ministry. Mary stood at the foot of the cross as Jesus died, and Jesus told the apostle John to look after her. We find her again in the upper room on the Day of Pentecost.
Matthew 1; Mark 6:3; Luke 1–2; John 2:1-11; 19:25-27; Acts 1

Joseph *"may (God) add"*
Joseph was "engaged" to Mary when they discovered that Mary was pregnant through the action of the Holy Spirit. Joseph married Mary and became foster father to Jesus. Being warned in a dream, Joseph took Mary and Jesus from Bethlehem to Egypt to escape Herod's massacre of baby boys in Bethlehem. After Herod's death, Joseph returned to his hometown of Nazareth, where he was a carpenter. After Jesus' visit to the Jerusalem Temple when he was twelve, Joseph is never heard of again, and it is assumed that he died when Jesus was still young.
Matthew 1–2; Luke 1:27–2:52

Elizabeth *"God is my oath"*
Elizabeth, wife of the priest Zechariah, was visited by her cousin Mary, the mother of Jesus, when they were both pregnant. Elizabeth greeted Mary with the words, "Blessed are you among women, and blessed is the fruit of your womb!" Elizabeth's son was John the Baptist.
Luke 1

John the Baptist *"the Lord is gracious"*
John the Baptist, son of Elizabeth and Zechariah, lived in the Judean wilderness. John wore clothes made from camel's hair, with a leather belt around his waist, as the prophet Elijah had done centuries earlier. He fearlessly preached a message of repentance, paving the way for his cousin, Jesus Christ, whom he baptized in the River Jordan. Speaking about himself and Jesus, John said, "He must increase, but I must decrease." John was imprisoned, and later beheaded, because he spoke out against Herod Antipas's marriage to his brother Philip's wife, Herodias.
Matthew 3; 11:1-19; 14:1-12; Mark 1:1-8; Luke 1; John 1:1-34; 3:30

Salome *"clothing"*
Salome was Herodias's daughter and Herod's step-daughter. At a great feast held on Herod's birthday, she danced a passionate dance, for which Herod promised her any gift she desired. At her mother's request, she asked for John the Baptist's head on a platter.
Matthew 14:6-11; Mark 6:21-28

Anna *"grace"*
Anna, a very elderly, widowed prophetess, spent her life worshiping God in the Jerusalem Temple. She recognized the baby Jesus as the Messiah when he was consecrated in the Temple.
Luke 2:36-38

Herodias *"heroic"*
While Herodias's husband, Herod Philip, was still alive, she married his brother-in-law, Herod Antipas. Herodias detested John the Baptist because he spoke out against this marriage. She had him thrown in prison and was responsible for his execution.
Matthew 14:1-12; Mark 6:14-29

Simeon *"he hears"*
A devout Jew who lived in Jerusalem, Simeon had been told by the Holy Spirit that, before he died, he would see the Christ. When Mary and Joseph brought the baby Jesus to the Temple, Simeon took him in his arms and praised God. His beautiful song of peace and joy is called the *Nunc Dimittis* and is sung regularly in many churches.
Luke 2:25-35

Tiberius *"son of the Tiber"*
Tiberius was Roman emperor from A.D. 14 to A.D. 37. (He was coregent beginning in A.D. 11.) He ruled during most of Jesus' lifetime.
Luke 3:1

Herod the Great *"heroic"*
Herod, the evil king of Judah from 34 to about 4 B.C., was visited by the "wise men," and subsequently ordered all male babies in Bethlehem under two years of age to be slaughtered. He was called "the Great" because the country was very prosperous during his long reign and he built many beautiful buildings, including the magnificent new Temple in Jerusalem. But he was loathed for his vicious cruelty and kept himself in power by fawning on the Romans and by killing all possible rivals.
Matthew 2; Luke 1:5

Augustus *"august"*
Augustus, the nephew and successor of Julius Caesar, took the title Octavian and became the first Roman emperor, ruling from 31 B.C. to A.D. 14. Augustus ordered the census which brought Joseph and Mary from Nazareth to Bethlehem for Jesus' birth.
Luke 2:1

Zechariah *"the Lord remembers"*
Old Zechariah, a godly priest and husband of Elizabeth, was told by an angel that they would have a son who must be called John, and who would bring many people back to God. Since Elizabeth was well advanced in years and had always been childless, Zechariah greeted this news with incredulity. For this he was struck dumb and remained unable to speak until the baby was born and named John.
Luke 1

Jesus teaching his disciples in the hills around Galilee

Jesus *"the Lord is salvation"*
Jesus Christ is portrayed in the New Testament as the Savior of the world, and the name "Jesus" itself means "Savior." As John wrote at the end of his Gospel, "These [miraculous signs] are written so that you may believe that Jesus is the Christ, the Son of God, and that by believing you may have life in his name."

Childhood
Jesus' mother, Mary, laid the baby Jesus in a manger at his birth in Bethlehem, where shepherds visited him. Jesus was presented in the Temple, and then Mary and Joseph, Jesus' foster father, fled to Egypt with Jesus after the wise men had visited them. They later returned to Nazareth, where Joseph worked as a carpenter. Apart from Jesus' visit at age 12 to the Temple, where he listened to the teachers and asked them questions, nothing else is known about his childhood.

Three years of ministry
When Jesus was about 30 years old, John the Baptist baptized him in the River Jordan, before Jesus went into the desert to be tempted by Satan. After

this, Jesus started his public ministry, choosing twelve disciples to be with him. Jesus performed many miracles, such as changing water into wine at Cana; and many healings, such as Jairus's daughter being brought back to life. He also preached often, as in the Sermon on the Mount, and told numerous memorable parables, such as the Good Samaritan and the Prodigal Son.

Final week
The four Gospel writers concentrate on the last seven days of Jesus' life. On the Sunday before his death, Jesus entered Jerusalem on a donkey, to the cheers of the crowds. The following Thursday, Jesus ate the Last Supper with his disciples, before going to pray in the Garden of Gethsemane, where Judas betrayed him. Jesus was arrested, given unfair trials, unjustly condemned to death, crucified like a common criminal, and buried. But Sunday his tomb was found to be empty, as he had been raised from the dead. Forty days later Jesus ascended into heaven, after many resurrection appearances, promising that he would one day return.
Matthew; Mark; Luke; John

The Twelve

Jesus chose twelve men to be with him during his three years' work of preaching and teaching. He called them "apostles," meaning "those who are sent."

Andrew *"manly"*
Andrew introduced his brother, Peter, to Jesus when they were disciples of John the Baptist. Andrew and Peter were fishermen on Lake Galilee. Andrew brought to Jesus a boy who had two small fish and five barley loaves, which Jesus miraculously used to feed 5,000 people.
Matthew 4:18-20; Mark 1:16-18; John 1:35-42; 6:8-9

Bartholomew *"son of Talmai"*
Nothing is known about Bartholomew. The only time his name appears is in the list of all of Jesus' apostles.
Matthew 10:3

James (form of Jacob, "supplanter")
James was a fisherman, working with his brother, John, and father, Zebedee, in the family business. He was mending nets when Jesus first called him, and he followed Jesus at once. Jesus gave John and James the nickname "sons of thunder" because they had stormy natures. They suggested, for example, that Jesus should ask God to rain down fire on an unbelieving village. James became one of Jesus' three closest apostles, whom Jesus chose to have with him at special moments, such as the transfiguration. James was beheaded for his Christian faith by Herod Agrippa I about ten years after the death of Jesus.
Matthew 4:21-22; 10:2; 17:1-13; 26:37; Mark 5:37; 10:35-45; Luke 9:51-56; Acts 12:2

James (form of Jacob, "supplanter")
There were two apostles called James. The James who was not John's brother was the son of Alphaeus, and nothing else is known about him.
Matthew 10:3; Acts 1:13

John *"the Lord is gracious"*
John, a fisherman and son of Zebedee, was one of Jesus' inner circle of three very close apostles; along with his brother, James, he was given the nickname "sons of thunder." John, who leaned on Jesus at the Last Supper, was Jesus' closest friend, and as Jesus was dying, he asked John to look after Mary, his mother. John wrote one Gospel, the book of Revelation (during his exile on the island of Patmos), and three short letters. In his Gospel, John never mentions himself by name, but uses the words "the disciple Jesus loved" instead. John became a leader in the early Church.
Matthew 4:21-22; 10:2; 20:20-23; John 13:23-25; 19:25-27; Acts 1:13; 3–4; Galatians 2:9; 1, 2 and 3 John; Revelation 1:1

Judas *"praise"*
The Judas who did not betray Jesus is called "Judas, not Iscariot," and is probably the same person as Thaddaeus.
Luke 6:16; Acts 1:13

Judas Iscariot
Judas Iscariot was the treasurer for the twelve apostles. For 30 silver pieces he betrayed Jesus with a kiss in the Garden of Gethsemane. When Judas saw that Jesus had been condemned to death, he was overtaken by remorse, and returned the silver to the elders, saying, "I have sinned by betraying innocent blood." Judas then hanged himself. Judas is always the last name in the list of the apostles.
Matthew 26:1–27:10; Acts 1:15-26

Matthew *"gift of the Lord"*
Matthew, also known as Levi, was called from being a tax collector to follow Jesus. He abandoned everything and held a feast in his house for Jesus and many tax collectors and sinners. He is the traditional author of the first Gospel.
Matthew 9:9-10

Nathanael *"God has given"*
Nathanael is most probably the same person as Bartholomew. Philip told Nathanael about Jesus. When Nathanael met Jesus, Jesus said of him, "Behold, an Israelite indeed, in whom there is no deceit!"
John 1:43-51

Thomas *"twin"*
Thomas, whose name is Didymus in Greek, showed

Jesus eats the Last Supper with the Twelve.

his courage when he was prepared to die for Jesus, before Jesus went to raise Lazarus. At the Last Supper, Thomas asked Jesus, "How can we know the way?" and Jesus replied, "I am the way, and the truth, and the life." Thomas is remembered as "doubting" Thomas because he said that he would never believe in Jesus' resurrection unless he saw Jesus for himself and touched his wounds. When the risen Lord Jesus did appear to him, Thomas immediately worshiped him and called him his Lord and God.
Matthew 10:3; John 11:16; 14:5-6; 20:24-28

Simon *"hearing"*
Simon, not to be confused with Simon Peter, is known as Simon the Zealot, because he was probably a member of a Jewish revolutionary group dedicated to driving the Romans from Israel.
Matthew 10:4

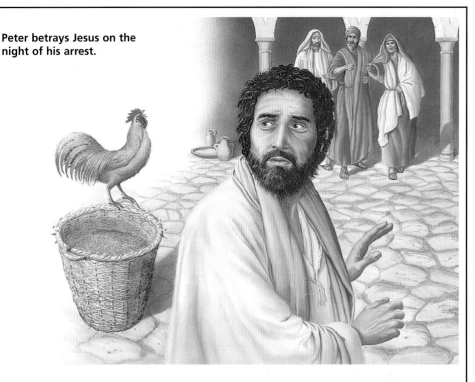

Peter betrays Jesus on the night of his arrest.

Peter *"rock"*
Peter, the outspoken and often brash leader of the twelve, always heads the lists of the apostles. With his brother, Andrew, Peter left his fishing at Christ's command and became one of Jesus' three closest disciples. At Caesarea Philippi, Peter told Jesus that he was "the Christ, the Son of the living God." Peter boasted that he would die for Jesus, but later denied him three times. After Jesus' resurrection, Jesus told Peter to be a shepherd and "feed my sheep." Peter led the first Christians, preaching fearlessly on the Day of Pentecost, when 3,000 people accepted his message and were baptized. With John, Peter healed a cripple outside the Temple gate called Beautiful. As the number of Christians swelled to over 5,000, Peter and John were thrown into prison for teaching that the resurrection of the dead comes through Jesus. Peter wrote two short letters, and much of Mark's Gospel is usually seen as a summary of his teaching. Jesus predicted that Peter would be martyred, and it is thought that he was executed by Nero in Rome.
Matthew 4:18-20; 10:2; 14:25-31; 16:13-23; 17:1-13; 26:31-35, 69-75; 1 and 2 Peter

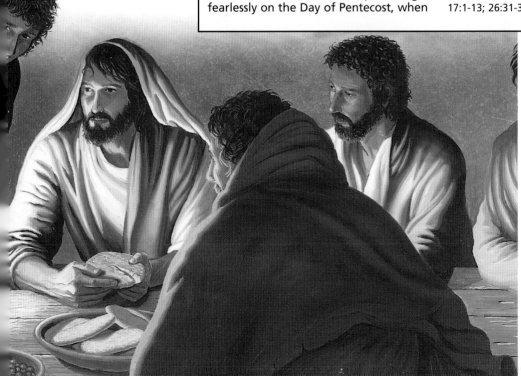

Philip *"lover of horses"*
Philip, who, like Andrew and Peter, was from Bethsaida, brought Nathanael (Bartholomew) to meet Jesus. When 5,000 hungry people needed food, Jesus tested Philip's faith. At the Last Supper, Philip asked Jesus to show them the Father, and Jesus replied, "I am in the Father and the Father is in me."
John 1:43-51; 6:5-7; 12:20-22; 14:8-9

Jesus' friends and foes

In addition to his twelve apostles, Jesus had many devoted followers and friends, although some of the religious leaders opposed him.

Zacchaeus *"pure"*
Zacchaeus, a wealthy, dishonest tax collector, climbed a tree to have a good view of Jesus as he passed through Jericho. Jesus told Zacchaeus to come down and then went to his house, where Zacchaeus called Jesus "Lord" and announced that he would give away half of his money to the poor and pay back four times over the money he had gained by cheating.
Luke 19

Mary Magdalene (form of Miriam) *"strong"*
Mary was named Magdalene after the town she came from, Magdala. Jesus drove seven demons from her, and she became his follower, standing close to his cross when he died. Mary Magdalene was the first person Jesus appeared to after his resurrection.
Matthew 27:55; 28:1-10; Mark 15:40; 16:1-8; Luke 8:2; John 19:25; 20:1-18

Nicodemus *"conqueror of the people"*
Nicodemus, a leading Pharisee, visited Jesus at night and was told that he needed to be born again. As a member of the Jewish ruling council, Nicodemus stood up for Jesus, saying that they ought to give him a hearing before they condemned him. Nicodemus helped Joseph of Arimathea to place Jesus in the tomb, and he brought myrrh and aloes to embalm him.
John 3:1-21; 7:45-52; 19:39

Simon *"he hears"*
On his way into Jerusalem from the country, Simon of Cyrene was pressed into carrying Jesus' cross as Jesus went to the place of execution.
Matthew 27:32; Mark 15:21; Luke 23:26

Bartimaeus *"son of Timaeus"*
As Jesus went through Jericho, a blind roadside beggar shouted out to him. Jesus stopped, called Bartimaeus to him, and healed him of his blindness. Bartimaeus then followed Jesus along the road.
Mark 10:46-52

Joseph of Arimathea *"may (God) add"*
Joseph of Arimathea, a wealthy Jewish member of the Sanhedrin council, was a secret follower of Jesus. As soon as Jesus had died on the cross, Joseph asked Pilate for permission to take Jesus' body for burial. Accompanied by Nicodemus, who brought the spices, Joseph took Jesus' body to a new tomb in which nobody had ever been laid, and wrapped the body with the spices in strips of linen. This was in accordance with Jewish burial customs.
Matthew 27:57-61; Mark 15:42-44; Luke 23:50-55; John 19:38-42

Jairus *"he will enlighten"*
Jairus, a ruler of the synagogue at Capernaum, asked Jesus to heal his sick twelve-year-old daughter. As Jesus was on the way to the house, news came that the daughter had died. Nevertheless, Jesus went with Jairus to his home, took the dead girl by the hand, and healed her.
Mark 5:21-43

Barabbas *"father's son"*
Barabbas had been condemned to death for murder. At the time of the feast of the Passover it was the custom for the governor to release one prisoner of the crowd's choice. Pilate wanted to release Jesus, but the crowd asked for Barabbas's release and for Jesus to be executed. Pilate gave in to their wishes.
Matthew 27:11-26; Mark 15:1-15; Luke 23:18; John 18:40

Jesus talks to Nicodemus.

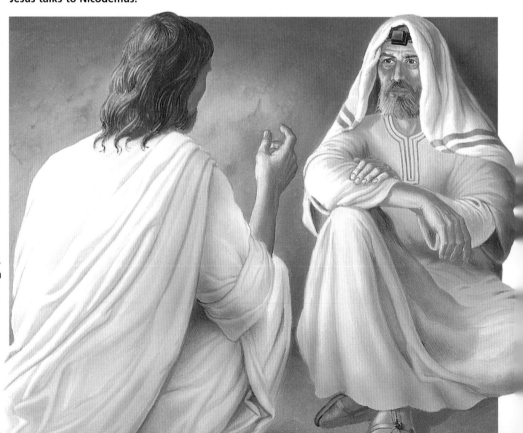

Annas *"grace"*

After Jesus was betrayed by Judas in the Garden of Gethsemane, he was arrested, bound, and taken to Annas for questioning. Annas, who had been high priest from A.D. 6 to 13, then sent Jesus to his son-in-law, Caiaphas, who was the high priest that year. After Jesus' ascension, Peter and John were also questioned before Annas because of their Christian preaching.
John 18:12-14, 19-23; Acts 4:6

Caiaphas *"depression"*

Caiaphas, son-in-law of Annas, held a dominant position among the Sadducees and the Jewish priesthood for many years, and was high priest in Jerusalem from A.D. 18 to 36. He masterminded Jesus' arrest, advising the Jewish authorities that one man, Jesus, should die for all the people. Caiaphas presided over the illegal trial of Jesus by the Sanhedrin, pronouncing Jesus guilty of blasphemy. Caiaphas, who had no power to enforce the death sentence, then sent Jesus to Pilate for sentencing. Caiaphas is referred to simply as the "high priest" in Acts and was responsible for persecuting the first Christians.
Matthew 26:3-5, 57-68; Mark 14:53-55; Luke 3:2; John 11:49-51; 18:12-14, 19-24; Acts 5:27

Pilate *"javelin carrier"*

As commander-in-chief of the Roman soldiers, Pontius Pilate was all-powerful as Roman governor of Judea (A.D. 26–36) and was the only person who could pass the death sentence. Caiaphas sent Jesus to Pilate, who recognized that Jesus was innocent, and even tried to release him as the one prisoner given free pardon each year. Pilate's wife told Pilate that he should have nothing to do with Jesus, for she had been troubled by a dream

Mary, Martha and Lazarus at their Bethany home

Lazarus *"God has helped"*

Lazarus, brother of Mary and Martha, was loved by Jesus. Lazarus died, and four days later Jesus came to his hometown of Bethany, wept with his two grieving sisters, and then brought Lazarus back to life, explaining, "I am the resurrection and the life." The Pharisees tried to kill Lazarus as well as Jesus because many people put their faith in Jesus on account of this miracle.
John 11:1–12:11

Mary (form of Miriam) *"strong"*

Mary, the sister of Martha and Lazarus, loved to sit at Jesus' feet and listen to his teaching. A short time before Jesus' death, Mary anointed his feet with expensive perfume, wiping his feet dry with her hair.
Mark 14:3-9; Luke 10:38-42; John 11:1–12:8

Martha *"lady"*

With her sister, Mary, and brother, Lazarus, Martha often entertained Jesus in her home in Bethany, some two miles from Jerusalem. Martha once complained to Jesus that Mary just sat and listened to Jesus while she was left to do all the work. Jesus, however, replied that Mary had chosen what was better.
Luke 10:38-42; John 11:1–12:8

about him and believed him to be innocent. But when the crowds shouted to Pilate that if he let Jesus go he would be opposing Caesar, he handed Jesus over to be crucified. Pilate had a notice prepared and fastened to the cross. It read, "JESUS OF NAZARETH, THE KING OF THE JEWS."
Matthew 27:11-26; Mark 15:1-15; Luke 22:66–23:25; John 18:28–19:22

The first Christians

The Acts of the Apostles describes people who became followers of Christ in the first exciting days of the early Church.

Stephen defends himself before the Sanhedrin.

Stephen *"crown"*
Stephen was the leading deacon of seven that the Jerusalem church appointed to care for the poor widows. Some Jews objected to Stephen's preaching and the miracles he performed, and so he was brought before the Jewish council of the Sanhedrin. They listened to Stephen's long defense until he accused them of killing "the Righteous One," which so angered them that they dragged him out of the city and stoned him to death. Stephen, the first Christian martyr, prayed for the forgiveness of those who stoned him. His death was witnessed by Saul (Paul).
Acts 6:1–8:2

Ananias *"protected by the Lord"*
Ananias, along with his wife, Sapphira, sold a piece of property and gave part of the proceeds to the apostles, while pretending that the money he gave was the total sale price.

Peter accused Ananias of lying to the Holy Spirit and to God, as well as to the apostles, at which Ananias fell down and died.
Acts 5:1-11

Sapphira *"beautiful"*
Sapphira, together with her husband, Ananias, tried to deceive the apostles by giving only part of the money they received for selling some land. When questioned about this by Peter, Sapphira lied and at once died.
Acts 5:1-11

Cleopas *"renowned father"*
Cleopas was one of two disciples who had a conversation with the risen Christ on their way from Jerusalem to Emmaus. Jesus warmed their hearts as he explained to them from the Old Testament that the Messiah had to suffer before he could be glorified. It was not until Jesus "broke bread" with them that they recognized him, as he vanished from

their sight. Cleopas and his friend returned to Jerusalem to report their experience to the eleven apostles.
Luke 24:13-49

Cornelius *"of a horn"*
Cornelius, a Roman centurion, was respected by the Jews at Caesarea, where he was well-known as a generous and devout man of prayer. An angel spoke to him in a vision, telling him to bring Peter from Joppa. As a result of Peter's visit and preaching, Cornelius and his household believed in Christ, received the Holy Spirit, and were baptized. They are the first Gentiles on record to become followers of Jesus.
Acts 10

Matthias *"gift of God"*
After Judas Iscariot's suicide, the remaining eleven apostles drew lots to choose between Barsabbas and Matthias, to see who would replace Judas. Both men had traveled with Jesus during his three-year public ministry. Matthias was chosen.
Acts 1:15-26

Rhoda *"rose"*
Rhoda worked as a servant in the house of Mary, the mother of John Mark. When Peter was miraculously delivered from prison and knocked on the door of Mary's house, Rhoda ran and announced to the praying Christians that Peter was outside. In her excitement she forgot to open the door for Peter.
Acts 12:1-19

Peter meets the centurion Cornelius.

James brother of Jesus (form of Jacob, "*supplanter*")
James was one of Jesus' brothers. During Jesus' lifetime, his brothers did not believe in him, but after Jesus' resurrection James became the leader of the church in Jerusalem. James probably wrote the letter of James.
Matthew 13:55; Mark 6:3; Acts 12:2; 15:13-21; 21:17-26; Galatians 1:19; 2:9

Agabus "*locust*"
Agabus, a prophet from Jerusalem, prophesied at Antioch about an impending famine that would spread across the Roman Empire. He also accurately pedicted that Paul would be "bound" if he went to Jerusalem.
Acts 11:27-30; 21:10-11

Simon (Magus) "*one heard*"
Simon Magus of Samaria astonished people with his magic. After hearing Philip preach about Jesus Christ, Simon himself believed and was baptized. However, when Simon saw that the Spirit had been given to believers after the apostles laid their hands on the people, he tried to buy this power from Peter and John. Peter rebuked Simon severely for this and told him to repent of his sin. Simon asked them to pray for him.
Acts 8:9-25

Jude *from* "*praise*"
Jude, one of Jesus' brothers, sometimes called Judas, believed in Jesus only after his resurrection. He was probably the writer of the letter of Jude, but never says he was Jesus' brother, preferring humbly to call himself "brother of James."
Matthew 13:55; John 7:5; Acts 1

Philip "*lover of horses*"
Philip, along with Stephen the martyr, was one of seven deacons appointed by the Jerusalem church. Philip became a leading evangelist among the Samaritans and Gentiles. He told a traveling Ethiopian official the good news about Jesus, which resulted in the man's immediate baptism.
Acts 6:5; 8:4-13, 26-40; 21:8

Ethiopian eunuch
The unnamed Ethiopian eunuch, Queen Candace's chief officer, who was in charge of all her treasure, was returning from worshiping in Jerusalem. In his chariot he was reading chapter 53 of the Old Testament book of Isaiah. He could not make sense of it until Philip joined him and explained that Isaiah's prophecies applied to Christ, whereupon the Ethiopian put his trust in Jesus. When they saw some water, Philip baptized him.
Acts 8:26-39

Philip explains the book of Isaiah to the Ethiopian.

Crippled beggar at Beautiful Gate
Each day "a man lame from birth" was carried to the Temple gate called Beautiful, where he was put to beg from those going into the Temple courts. Peter and John did not give him money, but healed him. He went into the Temple courts "walking and leaping and praising God."
Acts 3:1-10

Aeneas "*praise*"
Aeneas, a cripple who lived in Lydda, had been unable to get out of bed for eight years. Peter visited him and said, "Jesus Christ heals you." Immediately Aeneas was able to walk again.
Acts 9:32-35

Dorcas "*gazelle*"
Dorcas was a Christian widow who lived in Joppa. She was always doing good and helping the poor. When she fell ill and died, her friends sent for Peter. As soon as he arrived, the widows crowded around him, crying and showing him the clothes Dorcas had made for them. After praying, Peter brought Dorcas back to life.
Acts 9:36-43

Sergius Paulus
Paul and Barnabas visited the island of Cyprus, where Sergius Paulus, "a man of intelligence," was the Roman proconsul. After the sorcerer Elymas had been struck blind by Paul, Sergius Paulus believed, "for he was astonished at the teaching of the Lord."
Acts 13:4-12

Philippian jailer
When Paul and Silas were thrown into prison in the town of Philippi, little did they think that they would witness one of the most dramatic conversions in the early Church. "About midnight . . . there was a great earthquake so that the foundations of the prison were shaken." Their unnamed jailer woke up and drew his sword to kill himself, because he thought the prisoners had escaped. Paul assured him, "We are all here." At this the jailer asked Paul and Silas, "What must I do to be saved?" Paul and Silas told him about Jesus. Then the jailer and his whole family "believed in the Lord" Jesus Christ and were baptized.
Acts 16:22-40

Paul and his circle

Silas *"wood-dweller"*
A leader of the church in Jerusalem, Silas traveled with Paul on his second missionary journey, and was jailed with Paul at Philippi. When Paul traveled on to Athens, Silas stayed in Berea, rejoining Paul at Corinth. Silas is probably the "Silvanus" mentioned in several of Paul's letters, who also helped Peter write his first letters.
Acts 15–18; 2 Corinthians 1; 1 Thessalonians 1; 1 Peter 5

Titus *"honored"*
Titus was a Gentile Christian, and a friend and helper of Paul. We know he once visited Jerusalem with Paul, and he probably often traveled with him. Titus worked in Corinth, breaking down the bad feeling between the Christians and Paul. He also delivered Paul's second letter to the Corinthians and helped collect money in Corinth for poor Christians in Judea. Paul wrote his letter to Titus while Titus was working in Crete.
1 Corinthians 16; 2 Corinthians 7–8; Galatians 2; Titus

Tychicus *"fortunate"*
Tychicus, a friend of Paul, probably came from Ephesus, and it seems he was chosen by the churches of Asia Minor to take the money they collected to poor Christians in Judea. Tychicus was with Paul in prison in Rome and delivered Paul's letters to the churches at Colossae and Ephesus.
Ephesians 6; 1 Corinthians 4; 2 Timothy 4; Titus 3

John Mark *(Mark, "polite")*
Mark, writer of the second Gospel, lived in Jerusalem, where the first Christians met in his mother's house. Mark, cousin of Barnabas, accompanied Paul and

Barnabas on their first missionary journey, but he left them halfway, and Paul refused to take him on his second trip. But later Mark joined Paul in Rome and was described by Paul as "my son Mark." By tradition, Mark's Gospel is based on Peter's preaching.
Mark 14; Acts 12–15; 2 Timothy 4; Philemon

Barnabas *"son of encouragement"*
Barnabas, a native of Cyprus and member of the Jerusalem church, sold land to give money to poor Christians in Judea. When Paul came to Jerusalem after his conversion, Barnabas befriended him, although others were suspicious of him. The Jerusalem church sent Barnabas to Antioch to build up the church, and he asked Paul to join him. Barnabas accompanied Paul on his first missionary journey from Antioch, but on the second trip they disagreed over taking John Mark with them. They

John Mark and Barnabas in Asia Minor

separated, Barnabas taking Mark with him to Cyprus, but Paul always spoke well of Barnabas.
Acts 4, 9, 11, 12, 15; Galatians 2

Erastus *"desired"*
An assistant to Paul, Erastus joined Timothy to work in Macedonia while Paul remained in Asia Minor.
Acts 19; 2 Timothy 4

Timothy *"honoring God"*
Born to a Jewish Christian mother and Greek father in Lystra, Timothy became a friend and aide of Paul. He assisted on Paul's second missionary journey, staying in Thessalonica to help the persecuted believers there. Paul also sent Timothy from Ephesus to teach the church at Corinth. Although he

The theater at Perga, visited by Paul during his first missionary journey

lacked confidence and needed Paul's support, he became leader of the church at Ephesus; Paul's two letters to him are full of advice to leaders in the church.
Acts 16, 17; 1 & 2 Timothy

Paul

Paul *"small"*
The great apostle and pioneering missionary, whose letters form a large part of the New Testament, Paul was both a Jew and a Roman citizen. Born in Tarsus, he was given the name Saul and was educated by the rabbi Gamaliel in Jerusalem. Saul, who belonged to the Pharisee sect, was strongly opposed to the Christians, and he watched the stoning of Stephen.

On his way to Damascus to arrest Christians, Saul saw a dazzling light and heard Jesus ask: "Why are you persecuting me?" Blinded by the light, he was led into Damascus, where Ananias restored his sight. After Saul had been baptized, he started preaching the gospel; but when Jews in Damascus plotted to kill him, he fled to Jerusalem, where the Christians were at first frightened of him. But Barnabas befriended him and introduced him to the apostles. After another plot to kill him, Saul returned to Tarsus.

First mission
Some years later Barnabas brought Saul to help the church at Antioch in Syria. This church later sent them to Asia Minor to spread the gospel. Following their visit to Cyprus, Saul became known as Paul (the Greek form of his Hebrew name). He returned to Antioch and told the church what they had achieved. Paul also helped Jewish Christians in Jerusalem accept that Jesus is the Savior of all, not solely of the Jews.

On his second missionary journey Paul was accompanied by Silas, first visiting Christian converts in Galatia. They were joined in Lystra by a young man named Timothy, and sailed to Greece from Troas, where they were joined by Luke. They started a new church in Philippi, but Paul and Silas were beaten and jailed. After their release, they traveled on through Greece, Paul preaching in Athens and settling in Corinth for eighteen months. Paul then returned to Jerusalem, taking gifts for poor Christians from believers in Greece and Asia Minor.

Trial
Paul stayed a time in Syria before departing again for Ephesus, where he worked and preached for nearly three years, before revisiting Corinth, and returning, via Greece and Asia Minor, to Jerusalem. On arriving back in Jerusalem, Paul was arrested once more and sent to Caesarea for trial. After two years in jail, Paul appealed for trial before Caesar and was sent to Rome. His ship was wrecked off the coast of Malta, but no lives were lost. Paul eventually reached Rome safely, where he was kept under house arrest for two years, writing many of his letters from confinement. He was probably released following his trial, but rearrested and executed by the Emperor Nero around A.D. 67.
Acts 7, 9–28; Paul's letters

Luke, the physician

Gaius *"lord"*
A Macedonian Christian who joined Paul on his third missionary journey, Gaius was dragged into the amphitheater during the silversmiths' riot at Ephesus.
Acts 19

Luke *"light-giving"*
A Greek-speaking doctor who wrote the third Gospel, Luke was also a friend of Paul. He accompanied the apostle on some of his journeys and recorded his experiences in the book of Acts. Luke sailed to Rome with Paul, staying with him while he was a prisoner in the imperial capital.
Colossians 4; 2 Timothy 4; Luke–Acts

Artist's impression of Caesarea

Paul's converts and opponents

As a traveling missionary, Paul made many close friends who were eager to help him in the cause of Christ—as well as not a few opponents.

Aquila *"eagle"*
A godly Jewish Christian, husband of Priscilla, and friend and faithful supporter of Paul, Aquila was born in Pontus and was expelled from Rome by Claudius. Aquila met Paul in Corinth, where they were both tentmakers, and Paul worked and stayed with him. Aquila and Priscilla traveled with Paul to Ephesus. Later, after Claudius's edict had been revoked, they returned to Rome. In Ephesus and Rome the church met in their homes.
Acts 18; Romans 16:3; 1 Corinthians 16:19

Priscilla *"ancient one"*
Six out of the seven times Priscilla and Aquila are mentioned in the New Testament, Priscilla's name comes before Aquila's, and from this it has been concluded that Priscilla was exceptional in some way. They invited Apollos to speak in their home when they lived in Ephesus. Paul greatly valued Priscilla and Aquila, calling them his "fellow workers in Christ," who risked their lives for him and to whom all the Gentile churches were indebted.
Acts 18; Romans 16:3; 1 Corinthians 16:19; 2 Timothy 4:19

Apollos *"a destroyer"*
Apollos, a Jewish Christian from Alexandria, is described by Luke as a learned man, with a thorough knowledge of the Scriptures. He had been instructed in the way of the Lord, and he spoke with great fervor and taught about Jesus accurately. Priscilla and Aquila were able to teach him more about God. Apollos greatly encouraged the Christians of southern Greece and refuted the Jews in public debate, "proving from the Scriptures that Jesus was the Christ."
Acts 18:24–19:1 (NIV); 1 Corinthians 16:12

Crescens *"increasing"*
Crescens was a companion of Paul's during his imprisonment in Rome.
2 Timothy 4:10

Crispus *"curled"*
As a result of Paul's preaching in the synagogue in Corinth, where Crispus was the synagogue ruler, Crispus and his entire household believed in the Lord. Because of this, many people in Corinth believed and were baptized. Gaius, Crispus, and his household were the only people Paul baptized in Corinth.
Acts 18:7-11; 1 Corinthians 1:14

Demetrius *"belonging to Demeter"*
Demetrius was a silversmith in Ephesus who made silver shrines of the local goddess, Artemis. Such a trade was profitable in that city. Because Paul's preaching of the gospel threatened this trade, Demetrius organized a riot, with people chanting "Great is Artemis of the Ephesians!" Paul made a hasty exit for Macedonia.
Acts 19:23–20:1

Demas *"popular"*
Demas was one of Paul's friends and helpers but deserted Paul during his imprisonment in Rome because he was "in love with this present world."
Colossians 4:14; 2 Timothy 4:10; Philemon 24

Dionysius *"Bacchus"*
Dionysius was a member of the Areopagus council in Athens. After Paul spoke to this council about the resurrection of Jesus, Dionysius was one of the people who believed and became a follower of Paul.
Acts 17:34

Elymas *"sorcerer"*
Elymas, nicknamed Bar-Jesus, was a Jewish sorcerer and false prophet who opposed Paul and Barnabas at Paphos and attempted to turn the proconsul, Sergius Paulus away from the Christian faith. Because of his deceit and trickery, Paul struck him temporarily with blindness.
Acts 13:4-12

Epaphras *"charming"*
Epaphras was a leader, and possibly the founder, of the church at Colossae. Epaphras visited Paul while he was a prisoner in Rome, and was for some time imprisoned with him. Paul wrote his letter to the Colossians in response to what Epaphras told him about the church. Paul held Epaphras in high esteem, calling him a "dear fellow servant" and "a faithful minister of Christ."
Colossians 1:7; 4:12; Philemon 23

Onesimus *"profitable"*
Onesimus was a runaway slave who, through meeting Paul in prison in Rome, became a Christian. Paul sent Onesimus back to his master, Philemon, with a letter asking for Onesimus to be accepted back as a Christian brother.
Philemon

Philemon *"friendship"*
The letter to Philemon is the only surviving personal letter of Paul's. Paul entreats Philemon to receive back his runaway

Aquila and Priscilla earned their living making tents.

Onesimus with his master, Philemon

slave, Onesimus, as a fellow Christian, reminding Philemon that he himself owed his conversion to Paul.
Philemon

Epaphroditus *"handsome"*
Epaphroditus, a member of the Philippian church, was sent by his church to take a gift from them to Paul who was imprisoned in Rome. He worked so strenuously that he became ill and almost died. Paul wrote that he risked his life for the sake of the gospel.
Philippians 2:19-30; 4:18

Eutychus *"fortunate"*
During Paul's last day at Troas, the young man Eutychus fell asleep as Paul carried on speaking to the people until midnight. Eutychus fell to his death from a third-floor window. Paul immediately went down to him, put his arms around him, and miraculously brought him back to life.
Acts 20:7-12

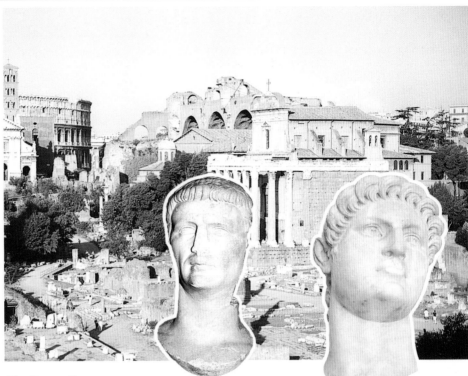

The Forum, Rome

Claudius

Nero

Claudius *"lame"*
Claudius, Roman Caesar A.D. 41–54, expelled the Jews from Rome for rioting.
Acts 11:28; 18:2

Nero
Although Nero is never mentioned by name in the Bible, he was the cruel Roman Caesar, successor to Claudius, who was responsible for the most horrific persecutions of Christians in Rome. Tradition has it that both Peter and Paul suffered martyrdom at the hands of Nero.

Felix *"happy"*
Felix was the Roman governor of Judea who tried Paul, keeping him in prison for two years, hoping to receive a bribe from him.
Acts 23:23–24:27

Festus *"swine-like"*
Festus succeeded Felix as Roman governor of Judea and continued Paul's trial.
Acts 25–26

Agrippa *"causing pain at birth"*
King Herod Agrippa II, as ruler of Galilee, had Paul brought before him by Festus, the Roman governor, and listened sympathetically to Paul's defense. Agrippa said Paul could have been released, if he had not appealed to Rome.
Acts 25

Jason *"healing"*
Jason looked after Paul and Silas during their stay in Thessalonica. Some zealous Jews went to Jason's house looking for Paul and Silas, but, not finding them, dragged Jason and some other believers before city officials and accused them of breaking Roman law. They forced Jason to pay before freeing them.
Acts 17:1-9

Lydia *"native of Lydia"*
Lydia, a businesswoman from Thyatira who traded in purple cloth, believed in the Lord through Paul's preaching and invited Paul and Silas to stay at her home.
Acts 16:11-15

Some Bible Facts and Figures

What's in the Bible?	222
Some ways into your Bible	224
When you are in need . . .	226
Animal, vegetable, and mineral . . .	228
Who are the heavenly beings?	230
Some Bible names and their meanings	232
The Last Days	233
The most popular English translations of the Bible	235

What's in the Bible?

A summary of the books of the Bible

OLD TESTAMENT

GENESIS
The beginnings, describing the creation, the rebellion and sin of man, and the early history of God's people, through whom he introduces his plan of redemption.

EXODUS
The history of Israel's departure from Egypt and the leadership of Moses; God's covenant with Israel and the giving of the Law; the construction of the Tabernacle.

LEVITICUS
The laws by which God's people can approach and maintain fellowship with their holy God.

NUMBERS
The census of the people, and their wanderings in the wilderness, during which God prepares them for the Promised Land.

DEUTERONOMY
Moses emphasizes the covenant and the Law to the people before his death.

JOSHUA
The story of Israel's conquest of Canaan and the division of the land among the tribes.

JUDGES
The continuing history of the Israelites as they learn that their turnings from God lead to oppression by enemies, which leads to repentance and deliverance through a judge.

RUTH
A story of tragedy and love in the lives of ordinary people who become ancestors of David and of Jesus.

1 SAMUEL
The history of Israel from the rule of Samuel, the last judge, to the reign of Saul, the first king.

2 SAMUEL
The record of David's reign.

1 & 2 KINGS
The last days of David's reign, to Solomon's reign and the division of the kingdom, after which the kings of both kingdoms are presented in historical order up to the release of Jehoiachin from prison in Babylonia, about 561 B.C.

1 & 2 CHRONICLES
The official histories of the kingdoms of Judah and Israel, including the genealogies and history from the reigns of David and Solomon to the captivity.

EZRA
The story of the return of the Jews from the Babylonian captivity, and the rebuilding of the Temple.

NEHEMIAH
A further account of the return from exile; the rebuilding of the walls of Jerusalem, and the renewing of the covenant.

ESTHER
The story of a Jewess who becomes Queen of Persia and saves the Jewish people from destruction.

JOB
The story of the sufferings and faith of a man who learns to accept the sometimes baffling will of God.

PSALMS
Poems, prayers, and praises written by David and others, expressing to God the emotion of personal experience.

PROVERBS
The wise and practical sayings of Solomon and other wise men.

ECCLESIASTES
A book revealing how the search for happiness and satisfaction in earthly things apart from God always ends in vanity.

SONG OF SOLOMON
A love song presenting the courtship and marriage of man and woman, and their God-honoring sexual relationship.

ISAIAH
Prophecies concerning Judah and Jerusalem, vivid messages of redemption for God's people, and the hope for a Messiah.

JEREMIAH
Prophecies predicting the fall of Judah, the people's sufferings, and the final overthrow of their enemies.

LAMENTATIONS
A lament expressing grief over the fall of Jerusalem and the destruction of the Temple.

EZEKIEL
Pronouncements of God's judgment on the Jews, and messages of comfort in their captivity.

DANIEL
A story of some of the events of the captivity, and prophecies of Christ and the end times.

HOSEA
Hosea's personal grief over his unfaithful wife illustrates God's relationship with Israel.

JOEL
Prophecies of God's judgment of Judah, and the blessings that will follow repentance.

AMOS
Predictions of judgment against Israel because of idolatry and oppressing the poor, and against surrounding nations, and glimpses of the Messiah's kingdom.

OBADIAH
Prophecies of the destruction of Edom and the deliverance that will be found in Zion.

JONAH
The story of the prophet Jonah and of God's concern and mercy toward nations who are willing to repent.

MICAH
The pronouncement of judgment on Israel and Judah; the prediction of restoration and the Messiah's reign.

NAHUM
Prediction of the downfall of Assyria.

HABAKKUK
A prediction of the Babylonian invasion, the destruction of the Babylonians, and the restoration of God's people.

ZEPHANIAH
A prediction of the overthrow of Judah because of idolatry, pride, and materialism; and a foreshadowing of the ultimate deliverance and restoration of God's people.

HAGGAI
Prophecies and exhortations concerning the rebuilding of the Temple.

ZECHARIAH
Prophecies relating to the rebuilding of the Temple and the coming of the Messiah and triumph of the kingdom of God.

MALACHI
Pronouncements of judgment for Israel's sins and predictions of blessings for the repentant, and of the coming of Christ.

NEW TESTAMENT

MATTHEW
A history of the life of Christ, emphasizing Jesus as the fulfillment of God's covenant with Israel and the importance of Jesus' teachings.

MARK
A history of the life of Christ, with special emphasis on the last week in Jerusalem, the crucifixion, and the resurrection.

LUKE
A history of the life of Christ, emphasizing the person of Jesus and the people whose lives he touched.

JOHN
The life of Christ, written to reveal that Jesus is the Christ, the Son of God.

ACTS
The giving of the Holy Spirit, and the development and spread of Christianity in the Spirit's power, told in terms of people and places.

ROMANS
Paul's explanation of the doctrine of justification by grace alone through faith alone in Christ alone.

1 CORINTHIANS
Paul's letter to the church at Corinth, correcting their errors, rebuking their sins, and exhorting them to practice Christ's love.

2 CORINTHIANS
Paul's letter revealing his concern for the Corinthians and guiding them into lives of love and unity.

GALATIANS
Paul's proclamation of Christian liberty, firmly maintaining that man's justification by God's grace is through faith alone, not through works of the Law.

EPHESIANS
Paul's treatise on the person of Christ and the Church, God's household, through which God's wisdom and grace are revealed.

PHILIPPIANS
Paul describes the joy and beauty of the Christian life.

COLOSSIANS
Paul combats errors and heresy by proclaiming the uniqueness and sufficiency of Jesus Christ as the only Savior of all.

1 THESSALONIANS
Paul's concern for the people and an exhortation to faith, purity, and holiness, waiting in hope for the Lord's return.

2 THESSALONIANS
Paul's letter concerning the second coming of Christ.

1 & 2 TIMOTHY
Letters from Paul concerning the Church, and the qualifications and duties of church officers.

TITUS
Paul's letter to Titus, emphasizing church order and sound doctrine.

PHILEMON
Paul's most personal letter, asking his friend to receive a runaway slave as a brother in Christ.

HEBREWS
A defense of the Christian faith, emphasizing the sufficiency and finality of Christ, and the superiority of the Christian faith over Judaism.

JAMES
A letter concerning the practical aspects of the Christian faith, and emphasizing that faith is shown to be alive and active by the works it produces.

1 PETER
A letter exhorting the people to a life of purity and spirituality, as God's chosen, a royal priesthood.

2 PETER
A reminder of the truth of Christ against heresies, and warnings to remain in this truth, looking toward the second coming of Christ.

1 JOHN
The fundamentals of the Christian faith revealed in Jesus Christ.

2 JOHN
The primary importance of love in Christian fellowship, and warnings against false teachers.

3 JOHN
A letter concerning hospitality toward traveling Christian teachers.

JUDE
Strong condemnation of false teachers, and admonitions to remain in the true faith of Christ.

REVELATION
A revelation stressing the lordship of Christ, the overruling sovereignty of God, and his final victory over all sin and evil.

Some ways into your Bible

Some fascinating Bible statistics

	Old Testament	New Testament
Number of books	39	27
Number of chapters	929	260
Number of verses	23,214	7,959
Number of words	592,493	181,253
Longest book	Psalms	Luke
Shortest book	Obadiah	3 John
Longest chapter	Psalm 119	Matthew 26
Shortest chapter	Psalm 117	Revelation 15
Longest verse	Esther 8:9	Revelation 20:4
Shortest verse	1 Chronicles 1:25	John 11:35 ("Jesus wept.")
Middle book	Proverbs	2 Thessalonians
Middle chapter	Job 29	Romans 13–14
Middle verse	2 Chronicles 20:13	Acts 7:7

Total number of verses in both Testaments: 31,173

Middle chapter of the Bible: Psalm 117

Middle verse: Psalm 118:5

Most mentioned character: David (1,118 times)

Longest word: Maher-shalal-hash-baz (*Isaiah 8:1*)

These figures are based on English Bibles and may vary according to the translation.

Bible translation facts
• More than 6,500 languages are spoken in the world.
• Of these, 2,167 languages have some or all of the Bible (355 complete Bibles, 850 New Testaments).
• About 4,333 languages are still without any part of the Bible.

The smallest Bible ever published was the Mite Bible published by Oxford University Press in 1896. Its pages were 28 x 41mm (1.62 x 1.12"); it was 900 pages long and 13mm (0.5") thick.

A Bible reading plan

If you would like to read the Bible systematically and carefully, the following reading order will be helpful. Although this plan does not include every book of the Bible, it will give you a good overview of Scripture if followed regularly.

New Testament
1. Mark
2. John
3. Luke–Acts
4. 1 Thessalonians
5. 1 Corinthians
6. Romans
7. Philemon
8. Philippians
9. Ephesians
10. 2 Timothy
11. 1 Peter
12. 1 John
13. Revelation (1–5 and 19:6–22:21)

Old Testament
14. Genesis
15. Exodus (1–24)
16. Numbers (10:11–21:35)
17. Deuteronomy (1–11)
18. Joshua (1–12 and 22–24)
19. Judges (sample)
20. 1–2 Samuel (sample)
21. 1–2 Kings (sample)
22. Nehemiah
23. Amos
24. Isaiah (1–12)
25. Jeremiah (1–25; 30–33)
26. Isaiah (40–55)
27. Ruth
28. Jonah
29. Psalms (some examples of the major types)
30. Job (perhaps 1–14 and 38–42)
31. Proverbs (1–9)
32. Daniel (1–6; sample chapters 7–12)

Noah's boat

The boat God told Noah to build (450 feet x 75 feet x 45 feet) was big enough to hold 432 double-decker buses.

There was plenty of room for the 35,000 or so animals that were saved from the flood with Noah and his family.

BIBLE VERSES FOR SPECIAL OCCASIONS

Birthdays
Joshua 1:1-9; Psalms 1; 23; 25; 37:3-7; 39:1-7; 90; 91; 139; Proverbs 3:5-8; 26:3-4; Lamentations 3:22-26; Luke 1:46-55; John 6:35; 8:12; 10:1-30; Romans 8:28-39; 11:33-36; Ephesians 1:3-14; Philippians 4:4-7; Hebrews 10:23; 1 John 1:7-9

Baptism, dedication of children, and confirmation
Joshua 1:5-9; 1 Samuel 1:27-28; Psalms 1; 23; 111; 121; Ecclesiastes 12:1; Matthew 3:11-17; 10:32-33; 28:18-20; Mark 10:13-16; John 3:1-21; 15:1-17; Acts 8:36-40; 16:30-33; 22:16; Romans 6:1-14; 1 Corinthians 12:12-13; Galatians 3:26-28; Ephesians 3:14-21; 4:1-6; Philippians 1:1-11; Colossians 2:6-14; 1 Timothy 6:11-16; Titus 3:4-7; 1 Peter 3:18-22; Jude 24

Thanksgiving
Deuteronomy 6:10-19; 8; Psalms 33; 65; 95; 100; 103; 104; 107; 111; 116; 126; 136; 145; 147; Isaiah 12; Luke 12:13-34; Acts 14:17; 1 Corinthians 3:5-9; Colossians 2:16-17; Hebrews 13:15-16; Revelation 5

Wedding day
Genesis 2:18-25; Ruth 1:16-17; Psalms 67; 84; 100; 118:24-29; 121; 127; 128; 139; Matthew 19:4-6; John 2:1-11; 1 Corinthians 7; 13; Ephesians 5:22-33; Colossians 3:12-21; 1 Peter 3:1-7

Retirement
Deuteronomy 33:27; Joshua 1:7-9; 1 Samuel 7:12; Psalms 23; 71:14-24; 93:12-15; Isaiah 26:3-4; 43:18-21; 46:4; John 14:27; 1 Corinthians 1:8; Philippians 3:7-16

CHRISTMAS AND NEW YEAR READING PLAN

December 20: *Luke 1:26-38*
Jesus' birth foretold

December 21: *Luke 1:39-56*
Mary and Elizabeth

December 22: *Luke 1:67-80*
Zechariah's song

December 23: *Colossians 1:15-20*
Who Jesus is

December 24: *John 1:1-18*
The Word became flesh

Christmas Day: *Luke 2:1-7*
The Savior is born

December 26: *Luke 2:8-20*
The shepherds and the angels

December 27: *Matthew 2:1-12*
The Magi worship Jesus

December 28: *Luke 2:21-32*
Jesus is presented in the Temple

December 29: *Luke 2:36-38*
The redemption of Jerusalem

December 30: *Matthew 2:13-18*
Jesus is kept safe

December 31: *Psalm 90*
Teach us to number our days

New Year's Day: *Exodus 33:7-23*
Show me your glory

January 2: *Philippians 3:7-14*
Pressing on to the goal

January 3: *Joshua 1:1-9*
Be strong and courageous

January 4: *Matthew 6:25-34*
Do not worry

January 5: *Romans 8:28-39*
More than conquerors

January 6: *Philippians 4:4-9*
Rejoice in the Lord

EASTER READING PLAN

Palm Sunday: *Luke 19:28-44*
The approach to Jerusalem

Monday: *Luke 19:45-48*
Jesus at the Temple

Tuesday: *Philippians 2:5-11*
Obedient to death

Wednesday: *1 Peter 2:21-25*
Christ suffered for you

Maundy Thursday: *Luke 22:7-71; John 17*
The Last Supper; Jesus' arrest

Good Friday: *Luke 23; Isaiah 53*
The crucifixion

Saturday: *Matthew 27:62-66*
The guard at the tomb

Easter Day: *Matthew 28:1-15*
The resurrection

Easter Monday: *John 20:24-31*
My Lord and my God!

Tuesday: *1 Corinthians 15:12-58*
Victory over death

Wednesday: *Acts 2:22-41*
Why Jesus died

Thursday: *Romans 1:1-7*
Jesus Christ our Lord

Friday: *Romans 6:5-14*
United with him

Saturday: *Colossians 3:1-4*
Raised with Christ

Sunday: *Revelation 1:4-18*
Alive forever and ever

Ascension Day
Luke 24:50-53; Acts 1:1-11

Pentecost *Acts 1:8; 2:1-2; 19:1-7; Ephesians 4:30*

If you want to have an idea of what's in the Apocrypha, here is a suggested reading plan.

Apocrypha
1. Tobit
2. Ecclesiasticus (sample chapters 1–23)
3. 1 Maccabees (1:1–9:22) or 2 Maccabees
4. Judith
5. The Wisdom of Solomon (1–9)
6. 2 Esdras (3–14)

When you are in need . . .

Bible verses to look at when you need help

The Bible includes many promises that can help and encourage us in times of sadness, difficulty, or stress. Here are some verses that show us God's help. Read and meditate over them:

• When you feel afraid
"I sought the LORD, and he answered me and delivered me from all my fears" *Psalm 34:4.*
See also Psalms 27; 46; 56; 91; Matthew 8:23-27.

• When you feel alone
"Fear not, for I am with you; be not dismayed, for I am your God" *Isaiah 41:10.*
See also Psalms 23; 73:23-24; Isaiah 49:14-16; John 14:15-21.

• When you are anxious or worried
"Casting all your anxieties on him, because he cares for you" *1 Peter 5:7.*
See also Isaiah 43:1-13; Matthew 6:25-34; 11:28; Philippians 4:4-7.

• When you are ill or in pain
"My grace is sufficient for you, for my power is made perfect in weakness"
2 Corinthians 12:9.
See also Psalm 103:1-4; Romans 8:18-25; 2 Corinthians 4:16-18.

• When you have been bereaved
"Blessed are those who mourn, for they shall be comforted" *Matthew 5:4.*
See also Psalm 23; John 11:21-27; 1 Corinthians 15:51-57; 1 Thessalonians 4:13-18; Revelation 21:1-5.

• When you feel discouraged
"Why are you cast down, O my soul, and why are you in turmoil within me? Hope in God" *Psalm 42:5.*
See also Psalms 34:18; 40:1-3; Lamentations 3:20-23; Romans 8:28-39; 2 Corinthians 4:7-18.

• When you have doubts
"I believe; help my unbelief!"
Mark 9:24.
See also Isaiah 40:27-31; Matthew 11:1-6; John 20:19-29; Acts 17:22-28.

• When you feel you have done wrong
"But God shows his love for us in that while we were still sinners, Christ died for us" *Romans 5:8.*
See also Psalm 51; Luke 15:11-24.

• When you feel distant from God
"Draw near to God, and he will draw near to you" *James 4:8.*
See also Psalm 139:1-18; John 10:29; Acts 17:24-31.

• When you need peace
"You keep him in perfect peace whose mind is stayed on you, because he trusts in you" *Isaiah 26:3.*
See also John 14:27; Romans 5:1-5; Philippians 4:4-7.

• When you are tempted
"For we do not have a high priest who is unable to sympathize with our weaknesses, but one who in every respect has been tempted as we are, yet without sin" *Hebrews 4:15.*
See also Luke 4:1-13; Ephesians 6:10-20; James 1:2-6, 12-18; 4:7-8; 1 Peter 5:8-9.

• When you are tired or weak
"Come to me, all who labor and are heavy laden, and I will give you rest. Take my yoke upon you, and learn from me, for I am gentle and lowly in heart, and you will find rest for your souls" *Matthew 11:28-29.*
See also Joshua 1:5-9; Isaiah 40:28-31; 2 Corinthians 4:16-18; 12:9-10; Philippians 4:12-13.

• When you need guidance
"In all your ways acknowledge him, and he will make straight your paths" *Proverbs 3:6.*
See also Psalm 48:14; John 14:16; 16:13.

Model prayers of the Bible

Complaint	*Numbers 14:13-19*
Confession	*Psalm 32; Psalm 51; Ezra 9:5-15*
Dedication	*2 Chronicles 6:14-42*
Dependence	*2 Chronicles 20:6-12*
Despair	*Psalm 73*
For believers	*Ephesians 1:16-23; Ephesians 3:15-21*
For blessing	*Psalm 90*
For deliverance	*Isaiah 37:14-20*
For healing	*Isaiah 38:3, 9-20*
For restoration	*Daniel 9:4-19*
For unity	*John 17*
In national crisis	*2 Kings 19:14-19*
Intercession	*Genesis 18:16-33; Exodus 32:11-13*
Petition	*Acts 4:24-30*
Praise	*Luke 1:46-55*
Recommitment	*John 2:2-9*
Thanksgiving	*1 Samuel 2:1-10; Psalms 16; 65*
The Lord's Prayer	*Matthew 6:9-13; Luke 11:2-4*
Trust	*Psalm 23*

Some key Bible passages

The creation story	*Genesis 1:1–2:7*
The fall	*Genesis 3:1-24*
The flood	*Genesis 6:1–9:17*
The call of Abraham	*Genesis 12:1-9*
The Ten Commandments	*Exodus 20:1-17*
The shepherd's psalm	*Psalm 23*
The birth of Jesus	*Matthew 1:18–2:23; Luke 1:26–2:40*
The golden rule	*Luke 6:31*
The Sermon on the Mount	*Matthew 5–7*
The Beatitudes	*Matthew 5:3-11*
The Lord's Prayer	*Luke 11:2-4*
The prodigal son	*Luke 15:11-32*
The good Samaritan	*Luke 10:29-37*
The Last Supper	*Matthew 26:17-30; Mark 14:12-26*
The death of Christ	*Luke 23:26-56; John 19:16-42*
The resurrection of Christ	*Matthew 28; Luke 24; John 20*
The ascension of Christ	*Acts 1:1-12*
The coming of the Holy Spirit	*Acts 2:1-21*
The conversion of Paul	*Acts 9:1-31*
The love chapter	*1 Corinthians 13*
The faith chapter	*Hebrews 11*

Where to find help in the book of Psalms

Psalms to read when you're feeling:

Afraid *3, 13, 27, 46, 56, 59, 64, 91, 118, 121*
Alone *9, 12, 13, 27, 40, 43*
Angry *17, 28, 36, 37, 109*
Burned out *6, 63*
Cheated *41*
Confused *10, 12, 73*
Depressed *27, 34, 42, 43, 88, 143*
Disappointed *16, 92, 102, 130*
Distressed *13, 25, 31, 40, 107*
Guilty *19, 32, 38, 51*
Impatient *4, 13, 27, 37, 40, 89, 123*
Insecure *3, 5, 12, 91*
Insignificant *8, 23, 86, 90, 139*
Insulted *41, 70*
Jealous *37, 73*
Joyful *96, 149*
Like giving up *29, 43, 145*
Lost *23, 139*
Overwhelmed *25, 69, 142*
Proud *14, 30, 49*
Purposeless *25, 39, 90*
Self-confident *24*
Sorry/repentant *51, 66*
Stressed *12, 31, 34, 43, 56, 62, 84*
Thankful *30, 33, 66, 96, 103, 104, 113, 118, 136, 138*
Threatened *143, 144*
Trapped *7, 17, 42, 88, 142*
Vengeful *3, 109*
Weak *13, 18, 23, 28, 29, 62, 70, 86, 102*
Worried *37*
Worshipful *19, 29, 148, 150*

Psalms to read when you're facing:

Competition *113*
Criticism *35, 56, 120*
Danger *11*
Death *23*
Decisions *1, 25, 62, 119*
Discouragement *12, 42, 55, 86, 107, 142*
Discrimination *94*
Doubts *34, 37*
Enemies *3, 25, 35, 41, 56, 59*
Evil people *10, 36, 49, 52, 109*
Hypocrisy *26, 50*
Injustice *7, 9, 10, 17, 56, 94*
Insults *35, 43*
Lies *5, 12, 120*
Old age *71, 92*
Persecution *1, 3, 7*
Poverty *12, 34, 146*
Punishment *6, 38, 39*
Sickness *6, 22, 23, 41, 116, 139*
Sorrow/grief *6, 23, 31, 71, 77, 94, 123*
Success *18, 112, 126, 128*
Temptation *38, 141*
Troubles *34, 55, 86, 102, 142, 145*
Verbal cruelty *35, 120*
Violence *46, 83*

Psalms to read when you want:

Acceptance *139*
Answers *4, 17, 119*
Confidence *46, 71*
Courage *11, 27*
Fellowship with God *5, 16, 25, 37*
Forgiveness *32, 38, 40, 51, 86, 103*
Friendship *16*
Godliness *15, 25*
Guidance/direction *1, 19, 32, 37, 89, 146*

Healing *6, 41, 103*
Hope *16, 17, 18, 23, 27*
Humility *19, 131, 147*
Illumination *19*
Integrity *24, 25*
Joy *9, 16, 33, 47, 84, 96, 97, 98, 100*
Justice *2, 7, 14, 26, 37, 82*
Knowledge of God *18, 19, 29, 65, 89, 97, 103, 145, 147*
Leadership *72*
Miracles *60, 111*
Money *15, 16, 49*
Peace *3, 4, 85*
Perspective *2, 11, 73*
Prayer *5, 17, 27, 61*
Protection *7, 16, 18, 23, 27, 31, 91, 125*
Provision *34, 81*
Reassurance *15, 23, 26, 112, 121*
Rest *23, 27*
Salvation *103, 146*
Security *34, 84, 91*
Vindication *9, 35, 109*
Wisdom *1, 16, 19, 64, 111*

Animal, vegetable, and mineral . . .

Why are some mountains of the Bible important?

Mount	Height (in feet above sea level)	Bible reference	Biblical significance
Ararat	16,946	*Genesis 8:4*	Noah's ark came to rest
Sinai (also called Horeb)	7,500	*Exodus 3,19* *1 Kings 19*	God revealed his name and his Law to Moses Elijah fled there from Jezebel
Ebal Gerizim	3,100 2,900	*Deuteronomy 11:29*	Moses reminded Israel of the Law's blessings and curses
Nebo	2,700	*Deuteronomy 32:49*	Moses died here
Halak	1,640	*Joshua 11:17*	Southern boundary of Joshua's conquest
Hermon	9,100	*Joshua 11:17* *Matthew 17:1*	Northern boundary of Joshua's conquest ?Jesus transfigured here
Tabor	1,900	*Judges 4:6* *Matthew 17:1*	Deborah's forces fought Sisera ?Jesus transfigured here
Gilboa	1,700	*1 Samuel 31:1*	Saul killed in battle
Carmel	1,750	*1 Kings 18:20*	Elijah defeated prophets of Baal
Moriah		*2 Chronicles 3:1*	Early name for Mount Zion
Zion		*Psalm 48:1-2*	Site of the Temple
Beatitudes (location uncertain)		*Matthew 5–7*	Jesus' Sermon on the Mount
Olives	2,600	*Zechariah 14:4* *Matthew 26:30*	Site of Bethany, Gethsemane, Jesus' ascension and his predicted return

The foothills of Mount Hermon, northern Palestine

Some animals in the Bible

Antelope *Deuteronomy 14:5*
Ape *2 Chronicles 9:21*
Bat *Leviticus 11:19*
Bear *1 Samuel 17:34-36*
Boar *Psalm 80:13*
Camel *Leviticus 11:4*
Cattle *Genesis 12:16*
Deer *Deuteronomy 12:15*
Dog *1 Samuel 17:43*
Donkey *Genesis 12:16*
Fox *Song of Solomon 2:15*
Gazelle *Deuteronomy 12:15*
Goat *Genesis 27:9*
Hare *Leviticus 11:6*
Horse *Genesis 47:17*
Hyena *Isaiah 34:14*
Ibex *Deuteronomy 14:5*
Jackal *Isaiah 34:13*
Leopard *Jeremiah 13:23*
Lion *Judges 14:5-6*
Mole *Leviticus 11:29*
Mouse *Leviticus 11:29*
Mule *1 Kings 1:33*
Ox *Deuteronomy 14:4*
Peacock *2 Chronicles 9:21*
Pig *Leviticus 11:7*
Rock badger *Deuteronomy 14:7*
Roe buck *Deuteronomy 14:5*
Sheep *1 Samuel 16:11*
Wild goat *Deuteronomy 14:5*
Wolf *Matthew 7:15*

Camels from an Assyrian relief

Musical instruments of the Bible

Instrument	Hebrew	Bible references
Wind		
Ram's horn	shophar, yobel	Exodus 19:13; Psalm 81:3; Joshua 6:4
Trumpet	hasoserah	Numbers 10:2-10; Psalm 150:3
Flute	'ugab	Job 21:12; 30:31; Luke 7:32
Double pipe	halil	1 Kings 1:40; Isaiah 5:12
String		
Lyre	nebel	2 Samuel 6:5; Psalm 33:2
Harp	kinnor	Genesis 31:27; Psalm 43:4
Percussion		
Tambourine	toph	Exodus 15:20; 1 Samuel 18:6; Psalm 149:3
Cymbals	selselim, mesiltayim	1 Chronicles 13:8; Psalm 150:5; Nehemiah 12:27

Some birds in the Bible

Crane *Isaiah 38:14*
Cormorant *Leviticus 11:17*
Dove *Genesis 8:8*
Eagle *Leviticus 11:13*
Falcon *Deuteronomy 14:13*
Gull *Leviticus 11:16*
Hawk *Leviticus 11:16*
Hen *Matthew 23:37*
Heron *Leviticus 11:19*
Hoopoe *Leviticus 11:19*
Kite *Leviticus 11:14*
Ostrich *Leviticus 11:16*
Owl *Leviticus 11:18*
Partridge *Jeremiah 17:11*
Pigeon *Luke 2:24*
Quail *Exodus 16:13*
Raven *Genesis 8:7*
Rooster *Matthew 26:34*
Sparrow *Psalm 84:3*
Stork *Leviticus 11:19*
Swallow *Psalm 84:3*
Swift *Isaiah 38:14*
Turtledove *Luke 2:24*
Vulture *Leviticus 11:13*
White owl *Leviticus 11:18*

Even the sparrow finds a home, and the swallow a nest for herself. . .

Psalm 84:3

Who are the heavenly beings?

What are the titles of Jesus in the Bible?

Anointed One *Psalm 2:2*

Author of life *Acts 3:15*

The beginning and the end (Greek *Alpha* and *Omega*) *Revelation 1:8*

Branch *Zechariah 6:12*

Bread of life *John 6:35*

Bright Morning Star *Revelation 22:16*

Christ (Greek "Anointed One," or Messiah) *Matthew 16:16*

Everlasting Father *Isaiah 9:6*

Gate *John 10:7*

Good shepherd *John 10:11*

Holy and Righteous One *Acts 3:14*

Holy One of God *Mark 1:24*

I am *John 8:58*

Immanuel *Isaiah 7:14*

Jesus (Hebrew "Yahweh saves") *Matthew 1:21*

King of kings *Revelation 17:14*

Lamb *Revelation 5:6-14*

Lamb of God *John 1:29*

Last Adam *1 Corinthians 15:45*

Light of the world *John 8:12*

Lion of Judah *Revelation 5:5*

Lord (Greek "Kyrios") *Philippians 2:9-11*

Lord of lords *Revelation 17:14*

Man of sorrows *Isaiah 53:3*

Master *Luke 5:5*

Messiah (Hebrew for the "Anointed One") *John 1:41*

Mighty God *Isaiah 9:6*

Morning star *2 Peter 1:19*

Nazarene *Matthew 2:23*

Prince of Peace *Isaiah 9:6*

Prophet *Acts 3:22*

Rabbi *John 1:38*

Resurrection and life *John 11:25*

Root of David *Revelation 5:5*

Root of Jesse *Isaiah 11:10*

Savior *Luke 2:11*

Son of David *Matthew 1:1*

Son of God *Mark 1:1*

Son of Man *Matthew 8:20*

True vine *John 15:1*

Way, truth, and life *John 14:6*

Wonderful Counselor *Isaiah 9:6*

Word (Greek "Logos") *John 1:1*

Word of God *Revelation 19:13*

What are some of the names for the Holy Spirit in the Bible?

Eternal Spirit *Hebrews 9:14*

Helper *John 14:16*

Holy Spirit *Luke 11:13*

Power of the Most High *Luke 1:35*

Spirit *Romans 8:26-27*

Spirit of Christ *Romans 8:9*

Spirit of his [God's] Son *Galatians 4:6*

Spirit of holiness *Romans 1:4*

Spirit of the LORD *Judges 3:10*

Spirit of sonship *Romans 8:15*

Spirit of truth *John 14:17*

How is the Church described in the Bible?

Believers *Acts 2:44*

Body of Christ *1 Corinthians 12:27*

Bride *Revelation 21:2*

Called *Romans 8:30; 1 Corinthians 1:2*

Children of light *Ephesians 5:8*

Chosen people *1 Peter 2:9*

Christians *Acts 11:26*

Church *Matthew 16:18; 18:17; 1 Corinthians 1:2*

Citizens of heaven *Philippians 3:20*

Disciples *Acts 6:1; 11:26*

God's building; God's field *1 Corinthians 3:9*

God's children *John 1:12; Romans 8:14-23*

God's elect *1 Peter 1:1*

God's fellow workers *1 Corinthians 3:9*

God's household *Ephesians 2:19*

God's temple *1 Corinthians 3:16*

Heirs of God *Romans 8:17*

Holy City *Revelation 21:10-27*

Holy nation *1 Peter 2:9*

Israel of God *Galatians 6:16*

Light of the world *Matthew 5:14*

Living stones *1 Peter 2:5*

People belonging to God *1 Peter 2:9*

Pillar and foundation of the truth *1 Timothy 3:15*

Royal priesthood *1 Peter 2:9*

Sanctified *1 Corinthians 1:2*

Saints *Ephesians 1:1, 15, 18; 3:18*

Salt of the earth *Matthew 5:13*

Sheep *John 10:3*

Soldiers of Christ *2 Timothy 2:3-4*

Strangers in the world *1 Peter 1:1*

Which Bible people saw God?

- Jacob dreamed of "a ladder set up on the earth, and the top of it reached to heaven. And behold, the angels of God were ascending and descending on it!" *Genesis 28:12-13*

- "Then Moses and Aaron, Nadab, and Abihu, and seventy of the elders of Israel went up, and they saw the God of Israel." *Exodus 24:9-10*

- Moses saw the back of God. *Exodus 33:23*

- Micaiah saw "the LORD sitting on his throne, and all the host of heaven standing on his right hand and on his left." *2 Chronicles 18:18*

- Isaiah saw "the LORD sitting upon a throne, high and lifted up; and the train of his robe filled the temple." *Isaiah 6:1*

- Ezekiel saw "the likeness of a throne, in appearance like sapphire; and seated above the likeness of a throne was a likeness with a human appearance." *Ezekiel 1:26*

- Daniel saw thrones "placed, and the Ancient of days took his seat; his clothing was white as snow, and the hair of his head like pure wool; his throne was fiery flames; its wheels were burning fire." *Daniel 7:9*

- Stephen looked up to heaven "and saw the glory of God, and Jesus standing at the right hand of God." *Acts 7:55*

- Paul wrote, "Last of all, as to one untimely born, he appeared also to me." *1 Corinthians 15:8*

- John wrote, "At once I was in the Spirit, and behold, a throne stood in heaven, with one seated on the throne." *Revelation 4:2*

Angels

The word "angel" literally means "messenger." As used in the Bible, it applies mostly to supernatural beings of the unseen world, used as messengers in the service of either God or Satan.

Angels played an important role in the life of Jesus:

- An angel announced the birth of John *Luke 1:11-17*.
- An angel named him *Luke 1:13*.
- An angel foretold to Mary the birth of Jesus *Luke 1:26-37*.
- An angel foretold to Joseph the birth of Jesus *Matthew 1:20-21*.
- An angel named him *Matthew 1:21*.
- Angels announced to shepherds the birth of Jesus *Luke 2:8-15*.
- They sang hallelujahs *Luke 2:13-14*.
- An angel directed the child's flight to Egypt *Matthew 2:13, 20*.
- Angels ministered to Jesus at his temptation *Matthew 4:11*.
- An angel came to Jesus in Gethsemane *Luke 22:43*.
- An angel rolled away the stone at his tomb *Matthew 28:2*.
- An angel announced to the women his resurrection *Matthew 28:5-7*.
- Two angels presented him to Mary Magdalene *John 20:11-14*.

Jesus talked about angels:

- Nathanael would see angels ascending and descending upon him *John 1:51*.
- He could have 12 legions of angels to deliver him *Matthew 26:53*.
- Angels will come with him *Matthew 25:31; 16:27; Mark 8:38; Luke 9:26*.
- Angels will be the reapers *Matthew 13:39*.
- Angels will gather the elect *Matthew 24:31*.
- Angels will separate the wicked from the righteous *Matthew 13:41, 49*.
- Angels carried the beggar to Abraham's side *Luke 16:22*.
- Angels rejoice over the repentance of sinners *Luke 15:10*.
- Little children have guardian angels *Matthew 18:10*.
- Jesus will confess his people before the angels *Luke 12:8*.
- Angels have no gender and cannot die *Luke 20:35-36; Matthew 22:3*.
- The devil has evil angels *Matthew 25:41*.

Artist's impression of Jacob's dream

Some Bible names and their meanings

Aaron *enlightened*
Abel *shepherd, meadow*
Abigail *source of joy, father's joy*
Abraham *father of a multitude*
Absalom *father of friendship, or of peace*
Adam *man*
Agrippa *causing pain at birth*
Ahaz *possessor*
Amos *burden, one with a burden*
Andrew *man, manly*
Anna *grace, gracious*
Apollos *destroyer*
Aquila *an eagle*

Balaam *foreigner, Lord of the people*
Barnabas *son of consolation*
Bartholomew *son of Talmai*
Bathsheba *daughter of an oath, or of seven*
Benjamin *son of the right hand*
Bernice *bringer of victory*
Boaz *fleetness, strength*

Cain *acquisition, possession*
Caleb *barker, dog*
Cephas *stone, rock*
Cornelius *of a horn*
Cyrus *sun, splendor*

Dan *judge*
Daniel *God is my judge*
David *dear, beloved*
Deborah *bee*
Delilah *dainty*

Ehud *the only*
Eleazar *God my helper*
Eli *God is exalted*
Elijah *Yahweh my God*
Elizabeth *oath of God*
Elisha *God as a Savior*
Enoch *teacher*
Esau *hairy*
Esther *myrtle*
Eve *life, living*
Ezekiel *God will strengthen*
Ezra *help*

Felix *happy*
Festus *joyful*
Gabriel *man of God*
Gad *good fortune, fortunate*
Gaius *lord*

Gideon *a hewer, tree-cutter, great warrior*
Goliath *expulsion, expeller*

Habakkuk *God is strength*
Haggai *festive*
Ham *hot, black*
Hannah *grace, prayer*
Herod *heroic*
Hezekiah *might of Yahweh*
Hosea *deliverance, salvation*

Immanuel *God with us*
Isaac *laughter*
Isaiah *salvation of Yahweh*
Ishmael *whom God hears*
Israel *soldier of God*

Jacob *supplanter*
James *supplanter*
Jason *healer*
Jehoiakim *set up by Yahweh*
Jehoshaphat *Yahweh judges*
Jehu *Yahweh is he*
Jeremiah *exalted by God*
Jesse *God exists*
Jesus *the Lord saves*
Jethro *preeminent*
Jezebel *chaste*
Joab *Yahweh is father*
Job *afflicted, persecuted*
Joel *whose God is Yahweh*

Judas betrayed Jesus for 30 pieces of silver.

John *God's gift, grace*
Jonah *dove*
Jonathan *God is given*
Joseph *he shall add*
Joshua *Yahweh is salvation*
Josiah *God supports*
Jotham *Yahweh is upright*
Judah *praise*
Judas *praised*
Jude *praised*
Judith *Jewess*

Laban *white, beautiful*
Lazarus *God my helper*
Leah *weary*
Levi *joined*
Lot *covering, veil*
Lucifer *light-bringer*
Luke *light-giver*
Lydia *contention*

Malachi *my messenger*
Manasseh *forgetting*
Mark *polite*
Martha *lady*
Mary *loved by God*
Matthew *gift of Yahweh*
Melchizedek *king of righteousness*
Micah *who is like God?*
Miriam *loved by God*
Moab *the desirable land*
Mordecai *consecrated to Merodach*
Moses *drawn out of the water*

Nahum *consolation, comforter*
Naomi *gracious, pleasant*
Nathan *gift (of God)*
Nathanael *gift of God*
Nebuchadnezzar *may the God Nebo defend the boundary*
Nehemiah *consolation from God*
Nicodemus *conqueror of the people*
Noah *rest*

Obadiah *servant of Yahweh*

Paul *little*
Peter *rock, stone*
Philemon *affectionate*
Philip *lover of horses*
Priscilla *ancient*

Rachel *ewe*
Rahab *gracious*
Rebekah *flattering*
Reuben *see, a son*
Ruth *friend*

Samson *distinguished*
Samuel *name of God, placed by God, heard of God*
Sarah *princess*
Saul *asked for*
Seth *sprout*

Ruth would not desert her widowed mother-in-law.

Simeon *one heard*
Simon *one heard*
Solomon *peaceful*
Stephen *crown*

Thaddaeus *man of heart*
Thomas *twin*
Timothy *honored by God*
Titus *honorable*

Uriah *light of Yahweh, Yahweh is my light*
Uzziah *power of Yahweh, strength of Yahweh*

Zechariah *remembered by Yahweh*
Zedekiah *justice of Yahweh*
Zephaniah *treasure of Yahweh*

Mary Magdalene, the first to see Jesus alive again

The Last days

Some Messianic prophecies

Prophecy	Old Testament reference	Fulfilled in Jesus
The woman's seed would bruise Satan's head	Genesis 3:15	Galatians 4:4
Messiah would be of Abraham's seed	Genesis 17:7	Galatians 3:16
Messiah would be of the house of David	2 Samuel 7:12-13	Acts 13:32-33
Messiah would be preceded by a messenger	Malachi 3:1	Mark 1:2-3
Messiah would be born of a virgin	Isaiah 7:14	Matthew 1:18, 21-23
Messiah would be born in Bethlehem	Micah 5:1-5	Matthew 2:1
Shepherd-Messiah	Isaiah 40:11	John 10:11-16
Prophet-Messiah	Deuteronomy 18:15	Acts 3:20-22
Priest-Messiah	Psalm 110:1-7	Hebrews 5:5-6
Messiah-King	Zechariah 9:9	John 18:33, 37
Redeemer-Messiah	Isaiah 59:20	Luke 2:11
Messiah would be a light to the Gentiles	Isaiah 49:6-10	Acts 13:47
Messiah would be a stumbling stone	Isaiah 8:14	Romans 9:32-33
Messiah would be reproached	Psalm 69:9	Romans 15:3
Messiah would be mocked	Psalm 22:7-8	Matthew 27:39-44
Messiah would be crucified	Psalm 22:16	John 19:18
Messiah would be our sin-bearer	Isaiah 53:4-6	John 1:29
Messiah would be resurrected	Psalm 16:10	Mark 16:6

What were Jesus' seven last sayings on the cross?

1. "Father, forgive them, for they know not what they do." *Luke 23:34*
2. (To Mary) "Woman, behold, your son!" (To John) "Behold, your mother!" *John 19:26-27*
3. (To the criminal on the cross) "Truly, I say to you, today you will be with me in Paradise." *Luke 23:43*
4. "I thirst." *John 19:28*
5. "My God, my God, why have you forsaken me?" *Matthew 27:46; see Psalm 22:1*
6. "It is finished." *John 19:30*
7. "Father, into your hands I commit my spirit!" *Luke 23:46*

The I Ams of John's Gospel

I am the bread of life 6:35-48

I am the living bread 6:51

I am the light of the world 8:12

I am from above; I am not of this world 8:23

I am the gate for the sheep 10:7

I am the good shepherd 10:11

I am the resurrection and the life 11:25

I am the way, and the truth, and the life 14:6

I am the true vine 15:1

The number of the beast?

In Revelation 13:18, "666" is given as the number of the beast. What does this mean? Any number of villains in history have been identified with the "beast": the infamous Roman emperor Nero, the wicked emperor Caligula, the persecuting Diocletian—or even the Roman emperors as a whole. Other candidates have included the Roman Empire itself, Muhammad, Napoleon, Hitler, and several popes!

The number 666 has also been used as the basis for calculating the year when the beast might appear.

However, it is possible that the number does not stand for any particular person or institution, but simply for "the beast."

In the Bible seven is the number of perfection, completion, and fulfillment (Genesis 2:2; Exodus 20:10; Leviticus 16:29-30; Revelation 1:12). However, six never reaches seven; it fails to attain perfection and forever misses the mark. Hence, the number of the beast—666—is failure after failure after failure—the mark of humanity.

What events will occur before Jesus' second coming?

- **Apostasy** *Matthew 24:10*
- **The rise of Antichrist** *Matthew 24:5, 23, 26*
- **Betrayal** *Mark 13:12; Luke 21:16*
- **Earthquakes** *Matthew 24:7; Mark 13:8*
- **False Christs** *Matthew 24:24; Mark 13:6, 21-23*
- **False prophets** *Matthew 24:11, 24; Mark 13:21-23*
- **False signs and miracles** *Matthew 24:24; Mark 13:22*
- **Famines** *Matthew 24:7*
- **Increase of evil** *Matthew 24:12*
- **International strife** *Matthew 24:7*
- **Persecution of believers** *Matthew 24:9; Mark 13:9-13*
- **Pestilence** *Luke 21:11*
- **Unparalleled distress** *Mark 13:17-19*
- **Wars and rumors of wars** *Matthew 24:6; Mark 13:7*
- **Worldwide proclamation of the gospel** *Matthew 24:14; Mark 13:10*

The most popular English versions of the Bible

Amplified Bible, The The unique feature of this translation is the addition of thousands of alternate (amplified) readings in brackets to help the reader understand the text. It was first published in 1964.

Douay-Rheims Bible A Roman Catholic translation produced in the early seventeenth century about the same time as the King James Version. For the most part it was translated from the Latin Vulgate. Until the 1970s, when the New American Bible was completed, the Douay-Rheims Bible was the standard English translation for the Roman Catholic Church.

English Standard Version (ESV) The English Standard Version seeks to maintain the historic KJV/ASV/RSV legacy of literal accuracy and readability, while also addressing various translation issues that have been a concern in evangelical churches. The ESV was published in 2001.

Good News Bible (GNB) *See* Today's English Version.

Holman Christian Standard Bible (HCSB) Published in 2004, this translation seeks a balance between the word-for-word and thought-for-thought styles of English Bible translation.

Jerusalem Bible (JB) Roman Catholic translation first published in 1966.

King James Version (KJV) Until recently, the King James Version was the most widely used English translation of the Bible. It was first published in 1611, authorized by King James I of England; in Britain it is called the Authorized Version (AV). Its stately language has had a great influence on spoken English and on English literature over four centuries. Most popularly known biblical phrases and quotations are from the King James Version. In recent years, modern translations have replaced the King James Version in many churches.

Living Bible, The (TLB) A paraphrase of the Bible, widely used since its initial publication in 1971. In the 1970s, it was the best-selling book in the United States.

New American Bible (NAB) A translation sponsored by the Roman Catholic Church. Sometimes called the Confraternity Bible, it was first published in 1970 and is the translation now mostly used by Catholics.

New American Standard Bible (NASB) First published in 1971, it gained popularity among evangelicals as an accurate word-for-word translation. It was updated in 1995.

New English Bible (NEB) A thought-for-thought translation published in 1970. It was more popular in Britain than in the United States.

New International Version (NIV) A popular translation that has been accepted by evangelicals since its publication in 1978. It has recently surpassed the King James Version as the most widely used English translation of the Bible.

New Jerusalem Bible. (NJB) Revision of the Jerusalem Bible first published in 1985.

New King James Version (NKJV) A popular revision of the King James Version, it was first published in 1982. Many difficult and archaic words have been updated, and the words "thee" and "thou" have been replaced with the contemporary "you."

New Living Translation (NLT) A complete revision of the Living Bible, first published in 1996.

New Revised Standard Version (NRSV) See Revised Standard Version.

Revised English Bible (REB) A revision of the New English Bible first published in 1989.

Revised Standard Version (RSV) Sponsored by the National Council of the Churches of Christ in the USA and first published in 1952. In 1990 a revised edition called the New Revised Standard Version (NRSV) was published to replace the former edition.

Today's English Version (TEV) This modern translation, published by the American Bible Society, has been popular since its publication in 1976. It uses simple English and tends to be a thought-for-thought style of translation. It is also called the Good News Bible.

Today's New International Version (TNIV) This is a new version of the best-selling NIV, which also remains in print as a separate translation. The TNIV is most noteworthy for its effort to achieve greater gender neutrality. The complete TNIV was published in 2005.

Index

A

Aaron 196
Abednego 206
Abel 194
Abiathar 201
Abigail 201
Abijah 202
Abimelech 199
Abner 201
Abraham 34–5, 45, 48, 195
    map 49
Absalom 200
Achan 197
Acts 96–7, 106–7, 223
Adam 194
Adonijah 201
Aeneas 215
Agabus 215
Agrippa 219
Ahab 61, 204
Ahasuerus 207
Ahaz 61, 202
Ahaziah 202, 204
Ahithophel 201
Albright, W. F. 27
Alexander the Great 67, 74
alphabet 8–9, 20–1
altars 54, 175
Amaziah 202
Amnon 201
Amon 203
Amos 71, 205, 222
Ananias 214
Andrew 210
angels 231
animals 229
Anna 208
Annas 213
Antioch, aqueduct 109
Antiochus IV 74
Antonia Fortress 140
Apocrypha
    New Testament 89
    Old Testament 6, 76, 225
Apollos 218
apostles 210–11
Aquila 218

Aramaic language 8
Ararat, Mount 228
archaeology 26–31
Ark of the Covenant 178–9, 183, 186
ark (Noah's) 224
armies 154–5
Artaxerxes I 65
Artemis 119, 192
Asa 202
ascension, of Jesus 104
Asherah 192
Ashtoreth 192
Assyria 61, 67
    map 66
Athaliah 202
Atonement, Day of 170
Augustus 209
Azariah 202

B

Baal 192
Baal-worship 61
Baal-Zebub 192
Babylon 61, 64, 67, 206
    map 66
Barabbas 212
Barak 198
bar mitzvah 146
Barnabas 216
Bartholomew 210
Bartimaeus 212
Baruch 76
Bathsheba 200
Behistun Rock 26
Bel and the Dragon 76
Belshazzar 206
Benjamin 196
Bethlehem 81
betrothal 144
Bible
    authorship 10
    contents 6, 11
    reading plans 224–7
    timeline 34–41
    verses 224–7
    versions 235
birds 229
birth 146
Boaz 199
Botta, Paul 26
bread 134, 148
breakfast 148
burial 165
burnt offerings 175

C

Caiaphas 213
Cain 194
Caleb 197
calendar 83, 170–1
camels 152
Canaan, maps 53, 54
Canaanites 61
canon 11
Capernaum 90, 98, 184
Carmel, Mount 228
carpenters 150
carriages 152–3
Castor and Pollux 192
Caxton, William 22
chained books 19
chariots 154
Chemosh 192
children 146
Chorazin 98, 122
Christ see Jesus; Messiah
Chronicles 222
church
    described 230
    maps 105, 120–1
cities of refuge 54
Claudius 219
Cleopas 214
cloaks 128
cloth 151
clothing 128–9, 134
Codex Sinaiticus 15
codices 14
Colossians 115, 223
Corinth 31
Corinthians 110–11, 223
Cornelius 214
covenants 47, 112–13
    see also Ark of the Covenant
creation 46
Crescens 218
Crispus 218
cuneiform writing 8, 26
Cyril 20–1
Cyrillic alphabet 20–1
Cyrus Cylinder 31
Cyrus the Great 64–5, 67, 206
Czech Republic 21

D

Dagon 192
Damascus 61
Daniel 71, 206, 222
Darius I 65, 106

dating 27, 29, 83
David 36–7, 56, 200
    and Jerusalem 136–7
    kingdom map 59
    and Tabernacle 178
Dead Sea Scrolls 12
death 165
Deborah 198
Delilah 198
Demas 218
Demetrius 218
Deuteronomy 222
Dionysius 218
disciples 210–11
diseases 147
doctors 147
Dorcas 215
dyeing 151

E

eating 148
Ebal, Mount 228
Ecclesiastes 73, 222
Ecclesiasticus 76
economy, map 32
Eden 46
Egypt 50–1
Eli 199
Elijah 69, 205
    map 70
Elisha 69, 205
    map 70
Elizabeth 208
Elymas 218
Enoch 194
Epaphras 218
Epaphroditus 219
Ephesians 115, 223
Ephesus 118, 119, 120, 126
Ephraim 196
Erasmus, Desiderius 22
Erastus 31, 216
Esau 195
Esdras 76
Essenes 12, 185
Esther 76, 207, 222
eunuch 215
Eutychus 219
Eve 194
Exile in Babylon 64–5, 138
Exodus 50–2, 197, 222
    maps 51, 177
Ezekiel 64, 71, 206, 222
Ezra 64, 207, 222

F

farming 160–2
feasts 144, 148
    see also festivals
Felix 219
festivals 170–1
Festus 219
Firstfruits, Feast of 170
fish 148
fishing 156–7
Flood 47
food 148
fruit 148, 149, 162
furniture 133

G

Galatians 108, 223
Galileans 185
Galilee 98
    map 81
Gehazi 205
Genesis 46–9, 222
Gerizim, Mount 228
Gideon 198
Gilboa, Mount 228
Gilgamesh 47
Glueck, Nelson 27
goats 158, 162
God
    character 168–9
    seen by men 231
gods 192
golden calf 52
Golden Gospels 19
Goliath 200
Gospels 86–8
grain 160–1, 162
grapes 148, 149
Greek Empire 74
    map 67
Greek language 8
    see also Septuagint
Gutenberg, Johann 22

H

Habakkuk 71, 203, 222
Hagar 195
Haggai 71, 207, 222
hairstyles 128
Halak, Mount 228
Ham 194
Haman 207

Hannah 199
Hanukkah 75, 140, 171
harvest 160, 162, 170–1
Hasmoneans 74–5, 82, 140
headgear 129, 144
health 147
Hebrew language 8
Hebrews 116–17, 223
Hebron 196
Hellenization 74
Hermes 192
Hermon, Mount 228
Herod Agrippa II 219
Herod the Great 83, 186, 209
    and Jerusalem 140–1
Herodians 185
Herodias 208
Herodion 30
Herodium 140, 186
Hezekiah 203
Hierapolis 118
hieroglyphics 26
high priest 116, 165, 182
Hiram 201
holiness 168
Holy Spirit 97, 230
honey 148
Hosea 71, 205, 222
Hoshea 205
houses 132–3
Huldah 69, 203
Hus, John 21

I

illuminated manuscripts 18
Ireland 18
Isaac 48, 195
Isaiah 71, 202, 222
Ish-bosheth 201
Ishmael 195
Israel
    kingdom 57
    kingdom divided 61–3
    maps 58, 59
    modern state 42
    tribal lands 54

J

Jacob 35, 45, 48, 195
Jael 198
Jairus 212
James 122–3, 210, 215, 223
Japheth 194

Jason 219
Jehoahaz 204
Jehoash 204
Jehoiachin 203
Jehoiakim 203
Jehoram 202, 204
Jehoshaphat 202
Jehu 31, 204
Jephthah 199
Jeremiah 71, 203, 222
    Letter of 76
Jericho 178
Jeroboam 204
Jeroboam II 63, 204
Jerome 17
Jerusalem 136–43
    archaeology 31
    and David 56, 136–7
    and Jesus 101, 103, 142–3
    plans 59, 103
Jesse 200
Jesus 78–81, 88, 90–5, 209
    and angels 231
    birthplace 96
    in Galilee 98
    in Jerusalem 101, 103
    last week 102–3
    map of journeys 101
    miracles 92
    parables 93
    resurrection and ascension 104
    sayings 234
jewelry 128, 129
Jezebel 61
Joab 201
Joash 202
Job 73, 194, 222
Joel 71, 205, 222
John 210
    Gospel 100–1, 223
    letters 118–19, 223
John the Baptist 80–1, 208
John Mark see Mark
Jonah 71, 205, 222
Jonathan 200
Jordan River 80
Joseph (son of Jacob) 35, 48–9, 196
Joseph of Arimathea 212
Joseph (husband of Mary) 208
Joshua 36, 196, 222
Josiah 61, 203
Jotham 202
Judah (kingdom) 57, 61–3
Judah (son of Jacob) 197
Judas 210
Judas Iscariot 210
Judas Maccabeus 74–5

Jude 122–3, 215, 223
Judea 74
judgment 47
judges 36, 53, 55, 198, 222
Judith 76
justification 112

K

Kells, Book of 18
kingdom of God 80
Kings 222

L

Lachish 44
Lamentations 222
lampstands 183
languages 8–9
    see also translation
Laodicea 124, 126
Latin language 17
Law 52, 166–7
Layard, Austen 26, 27
Lazarus 213
leather 150
Levi 197
Levites 165
Leviticus 222
Lindisfarne Gospels 19
looms 151
Lot 195
Luke 106–7
    Gospel 96–7, 223
    see also Acts
Luther, Martin 23
Lydia 219

M

Maccabees 74, 76
    map 75
Machpelah, Cave of 196
Magdala 98
Malachi 71, 207, 222
Manasseh 76, 197, 203
manna 52
manuscripts 16–19
    see also scrolls
Marduk 192
Mark 216
    Gospel 87, 223
marriage 144–5
Martha 213

Mary 89, 208, 213
Mary Magdalene 208, 212
Masada 31, 140, 186
Matthew 90–1, 210
    Gospel 223
Matthias 214
meat 148
medicines 147
Melchizedek 195
Mesopotamia, map 32–3
Messiah 79, 80, 94, 233
Methodius 20–1
Methuselah 194
Micah 71, 203, 222
Michal 200
milk 148
millennium 125
milling 134, 135
miracles, of Jesus 92
Miriam 196
Molech 192
monks 16
Mordecai 207
Moriah, Mount 182, 228
Moses 36, 45, 50–2, 197
music 72, 165, 229

N

Naaman 205
Nabal 201
Naboth 205
Nahum 71, 203, 222
names 146, 232
    of God 169
    of Jesus 230
Naomi 199
Nathan 69
Nathanael 210–11
Nazareth 80
Nazirites 185
Nebo 192
    Mount 228
Nebuchadnezzar 67, 206
Nehemiah 64, 138–9, 207, 222
Nergat 192
Nero 219
New Testament 77–126
    authors 89
    contents 223
Nicodemus 212
Noah 194
number of the beast 234
Numbers 222
nuts 148

O

Obadiah 71, 203, 222
Old Testament 43–73
    contents 11, 222
    time chart 45
    see also Septuagint
olives 148, 149
Omri 204
Onesimus 218
oral tradition 10
ovens 134

P

Palestine
    maps 32–3, 86, 99
    under Maccabees 75
Papiasa 119
papyrus 7, 9
parables 93
parchment 18
Passover 80, 170
Paul 217
    conversion 105, 107
    journey to Rome 112
    letters 108–17
    missionary journeys 107, 109,
    110
Pekah 205
pens 18
perfume 129
Pergamum 124, 126
Persia 64–5
    map 67
Peter 105, 211
    letters 118–19, 223
    and Mark's Gospel 87
Petrie, Flinders 27
Pharaoh 196
Pharisees 74, 91, 185
Philadelphia 126
Philemon 115, 218–19, 223
Philip 105, 211, 215
Philippians 114, 223
Pilate 213
plagues 50
plowing 160
poetry 72–3
Pompey the Great 74
Pontius Pilate 213
Potiphar 197
potters 150
pottery, dating 27
poverty, in Luke's Gospel 97
prayer, in Luke's Gospel 97

Prayer of Manasseh 76
prayers 226
priests 165
printing 22
Priscilla 218
Promised Land 48–9, 53–4, 178
prophets 68–71
proselytes 185
Proverbs 73, 222
Psalms 72–3, 222, 227
Ptolemy 74
publicans 185
Purim 171

Q

quail 52
Qumran 12–13

R

rabbis 8, 79
Rachel 195
Rawlinson, Henry 26
Rebekah 195
Rehoboam 56, 202
religion 163–92
repentance 80
resurrection, of Jesus 78, 104
Reuben 197
Revelation 124–6, 223
Rhoda 214
Rimmon 192
Roman army 154–5
Roman Empire 74, 82–3
    map 84–5
Romans 112–13, 223
roofs 132–3
Rosetta Stone 26
Rosh Hashanah 170
Russian language 20–1
Ruth 53, 199, 222

S

Sadducees 185
Salome 208
Samson 198
Samuel 56, 199, 222
Sanballat 207
sandals 129
Sapphira 214
Sarah 195

Sardis 124, 126
Saul 56, 200
    kingdom maps 58, 59
Schliemann, Heinrich 26–7
schools 8, 146
scribes 10, 16, 185
scrolls 9, 13
Seleucid kingdom 74–5
Sennacherib 206
Sennacherib's prism 30–1
Septuagint 11, 16
Sergius Paulus 215
Sheba, Queen of 60
sheep 158–9, 162
Shem 194
shepherds 158–9
ships 153
shopping 134
sieges 154
Silas 216
Simeon 197, 208
Simon of Cyrene 212
Simon Magus 215
Simon the Zealot 211
Sinai 52
    Mount 176–7, 228
Sisera 198
Smyrna 124, 126
soldiers 154–5
Solomon 56, 201
    kingdom map 60
Son of Man 94–5
Son of God 94–5
Song of Solomon 222
Song of the Three Holy Children 76
spinning 151
star of Bethlehem 81
Stephen 105, 214
Story of Susanna 76
Succoth 170
Susanna 76
synagogues 90, 95, 122, 146, 184

T

Tabernacle 117, 172–9
Tabernacles, Feast of 170
Tabgha 98
Tabor, Mount 228
Tammuz 192
teaching 8
Temple 186
    and the Tabernacle 173
    built by Solomon 180–3
    rebuilt after Exile 64
    plundered by Antiochus 74

rebuilt by Herod 186–9
restored under Hasmoneans 75, 140
destroyed by Romans 190–1
Ten Commandments 167
tens 130–1
Terah 195
textiles 151
Theophilus 96
Thessalonians 108–9, 223
threshing 160
Thyatira 126
Tiberius 209
time charts 34–41, 45
Timothy 115, 216, 223
Titus (New Testament) 115, 216, 223
Titus (Roman general) 190, 191
Tobiah 207
Tobit 76
translation 17, 20–1, 23, 24, 224, 235
travel 152–3
tribes of Israel 54, 56
Troy 26–7
Trumpets, Feast of 170
tunics 128, 129
Tychicus 216
Tyndale, William 23

U

Uriah 201
Uzziah 63

V

vegetables 148
vellum 18
verses of the Bible 224–5
Vulgate 17

W

Waldo, Peter 20
war 154–5
water supply 134
wealth, in Luke's Gospel 97
weapons 154–5
weaving 151
weddings 144–5
wilderness 176–7
windows 132
wine 148, 149

winnowing 161
Wisdom 73
Wisdom of Solomon 76
women, in Luke's Gospel 97
worship 164–5
Wright, G. Ernest 27
writing 7, 8, 10
see also hieroglyphics; manuscripts
Wycliffe, John 20–1

X

Xerxes 207
Xerxes I 65

Y

Yom Kippur 170

Z

Zacchaeus 212
Zadok 201
Zealots 185
Zechariah 71, 207, 209, 222
Zedekiah 203
Zephaniah 71, 203, 222
Zerubbabel 207
Zeus 192
Zion, Mount 228
Zipporah 196